MW00441834

The Artistry of Neil Gaiman

Critical Approaches to Comics Artists
David Ball, Series Editor

The Artistry of
NEIL GAIMAN

FINDING LIGHT IN THE SHADOWS

Edited by Joseph Michael Sommers
and Kyle Eveleth

UNIVERSITY PRESS OF MISSISSIPPI | JACKSON

The University Press of Mississippi is the scholarly publishing agency of
the Mississippi Institutions of Higher Learning: Alcorn State University,
Delta State University, Jackson State University, Mississippi State University,
Mississippi University for Women, Mississippi Valley State University,
University of Mississippi, and University of Southern Mississippi.

www.upress.state.ms.us

Designed by Peter D. Halverson
Frontispiece illustration by Kristi Williams Olson

The University Press of Mississippi is a member of
the Association of University Presses.

Copyright © 2019 by University Press of Mississippi
All rights reserved

First printing 2019
∞

Library of Congress Cataloging-in-Publication Data

Names: Sommers, Joseph Michael, 1976– editor. | Eveleth, Kyle, editor.
Title: The artistry of Neil Gaiman: finding light in the shadows / edited by
   Joseph Michael Sommers and Kyle Eveleth.
Description: Jackson: University Press of Mississippi, [2019] | Series:
   Critical Approaches to Comics Artists | Includes bibliographical
   references and index. |
Identifiers: LCCN 2018042196 (print) | LCCN 2018047946 (ebook) | ISBN
   9781496821669 (epub single) | ISBN 9781496821676 (epub institutional) |
   ISBN 9781496821683 (pdf single) | ISBN 9781496821690 (pdf institutional)
   | ISBN 9781496821645 (cloth) | ISBN 9781496821652 (pbk.)
Subjects: LCSH: Gaiman, Neil—Criticism and interpretation. | Comic books,
   strips, etc.
Classification: LCC PN6737.G3 (ebook) | LCC PN6737.G3 Z27 2019 (print) | DDC
   741.5/942—dc23
LC record available at https://lccn.loc.gov/2018042196

British Library Cataloging-in-Publication Data available

CONTENTS

The Lighter Side of Neil Gaiman

"No Light, but Rather Darkness Visible": Illuminating Gaiman's Murkier Pages

Gaiman's Brumous Boundaries and the Liminal Space

"The World Always Seems Brighter When You've Just Made Something That Wasn't There Before": Afterthoughts, Fitters, and Interviews

Interviews

ACKNOWLEDGMENTS

A work of this breadth and scope does not come about without significant support and structure. This is not to mention a cast of outstanding writers, and it is that group, assembled and culled from an even larger group of potential writers, that we would like to thank first. For your patience, your traction, your endless capacity to suffer through our requests, demands, and incessant moaning, we would both like to thank all the contributors to this collection. Notably, we drew upon Annette Wannamaker for guidance and strength as a critic and friend. She's an editor's editor, and the well of her generosity knows no bottom.

Likewise, we would be both remiss and horrible human beings if we did not thank two people in particular: P. Craig Russell and, of course, Neil Gaiman. Craig took our call and quite literally welcomed us into his home for several hours to do nothing more than have a conversation about comics and let us tour his home and gallery with hot coffee and warm considerations. Neil made the time. He has no time, but he made it anyway. And along those lines, the editors would like to express their extreme gratitude to Neil's assistants, Cat Mihos and Stephanie Bryant, two incredible women who made the conversation with Neil possible (and likely also managed his calendar in a manner to sneak Joe into his schedule). You are both simply class personified and angels of grace and mercy.

This book would not exist as a published thing if it were not for the support, care, and guidance of more than a few people at the University Press of Mississippi. Craig W. Gill, the director, and Vijay Shah (alongside his assistant, Lisa McMurtray), in particular, are owed a degree of thanks that we simply don't have the word count for (short a subvention). Their willingness to work with us and patience to *deal* with us gave us the steel to push forward through the thousands of words you are reading at present. UPM is now and continues to be the finest university press operating in the field of comics studies, and it is due in no small part to the leadership of that press and the fine human beings who work for it and craft our words to be read by all. We are grateful for the decades and decades of scholarship coming from this grand institution.

Individually, the authors have a few people they would like to thank.

As Gaiman does in his acknowledgments for *Miracleman* (2016), **Kyle** wonders if it is appropriate to acknowledge a person who is responsible for at least 50 percent of a project. Social codes be damned; Joseph deserves more acknowledgments than I can write. This project exists because of him, and it would not have aspired to the heights it has without his energetic dedication. He is a model academic, a model fan, and a model family man. Joseph: thank you for including me as your peer on this wild ride.

None of this would have been possible without the enduring tolerance and support of my friends and family. They quietly listened while the project was still in babbling stages, endured as I made pots and pots of coffee and became a nearly permanent fixture at their kitchen tables, editing and puzzling over what would become this book. I owe deep debts to those who have pushed me throughout my career including William Wandless, Ted Troxell, Jeffrey Weinstock, and the others at Central Michigan University; Pearl James, Carol Mason, Michelle Sizemore, and everyone at the University of Kentucky; my deepest friends, Jonathan and Trisha Barefield, Justin and Samantha Leigh, Regan Schaeffer, and all those who assisted and listened during the course of this project.

Finally, the most tolerant, wonderful, and upbeat member of my support system, however, has been my partner in crime, Alex. She is my inspiration, my joy, my resilience, and my guidance.

Joseph, first and foremost, would like to thank his family: his wife and better nine-tenths, Sulynn, and his children, *especially* his children, Maggie and Gwendolyn.

Books such as these don't come pre-assembled out of the box. They take time and effort that, regardless of how many predawn mornings one consumes so as to not interfere with the time one spends with one's children, eventually, and repeatedly, cuts into that family time. As I type this, my children are painting for me because they think I need the strength.

They are my strength. And this work I do, I do for them.

Likewise, I have the finest colleagues a boy could ask for. My co-editor, my colleague, and my friend Kyle first among them because if it had not been for his willingness to take me up on co-editing this project, it would not exist. As willing as the mind is, sometimes you need a body ten to fifteen years younger; it doesn't hurt that he's pretty smart as well. Annette Wannamaker, thanked at onset and thanked again, continues to be a muse to my work, and her paper delivered some years ago at the Children's Literature Association Conference (which eventually became a chapter in another collection of mine) was the germ of thought that led to this book's focus. She is simply one of the finest academics in the world, and she is a wonderful human being just the same. There are others, the "Gaimanites," I have come to think of them, simply because it's shorter than saying, "devotees of the work of Neil Gaiman": Laura Nicosia, Lisa Von Drasek, Collette Drouillard, and Kelly Murphy all listened to my endless ramblings and thought babies on the road to this work's completion. Thank you all.

And, of course, to my students, young and old, but particularly my students at Central Michigan University who have sat through more classes talking about Gaiman and his work than I can recall—you're not *my* children, but you're the folks who speak with me on a regular basis and feed my mind the stuff that make things like this possible. You are all better than I deserve, and I am grateful to be your professor.

INTRODUCTION
Lux in Tenebris: Finding the Light in the Darkness and the Child in the Adult

> "'I'm going to tell you something important. Grown-ups don't look like grown-ups on the inside either. Outside, they're big and thoughtless and they always know what they're doing. Inside, they look just like they always have. Like they did when they were your age. The truth is, there aren't any grown-ups. Not one, in the whole wide world...'

> "We sat there, side by side, on the old wooden bench, not saying anything. I thought about adults. I wondered if that was true: if they were all really children wrapped in adult bodies, like children's books hidden in the middle of dull, long books. The kind with no pictures or conversations."
>
> NEIL GAIMAN, *The Ocean at the End of the Lane* (112–13)

Lux in tenebris can be translated literally as "light in darkness," but it is a phrase that has multiple other meanings, making its use here somewhat ironic. While it is the title of a one-act farce composed by German dramatist Bertolt Brecht, we use it here as a call back to the Gospel of John where it was written (as composed by Jerome) *"et lux in tenebris lucet et tenebrae eam non comprehenderunt"* (John 1.5), or "the light shines in the darkness, and the darkness does not comprehend it." As regards a collection of scholarship about a man who wears black almost exclusively and who is known best, perhaps, for comics that rely greatly upon remarkable, demonstrative, and colorful images, the phrase is as much about Gaiman's aesthetic as it is a nod to the themes and subject matter in his works. It is also a phrase that hints at Gaiman's complex and ambivalent views about childhood and adulthood, which are most clearly illustrated through the depiction of the Hempstock family from *The Ocean at the End of the Lane*.

There's something peculiar about the name "Hempstock" in the works of Neil Gaiman; as an analogue, and certainly a family, they are almost akin to the Snopes family which populates the fictitious Yoknapatawpha County in the works of William Faulkner. As Marlyn Thomas notes, their existence spans from Gaiman's children's work, where one will find ethereal Liza Hempstock in *The Graveyard Book*, to his more adult works like *Ocean*, and to his odd, rather indefinable works that fall some odd place in between, such as the fairy-tale-esque *Stardust*'s Daisy and her mother (96, 109). *The Ocean at the End of the Lane* features no less than three Hempstocks: Gran, Ginnie, and Lettie. Supposedly a derivation of the name "Henstock," itself a derivation of "Hinstock," the Hempstock name is, etymologically speaking, oft found in connection with the servants of a religious society or a "monastic community" (Holden), an origin that adds layers of meaning to the fact that all the Hempstocks found in Gaiman's work appear to be women of a certain mystical or supernatural repute. Gaiman himself notes that he doesn't recall why he called his clan the Hempstocks (Lough) but remembers assigning various fictional women that name when he was, himself, but a teen. Over the years, he has continually revisited Hempstocks, conferring them with varying degrees of significance along the way. Daisy, the eldest in print from *Stardust* (1999), is little more than a young domestic. Liza from *The Graveyard Book* (2008), who is the ghost of a witch burned alive some five hundred years prior to the story itself, aids young Bod's mischief of one sort or another throughout the novel. The Hempstocks of *The Ocean at the End of the Lane* (2013) occupy a far more mysterious place than old Liza; witches they are, for sure, yet they are also the kindly saviors of the unnamed protagonist, and one of them in particular, Lettie, does so at a considerable expense to her own person.

Which brings us to the rather lengthy epigraph that leads this introduction—Lettie, in her conversation with the unnamed protagonist, elucidates (quite literally throws a light on) the nature of humanity for the young boy. That is to say, she reminds him that simple binaries are just not the nature of humanity by explaining that people are monsters, and monsters are people just the same. But there's more to it than that. "Nobody actually looks like what they are on the inside. You don't. I don't," she says (112). "Monsters come in all shapes and sizes. Some of them are things that look like things people used to be scared of a long time ago. Sometimes monsters are things people should be scared of but they aren't" (112). And *that* statement underpins one of the tensions at the heart of this anthology, Gaiman's uncanny ability to write liminal characters and spaces that disturbingly and delightfully dismantle comfortable binaries like human/monster, light/dark, and adult/child.

In her essay, "Guilty Pleasures: Neil Gaiman's Books for Children for Adults," Annette Wannamaker notes this tension going back to remarks Gaiman made at the 2012 Zena Sutherland Lecture at the Chicago Public Library, "What the (Very Bad Swearword) is a Children's Book Anyway?" where Gaiman, she notes, discussed crafting a delightful little book about a panda (*Chu's Day*) "because he wanted to mess with people, specifically adult readers of children's books" (67). Since preliterate children often obtain the written word through the interlocution of adults, those adults are essentially a secondary audience for all books ostensibly for children. Authors adept at writing for children regularly address a dual audience consisting of a child reader and the adult who buys the book and reads the book to the child, oftentimes filtering, interpreting, or censoring its contents. Wannamaker states that because Gaiman has written for just about every age range, he is a master not only at addressing this dual audience, but also at interrogating it:

> Gaiman [. . .] is a trickster of a writer who enjoys challenging himself and his readers. He manages, again and again, to discomfort us, to unsettle us, not only by writing strange and frightening works of horror, science fiction, and fantasy but also by nudging at boundaries of literary categories in ways that destabilize our readerly selves in both distressing and pleasurable ways. (67)

"Distressing and pleasurable"—Wannamaker claims that one of the aspects of Gaiman's work that makes it especially uncanny for readers is his ability to make us question which bodily and psychic borders are permeable, fluid, or perhaps even nonexistent: If humans are monstrous, are monsters more human than we want to admit? Are we really the adults we think we are or are we just pretending? Later in her chapter from this collection, Tara Prescott asserts that Gaiman essentially rejects the hierarchy "that distinguishes adult fiction from children's literature, high culture from low" (6). And, as might be expected of a boy seemingly raised in a West Sussex library, one of his greater advocacies as an adult became the promotion of literacy, particularly for children.

Gaiman's Literary Life, Briefly

Unlike the uncharted pasts of many of his characters discussed in this volume, Neil Richard Gaiman's life is not one especially shrouded in mystery. Born to a grocer and a pharmacist in Portchester, Hampshire, United Kingdom in 1960, arguably the most salient development in Gaiman's professional life occurs just five years after his birth. In 1965, Gaiman's family moved to West Sussex, and an impatient Neil, who had learned to read independently a year prior, quickly became a "feral child" brought up in the stacks of the local reading room by "patient librarians" and nourished on the works of world-builders such as J. R. R. Tolkien and C. S. Lewis (Prescott 18). It was here, in a library, where Gaiman fostered his love of the written word, and it was also here, unencumbered by adults who might tell him otherwise, where Gaiman discovered library sections segregating those books that were designated for adults from those that were designated for children. And he read from them both. There, in the recesses of fiction catalogues, Gaiman drank deeply from the well of all the forbidden fruits of childhood: stories of magic, ghosts, witches, and heroic battles between wizards good and evil (29). Impressed upon by the fantastic realms of such masters as Tolkien, Lewis, Dennis Wheatley, and others, Gaiman's taste for the magical, the supernatural, and the fantastic blossomed early in his young life.

His thirst for the fantastic inevitably led him to American comic books, which, during his youth in the late 1960s and early 1970s, enjoyed a resurgence in both Great Britain and the United States. Gaiman consumed iconic stories from some of the form's most important authors and illustrators, like Jack Kirby's *Fantastic Four* and *Silver Surfer*, Stan Lee and Steve Ditko's *Spider-Man* (Campbell 26), and Will Eisner's seminal *The Spirit* (Gaiman, "Neil Gaiman on Will Eisner"), not to mention emerging names in the medium such as Denny O'Neil and Neil Adams's *Green Lantern* and *Batman* and Len Wein's *Swamp Thing* (Campbell 26). The measure and scope of high fantasies like *The Chronicles of Narnia* and *The Lord of the Rings* combined with the more accessible concepts of *The Spirit* and *Batman* affected Gaiman so powerfully that, in 1976, he declared to a guidance counselor that he wanted to become a comics writer. As one might imagine, his dreams were rebuffed (Wagner, Golden, and Bissette 228).

Gaiman remained unfazed by suggestions that he become an accountant or something more practical than a writer (228). Rather, he began writing professionally immediately after leaving preparatory school in 1977, foregoing college. Upon having difficulty selling his initial manuscripts, Gaiman turned instead to journalism, using the job as an opportunity to network and interview authors he idolized, including Clive Barker, Arthur C. Clarke, Terry Jones, and others. His first "successful" book was actually a commissioned biography of the band Duran Duran, and while the book was, in Gaiman's opinion, hastily written and poorly executed (Elder 76), it sold out its first print run and established Gaiman as a writer for popular audiences. This success translated to an opportunity to publish his first comics in 1986 with the British magazine *2000 AD* (Campbell 72). Read in conjunction with his collaboration with Dave McKean on *Violent Cases* (1987), Karen Berger, then an editor at DC Comics, reached out to Gaiman to publish what would become *Black Orchid* (1988–89), again with McKean). 1988 would prove to be a watershed year for Gaiman with the revival, or more properly, reconsideration, of a Golden Age hero of small renown with the first issue of *The Sandman*, published in November. Gaiman and his many illustrators' treatment of *The Sandman* would ultimately prove to be one of the most popular, profitable, and prized comics in DC's history. By the end of *The Sandman*'s run in 1996, Gaiman's place in the canon of comics was solidified alongside the very names he had idolized in his youth. Perhaps more importantly, though, these early works, undertaken most often in the spirit of continuation and collaboration, proved impactful to his career as they allowed Gaiman to work with some of the illustrators and industry professionals he would revisit throughout his career: Buckingham and McKean certainly, but also Mike Dringenberg, Sam Kieth, letterer Todd Klein, Chris Riddell, Mike Allred, P. Craig Russell, among so many others.

Of course, Gaiman's production is not limited to comic books. In fact, in this moment, he may be more renowned for his work *outside* the medium of comics and graphic novels. Even as his comics career was booming, Gaiman sold short stories and worked on early drafts of what would become his most famous novels. A fumbling draft of *Good Omens*, sent to eventual co-author Terry Pratchett in 1985, turned into Gaiman's "apprenticeship" with someone who he considered to be a master craftsman (Wigard xxxi). The novel, and an entirely reconfigured writer in Gaiman, emerged in 1990. Though his career was primarily dominated by *The Sandman* throughout the early 1990s, punctuated by short stories and collections, Gaiman set out on his own novels. First, with a reconceptualization of his BBC scripted televised serial *Neverwhere* (1996), but, more prominently, in 1999, Gaiman published his novelized fairy tale, *Stardust*, following it up with a string of what would be regarded as classics including *American Gods* (2001), *Coraline* (2002), *Anansi Boys* (2005), *The Graveyard Book* (2008), and *The Ocean at the End of the Lane* (2013). Even as he published these award-winning novels—both *American Gods* and *Coraline* were joint Hugo and Nebula winners in consecutive years, and *The Graveyard Book* remains the only book ever to win both the Carnegie and Newbery medals—Gaiman continued to work prolifically on other projects, completing screenplays for *MirrorMask*

(2005) and *Beowulf* (2007), the short fiction collections *Fragile Things* (2006) and *Trigger Warning* (2015), and, most recently, the short nonfiction collection *The View from the Cheap Seats* (2016) and the collection of Norse tales appropriately enititled *Norse Mythology* (2017). Amidst that work for an older audience, Gaiman produced considerable children's fare as well, including such works as *The Day I Swapped My Dad for Two Goldfish* (1997), *Wolves in the Walls* (2003), *Blueberry Girl* (2009), and *Chu's Day* (2013), among others.

Gaiman's oeuvre covers a breadth of variegated projects and articulates the uncategorizability of his work. He writes not merely as a high fantasist but also as an advocate for the disenfranchised and downtrodden. He will compose just as readily of the biography of real people as he will construct the complete life of an endless host of characters. He can scare and bedazzle children just as readily as he can adults, and he can do it in as little as a twenty-page comic or over several hundred pages detailing the lives of gods new and long-forgotten. In every case, Gaiman has been singled out time and again for the cultural value of his works, evidenced by the numerous awards his books have garnered. Looking only at his comics production, Gaiman's comics have been awarded twenty-six Eisner awards, three Harvey awards, two Bram Stoker awards, a Hugo award for *The Sandman: Overture*, a British Fantasy Award for *Whatever Happened to the Caped Crusader?*, and an Angoulême award. *The Sandman* no. 19, "A Midsummer Night's Dream," remains the only comic ever to win the World Fantasy Award for short fiction.

Gaiman in The Library, Briefly

In his Reading Agency Lecture, "Why Our Future Depends on Libraries, Reading, and Daydreaming," Gaiman elucidates quite clearly his *modus operandi* as an author:

> I'm going to suggest that reading fiction, that reading for pleasure, is one of the most important things one can do. . . . I write for children *and* for adults. . . . I don't think there is such a thing as a bad book for children [and] well-meaning adults can easily destroy a child's love of reading. . . . [A]ll writers—have an obligation to our readers; It's the obligation to write true things, especially important when we are creating tales of people who do not exist in places that never were—to understand that truth is not what happens but in what it tells us about who we are. Fiction is the lie that tells the truth. (emphasis ours, 5, 7, 13)

"The lie that tells the truth" is as nice and accurate a paradox that describes the important role fiction plays in explaining the human condition: that being a symbiosis between black and white, the verity in falsehoods, and all the other false binaries that need to be muddied lest they simplify life's rich complexities and, in turn, dehumanize us. Significantly, Gaiman points out that, despite the dominant assumption that children's fiction should be simple, children's writers are, or should be, the first to free the mind from the prisons of false binaries and other such supposed realities (9). And adult writers? Perhaps they are those folks who take us back to the pleasures of reading we first encountered as children.

But what if, as Gaiman muses, there's not really a meaningful difference between things written for adults and things written for children—*The Ocean at the End of the Lane* certainly calls these categories into question. Written for his wife, Amanda Palmer, from a place in his own childhood, Gaiman said the novel was an attempt to explain his childhood self to a woman who "doesn't really like fantasy, but she likes me. She likes honest stuff and feelings" (Liegl). It is written from the point of view of an adult reflecting on a troubling experience from his youth, providing the reader with a child protagonist with the cognitive and emotional reflections of an adult. *Ocean* defies simple categorizations. Against established norms and expectations of a child or adult reader, it resists being placed on any particular shelf of the library: it's reflective of an autobiographical moment in the author's life where a lodger at the Gaiman family residence committed suicide in their new car, an event recalled in the novel (Martin). It is also, though, assuredly a fantasy loaded with witches, hunger birds, and oceans concealed in puddles. It houses the same family, the Hempstocks, who populate his earlier works of children's fantasy, giving them a history the author always wanted to write for them. Reflecting on the book, Gaiman recalls:

> When I started [*Ocean*], I was writing a short story. At short story length you don't really have to worry that much about the potential audience. . . . I remember reading it to my agent—reading what there was of it, maybe the first three chapters—and saying, "Well, look, this is what I've got. I'm not even sure what it is yet. I think it might be a kids' story, but I don't want it to be that, I want it to be about an adult." And she said, "Well just write it, and don't worry." (Filgate)

Fair enough critique—it is the agent's job to solicit words from the writer, not to define them by genre or audience—but, for Gaiman, it still didn't settle the debate for him. Later, Gaiman gave the Zena Sutherland Lecture and, as he was composing that speech, he reflected over the corpus of his work and this new work he was in the process of writing, musing:

> As I was writing the speech and I was working on the book I was start-ing to think more about what makes something a children's book and what doesn't. And eventually, the conclusion I came to was that *Ocean* probably isn't a children's book, for reasons that have much more to do with how much hope I offer than anything else. You know, people grumble that *Coraline* is too scary for kids, but I don't think it is. But I also know that fundamentally *Coraline* is a book about being brave and about coping with adversity. (Filgate)

In that same reflection, he later went to describe himself in ways many chil-dren's authors do. Noted children's author and illustrator Maurice Sendak fa-mously once said to a somewhat incredulous Stephen Colbert that "I don't write for children. No, I write, and then someone says, 'That's for children.'" Not without coincidence, the epigraph to *The Ocean at the End of the Lane* is a quote from Sendak about childhood and the inescapable horrors encountered in one's youth. In conversation with comics author and illustrator Art Spiegel-man, Sendak said, "I remember my own childhood vividly. I knew terrible things. But I knew I mustn't let adults know I knew. It would scare them" (*Ocean*, Gaiman 1).

Critical Conversations Surrounding Gaiman

Sendak's observation concerning adults seems prescient concerning critical analysis regarding Gaiman. Despite Gaiman's increased exposure—particu-larly now as his works are readily being adapted in television, film, and ra-dio—scholarly work on one of comics' finest writers remains relatively in-consequential by comparison to his peers, titans like Alan Moore and Art Spiegelman. In a 2008 special issue of *ImageText*, dedicated to Gaiman's com-ics work, editors Philip Sandifer and Tof Eklund mused that:

> the question of introducing a special issue on Neil Gaiman seems almost incidental. Gaiman is one of those comics creators, along with Spiegel-man, Moore, Crumb and a few others, who one could assemble a special issue on without having to justify the worth of the endeavor. (1)

While critical engagement with his works has been sprinkled throughout literary criticism, comics scholarship, and philosophy for the better part of two decades, even now in 2018, Sandifer and Eklund's observation from that special issue still rings true:

> Everybody knows that Gaiman is a touchstone of comics scholarship. If anything the question seems to be "Why do we need more scholarship about Gaiman?" [. . . .] But that's where the problem comes up—the question is not why we need to say more about Gaiman. It's why, despite his iconic status, comics scholarship has said so little. (2)

Since that 2008 special issue, only a scant few book-length critical examinations of Gaiman have been published: Tracy L. Bealer, Rachel Luria, and Wayne Yuen's *Neil Gaiman and Philosophy: Gods Gone Wild!* (2012), part of Open Court Press' long-running "Popular Culture and Philosophy" series; Tara Prescott and Aaron Drucker's *Feminism in the Worlds of Neil Gaiman* (2012), a valuable popular-press edited collection; and Prescott's *Neil Gaiman in the 21st Century* (2015). Popular treatments have been equally sparse, composed of Hank Wagner, Christopher Golden, and Stephen R. Besette's *Prince of Stories: The Many Worlds of Neil Gaiman* (2008), and Hayley Campbell's *The Art of Neil Gaiman* (2014). The latter of that list, while not necessarily an academic investigation of Gaiman, is priceless due to the access to Gaiman's material given to Campbell who, a journalist herself, catalogued with a biographical and contextual investigation not seen before or since.

There remains a dearth of scholarly treatments at the level of the monograph or even anthologized collection examining the long-running concept of Gaiman's voice and authorial tone, let alone the construction of them within his visual narratives—and, aside from Campbell's recent work, of what there is, mostly focuses on *The Sandman*. From Joe Sanders's anthology *The Sandman Papers* (2006) to Alisa Kwitney's *The Sandman: King of Dreams* (2003) to Hy Bender's *Sandman Companion* (1999) to Steven Rauch's *The Sandman and Joseph Campbell* (2003), *The Sandman* is continually the primary locus of Gaiman scholarship. As such, this anthology tries to open up discussion on the many of his texts that have been left critically undiscovered. Of course, our writers *do* cover the touchstones like *The Sandman*, but we selected work that allowed us to expand access to those worlds by examining *The Sandman: Overture* and ancillary additions to that universe such as *The Sandman: The Dream Hunters*. At the same time, we have tried to demonstrate the breadth of scholarly lenses one could bring to bear on Gaiman's comics work, ranging from relatively strict formalism to queer theory and even, amazingly, mathematical theory and quantum entanglement. But we also understand that discussions of Gaiman, as with many comics creators, are also discussions about the collaborative work of putting both words and images on the page. To that end, we have included an interview with P. Craig Russell, who granted us a fresh perspective to the criticism through his insights into the design and adaptation of Gaiman's mostly verbal materials. It is through his viewpoint that we illuminate upon the existing criticism from the artist's vantage, a perspective that is often forgotten by standard volumes of literary criticism.

This anthology explores Gaiman's texts along three trajectories—deceptively lighter work, seemingly darker texts, and the liminal ones, those texts that exist somewhere between the poles like *Ocean*—often associated with his work and then interrogating those staid categorizations. It is here in the interstitial spaces between the expected or the obvious where we feel the trajectory of Gaiman's life's work has arrived. Undoubtedly, there are exceptions. We are not proposing a grand unifying theory of Gaiman's publishing career that somehow upends *Chu's Day* as a deceptively terrifying thought experiment. Our suggestion is that one of the major prohibitions to the larger cataloguing of Neil Gaiman's work, aside from such things as *Coraline* and *The Sandman*, might be that the collected body of his work occupies difficult and contrasting paths that resist longitudinal arguments. How, for example, does one reconcile the gentle gestures of *Crazy Hair*, a simple poem Gaiman composed for his daughter during a quiet moment at an academic conference, with the terrifying visions of a mother who has lost her son by abominable fashion in the 2013 short story "Down to A Sunless Sea"? Normally, we'd suggest, one would not place either of those two texts on the same scale let alone in juxtaposition. One is a children's book, a picture book at that, and one is a short fiction published in the *Guardian*. Ostensibly, they are two different texts for two different audiences in two distinctly different time periods.

Comics and comic books and even the concept of the graphic novel have moved and careened and sometimes been overtly thrust upon different audiences and into different mediums throughout their lengthy history. Quite often this has been done with arbitrary designators assigning some of these texts as "for adults" or "for young children" or as things indefinable unless someone chooses to place a designation upon them. The culturally imposed terminology of comics itself engenders this tension: children read *comic strips* and *comic books*, with emphasis placed on the humorous aspect of the term "comic." Meanwhile, *graphic novels*, prickly a term as it is, are misconstrued as the dead-serious fare of more mature tastes. But these categories and their attendant connotations are markedly contentious in practice. As Michelle Abate and Gwen Athene Tarbox showed in their anthology *Graphic Novels for Children and Young Adults* (2017), graphic novels are often designed *specifically* for children and teens, and the most celebrated comics arriving today are often deeply concerned with adult interests. Moreover, artists—a term we use loosely here to designate writers, illustrators, inkers, letterers, etc.—rarely seem to have interest in being exclusive to one audience in one genre in one mode or media. Arguably, the same Neil Gaiman and Dave McKean who crafted *Violent Cases* in 1987, showcasing a boy in Great Britain who was thrust into situations adult and possibly terrifying, are the same Neil Gaiman and Dave McKean who, in 2008, crafted another tale about a boy in Great Britain thrust into an unimaginably horrifying situation involving death, terror, and violence. Except that book, a clever retelling of *The Jungle Book*, won both Newbery and Carnegie Medals for the most outstanding work in children's fiction that year. Even though *Violent Cases* and *The Graveyard Book* are by the same two men using art and words, no one would find those two books as interchangeable by way of audience, book type, or, again arguably, even authorship, as would it not be fair to suggest that both Gaiman and McKean evolved in their art over the course of thirty years?

At the heart of this collection rests ideas and questions such as these. We would not suggest that we have filled all the gaps and chasms in the scholarship on Neil Gaiman. However, we would suggest that this book exists to not try and reconcile Neil Gaiman as a writer; instead, this collection serves to further tease out the threads of his career, exploring opportunities when he sought to be more overt in his authoritative motivations, be they more explicit or murky, into what we would argue becomes the more shadowy Neil Gaiman that catapulted him into the realms or superstardom by both audiences and critics alike. When Gaiman chose to stop being a writer who imitated the voices of the authors he idolized, he became an author comfortable with the voice he grew into. That voice articulates itself in sharp, terse prose, but it also edges its way between the boundaries of expectations. That voice knows where it is going, but it is also not afraid to take a few detours along the route to getting there, wherever that may be. Likewise, that voice might intone one way for a child and otherwise for a teen and certainly differently as an adult. That voice intentionally cradles valences and layers that can be peeled back like a narrative onion or left whole and read absently. In some cases, the further one peels down, the more mature a thing Gaiman composed might become, and the less appropriate for a younger reader it may be. That does not, however, preclude a child from reading it, or even an adult for that matter.

Methodology and Organization

We organized the essays in this volume focusing on three major criteria our contributors noted in Gaiman's body of work: the light, the dark, and the shadowy or liminal. Within Gaiman's works, these concepts signify many things, including questions of knowledge and ignorance, concerns about a diverse representation of audiences and ideas, or ways of seeing and failing to see the world. The first section is entitled "The Lighter Side of Neil Gaiman," because it brings together essays focused on texts from the prerogative of arising from good intentions, youthfully optimistic privilege, or even from a critical perspective, supposedly "lighter" genres. The writers examine ways in which the evolution of Gaiman's thinking on writing can be used to examine and reexamine the totality of his work, or the impact his work has on the genres and forms it takes. Ironically, in a book dedicated to visual literature, we chose to lead with an essay that discusses a book with no pictures.

Tara Prescott's essay, "Perspective, Empathy, and Activism: Neil Gaiman's *The View from the Cheap Seats*," asks a unique question: How does Gaiman's writing construct images in moments where no visuals are presented? An analysis of Gaiman's most recent nonfiction collection, *The View from the Cheap Seats*, it takes as its starting point the notion of situatedness *vis-à-vis* points of view, contending that it is precisely Gaiman's disarming "view from the nosebleed section" that allows him to make his incisive, meaningful interventions into the world outside his writing through his writing, activism by any other measure. The visual inflections in Prescott's reading of *View* are metaphorical as it examines the concepts of sight and blindness, position and disposition, visibility and invisibility. However, as Prescott reminds us, Gaiman's work, fictional and nonfictional, is intently focused on the project of "seeing further by building doors instead of walls" (16). In a similar manner, Kristine Larsen's essay, "Dreaming the Universe: *The Sandman: Overture*, Creation Myths, and the Ultimate Observer," notes how Gaiman's work flits between the mythic, the real, and the mythopoeic, drawing upon physics and mathematics to analyze the spooky action (at a distance) paradox that Gaiman constructs in *Overture*. The other works in this section, Krystal Howard's "Comics Grammar in Neil Gaiman and Dave McKean's Picture Book Collaborations" and Darren Harris-Fain's "Neil Gaiman and the Multifarious Approach to the Superhero," firmly locate the reader in the realm of comics discourses, conventions, and, in Harris-Fain's case, books, as two unique takes on Gaiman's approach to visual media. Howard reflects upon how Gaiman's picture books borrow the grammar of comics in ways that demonstrate his high esteem for the young reader, while Harris-Fain performs some much-needed classification of styles and approaches Gaiman has taken to the superhero genre over the course of his career, touching upon keystone works within it.

The second section, "'No Light, but Rather Darkness Visible': Illuminating Gaiman's Murky Page," delves into the more ill-lit recesses of Gaiman's work through articulating the paradox of making the darkness visible and visualizing that which can't otherwise be seen. The authors, here, work towards demystifying the less frequently observed aspects of Gaiman's narrative and bringing them to front and center of the reader's perception to see what underpins these texts. The first of these chapters traces how the unspeakable manifests in Gaiman's work. Christopher Kilgore's "At the Edge of the Barely Perceptible: Temporality and Masculinity in *Mr. Punch* and *Violent Cases*" analyzes venomous and abusive masculinities as drawn-out temporal trauma in some of Gaiman and McKean's darker works, *Violent Cases* and *The Tragical Comedy or Comical Tragedy of Mr. Punch* (1994). Likewise, in "'Evil Witch! I'm Not Scared!': Monstrous Visualizations of the Other Mother in Multimodal Adaptations of Neil Gaiman's *Coraline*," Justin Wigard examines the idea of the monstrous with three different representations of the Other Mother in *Coraline* and its many adaptations. Both essays comment upon the murky temporalities involved in trauma. While Kilgore's efforts demonstrate trauma's ability to reinscribe the present with past pain, Wigard's essay exemplifies the snowball effect that terror can have over time. Andrew Eichel's chapter, "Between Mimesis and Fantasy: Illuminating *The Books of Magic* through Kathryn Hume," explores the darkness of perception and representative modes, contending that through the genre of the fantastic, Gaiman attempts to resuscitate human pleasure in non-mimetic discourse. Reading Gaiman through Kathryn Hume, Eichel examines *The Books of Magic* (1990–91; second series 1994–2000) as a classic false-choice narrative, one which collapses the divide between mimesis and fantasy by demonstrating that life and fantasy, whether literary or extra-literary, are contingent upon being meaningful; that is, life matters only if is meaningful. For Eichel, magic and the fantastic are the tools that Gaiman wields to show how meaning can be made. Conversely, in "Inverted Spaces: Rising from the London Below and the Dark Lands in *Neverwhere* and *MirrorMask*," Züleyha Çetiner-Öktem contends that Gaiman constructs worlds that are not real, but are invesions of them with this inversion becoming the source of so much of his characters' power. Çetiner-Öktem suggests that arrival in "dark spaces," like the London Below of *Neverwhere* or the Brighton of Gaiman/McKean's *MirrorMask* (2005), enables otherwise marginalized and disempowered characters to find opportunities where they can thrive. These dark places defy the usual rules of mimetic space, fully embracing the fantastic, and this full embrace signals liberation for Gaiman's protagonists.

The third section of essays, "Gaiman's Brumous Boundaries and The Liminal Space," embraces the interstitial spaces and embodiments so frequently seen operating in Gaiman's work. Liminality, or a state of in-betweenness, is the keyword for this section. We begin with another examination of the non-fictional Neil Gaiman, or at least his online avatar, with Lanette Cadle's "The Shadow or the Self: The Construction of Neil Gaiman on Social Media." Cadle argues that Gaiman's construct of a ubiquitous online presence creates a very attractive and appealing character for Gaiman's audience. That character just happens to be Neil Gaiman (or @neilhimself). As such, Gaiman's fanbase and readership have seemingly become infatuated more with the avatar than the man himself, and in their desire for interaction with @neilhimself, the audience actually prohibits the author from crafting more of what attracted them to him in the first place. Then, in "Damsels in Deep Rest No More: The Coalescence of Light and Dark in *Blueberry Girl, The Wolves in the Walls, and The Sleeper and the Spindle*," Danielle Russell illuminates Gaiman's approach to feminism by reading his works for ladies of light, dark, and never-you-mind. Using *Blueberry Girl* (2009) as a method of reading *The Wolves in the Walls* (2003) and *The Sleeper and the Spindle* (2014), Russell suggests using Gaiman's more self-reflexive work as a cypher to decoding his literary fictions. She concludes that Gaiman incites his young women readers to be the fearless, confident blueberry girls he sees in his children and friend's children. Erica McCrystal then echoes Andrew Eichel's approach of utilizing classic approaches to literary criticism in "Liminality and the Gothic Sublime of *The Sandman*," reading *Sandman* as an example of the Gothic sublime. For McCrystal, liminality and subliminality interweave, infusing the text with fantastic opportunity and subversive potential. The collaboration of Renata Lucena Dalmaso and Thayse Madella pick apart the layered spaces in several of Gaiman's visual works in the chapter "Queering Space in Neil Gaiman's Illustrated Works." Ultimately, they note that much of his writing pushes toward a queering of space, that is, a rendering of it as illegible to traditional modes of representation. The closing chapter, "Weaving New Dreams from Old Cloth: Conceptual Blending & Hybrid Identities in Neil Gaiman's Fairy-Tale Retellings" by Anna Katrina Gutierrez, tracks the disparate flows of narrative cloth Gaiman selects and braids. Noting that he pulls from classic storytelling schematics, Gutierrez identifies a paradoxical mesh of innovative and traditional threads. She notes that Gaiman's work, even at its most new and subversive, looks so much like historical fact or tried-and-true mythology that it is difficult to disentangle fact from myth.

In our closing section, "'The world always seems brighter when you've just made something that wasn't there before': Afterthoughts, Filters, and Interviews," we close in the spirit of a Neil Gaiman collection focused intently on work which is almost entirely collaboration: collaborative examinations of the collection itself. Joe Sutliff Sanders's coda provides a reading of the critical work these essays undertake and offers a glimpse of possible avenues of inquiry aspiring scholars might consider as Gaiman's body of work continues to grow and evolve. Then, in interviews with frequent Gaiman collaborator P. Craig Russell (with Kyle and Joe) and, of course, Gaiman himself (with Joe), we take the rare opportunity to speak with the creators and get their views on their work and the scholarly thought surrounding it.

At introduction's close, we want to be explicit: Latin or no Latin, these words are meant to be read and are meant to start a conversation, perhaps one that's long overdue. Certainly, as Tara Prescott smartly reminded us in the introduction to *Neil Gaiman in the 21st Century*, "to be a scholar or fan of Neil Gaiman is to become okay with the fact that you cannot cover it all" (1). And we did not cover it all. But we did tax the limits of what one could fit between two covers and roughly 100,000 words. We hope that this conversation, like Gaiman's works, continues and evolves as more and more people find their way to his writings. It is our hope that this collection brings the reader some inspiration to speak forth and continue the dialogue. It was in that spirit of collaboration that this book was crafted, and it is in that spirit that we wish to leave you.

JOSEPH MICHAEL SOMMERS AND KYLE EVELETH, 2018

WORKS CITED

Campbell, Hayley. *The Art of Neil Gaiman*. HarperCollins, 2014.

Colbert, Stephen. "Grim Colberty Tales with Maurice Sendak Pt. 1—The Colbert Report." *The Colbert Report*. Comedy Central, n.d.

Gaiman, Neil. *Ocean at the End of the Lane*. William Morrow, 2016.

Gaiman, Neil. *Smoke and Mirrors*. William Morrow, 1998.

Gaiman, Neil. "Neil Gaiman on Will Eisner: 'He Thought Comics Were An Art Form—He Was Right." *Guardian*, 7 March 2017. Accessed 1 February 2017.

Gaiman, Neil. "Why Our Future Depends on Libraries, Reading, and Daydreaming: The Reading Agency Lecture," *The View from The Cheap Seats*. HarperCollins, 2016, pp. 5–16.

Gaiman, Neil. "The Zena Sutherland Lecture: What the (Very Bad Swearword) is a Children's Book Anyway?" *The View from The Cheap Seats*. HarperCollins, 2016, pp. 77–94.

Filgate, Michele. "Locked in the Sweetshop: Seven Questions for Neil Gaiman." *Poets & Writers*, n.p., n.d. Accessed 25 August 2017.

Jerome. *Vulgate* Gospel of John. 1.5.

Holden, Desmond. "What's in a Name, HENSTOCK?" *Peak Advertiser*, n.p., n.d. Accessed 25 August 2017.

Liegl, Andy. "Gaiman Talks *Sandman*, Walks to *The Ocean at the End of the Lane*." *Comic Book Resources*, n.p., 11 August 2016. Accessed 25 August 2017.

Lough, Chris. "This Doesn't Have to Be the World You Live In. Neil Gaiman on 'Why Fiction Is Dangerous.'" *Tor*, n.p., 14 December 2014. Accessed 25 August 2017.

Martin, Tim. "Neil Gaiman: 'I Wanted to Write My Wife a Story.'" *Telegraph*, 8 June 2013.

Prescott, Tara. "Introduction." *Neil Gaiman in the 21st Century: Essays on the Novels, Children's Stories, Online Writings, Comics and Other Works*. McFarland, 2015, pp. 1–8.

Prescott, Tara. "Visual Perspective, Empathy, and Activism: Neil Gaiman's *The View from the Cheap Seats*." *The Artistry of Neil Gaiman*. Joseph Michael Sommers and Kyle Eveleth, eds. University Press of Mississippi, 2019, pp. 3–20.

Sandifer, Philip, and Tof Eklund. "Editor's Introduction." *ImageText* vol. 4, no. 1, 2008.

Thomas, Marlyn. "'What is She?': Neil Gaiman's Intertextual Conversation on Female Artistry in *Coraline* and *The Ocean at the End of the Lane*." *Critical Insights: Neil Gaiman*. Joseph Michael Sommers, ed. Salem/Grey House, 2016, pp. 96–111.

Wagner, Hank, Christopher Golden, and Stephen R. Bissette. *Prince of Stories: The Many Worlds of Neil Gaiman*. St. Martin's Press, 2009.

Wannamaker, Annette "Guilty Pleasures: Neil Gaiman's Books for Children for Adults." *Critical Insights: Neil Gaiman*. Joseph Michael Sommers, ed. Salem/Grey House, 2016, pp. 67–80.

Wigard, Justin. "Biographical Sketch of Neil Gaiman." *Critical Insights: Neil Gaiman*. Joseph Michael Sommers, ed. Salem/Grey House, 2016, pp. xxix–xxxvi.

The Lighter Side of Neil Gaiman

PERSPECTIVE, EMPATHY, AND ACTIVISM
Neil Gaiman's *The View from the Cheap Seats*

TARA PRESCOTT

In 1981, folk singer Harry Chapin was performing his 2,000th concert in front of a live audience in New York. As he neared the end of "30,000 Pounds of Bananas," his tragicomic vehicular ballad, Chapin re-energized, escalating, singing faster and faster until reaching a feverish crescendo that matched the pace of an out-of-control semi-truck burdened with bananas careening towards Scranton, Pennsylvania. "Almost 30,000 pounds," Chapin sang, then invited the people "upstairs in the cheap seats" to call out the rest of the line. "Of bananas!" they crowed in return. With a laugh, Chapin noted, "You can always count on the cheap seats" (Chapin).

Chapin, of course, was not the first entertainer to appreciate the undying loyalty (and gleeful, drunken participation) of the people who can only afford the cheapest tickets and the worst views. As an American folk musician, he would seem a far cry from a soft-spoken *New York Times* bestselling British author. But as Neil Gaiman notes in *The View from the Cheap Seats*, references to other artists lead readers to new discoveries, so if reading this chapter leads you to Google "30,000 Pounds of Bananas," you may well find a serendipitous synchronicity between a singer playfully memorializing the final moments of a blue collar truck driver and an author known for writing about an ex-con roadtripping with gods across America.[1]

Gaiman's first collection of nonfiction is titled, appropriately enough, *The View from the Cheap Seats*. The dozens of works gathered in *Cheap Seats* are diverse, culled from public speeches and book introductions, often in celebration of librarians, authors, artists, and musicians, offering Gaiman's view of events and popular culture. The individual pieces are nearly all stand-alones, which can lead to a fractured reading experience. And, in many ways, thinking critically about *The View from the Cheap Seats* entails a similarly disjointed process.[2] Nonetheless, when the essays in *Cheap Seats* are analyzed together, a trajectory emerges. First, Gaiman emphasizes perspective in several ways throughout the collection, mainly by drawing on the arts. Second, he builds on the perspectival nature of the arts in general, and literature specifically, to adopt the perspective of another as a means of building empathy. Finally, acknowledging what it means to inhabit the perspective of another, he utilizes empathy as a catalyst for social change, compelling the reader to take action. Collectively, Gaiman emphasizes vision and point of view in *The View from the Cheap Seats* as a strategy to inhabit the position of the vulnerable or disenfranchised, including children and refugees, to draw attention to unheard voices and propel the reader into taking action.

Seeing Through Gaiman's Eyes: *The View from the Cheap Seats*

As a running metaphor, Gaiman crafts the collection from his perspective—the "cheap seats" in the title references his experience as a mildly clumsy author hidden amidst movie stars at the 2010 Academy Awards, where he admired, then accidentally stepped on, Rachel McAdams's dress. The title essay is a comedic but thoughtful piece about Gaiman privately mourning on the anniversary of his father's death while begrudgingly participating in such a surreal public spectacle. The title is a reminder of a collective vision of regular people—that even someone who has been invited to the Oscars can feel like an outsider. In an interview with Tyler Malone, Gaiman confesses, "What I like about 'The View from the Cheap Seats' as the title for the collection is that most of the things that I'm talking about are not exactly pop culture nor exactly low culture, but they are the areas of culture that don't often get commented on" (Malone). This includes science fiction, fantasy, horror, comics, and alternative music, but also, by the end of the collection, the plight of Syrian refugees. The cheap seats are far from the action, on the periphery, but general admission is the perspective that many audiences and readers share. "I tend to write about things from wherever I am standing," Gaiman notes in the introduction (xvii). This concept is often quite literal—such as staying at Jim Henson's home in England while writing the script for the *Labyrinth*-inspired film *MirrorMask* (*Cheap Seats* 206), but it can also be figurative. Gaiman immerses himself in particular places, both physical and emotional, writing from where he is.

Devoted readers of Gaiman's fiction are likely familiar with the experience of identifying with his characters' points of view and the challenges they face. But what is unique and revealing about *The View from the Cheap Seats* is that it shows that Gaiman sees his work not just as a source of enjoyment and storytelling pleasure but also as a call to action. In his nonfiction, Gaiman can be more direct with his readers about the actions he wants them to take in the real world. Like much of Gaiman's work, *Cheap Seats* heavily emphasizes perspective, vision, and view. Many of Gaiman's novels are marked with playful, almost superfluous details that gives them a cinematic texture, and this quality has no doubt figured into why so many of his works have been made into successful audio, illustrated, and filmed adaptations. Gaiman paints his scenes with words, and what characters see—or think they see—is of utmost importance in his texts. Analyzing the multilayered ways that Gaiman utilizes vision and perspective in his nonfiction essays shows how he uses this genre to motivate audiences to take particular actions dependent on the subject matter or concern. Whereas Gaiman's fiction encourages reader identification as part of a pleasurable, immersive reading experience, his nonfiction goes one step further to compel the readers to take action and effect change in their own lives. Examining his use of vision and the arts—both as metaphors and literally in his fiction (as described in *Cheap Seats*) and in his nonfiction (as collected in *Cheap Seats*)—shows Gaiman's complex, polyvalent approach to crafting perspective and weaponizing an audience through its employ.

In considering the visual elements in Gaiman's works in terms of their connections to perspective, his early, famous examples from comics immediately come to mind, such as his collaborative efforts on *Black Orchid*, *The Sandman*, and *Marvel: 1602*. It is not surprising that Gaiman made the leap to visual forms of storytelling so successfully, since he was raised on comics from a young age. Gaiman's early forays into literature as a young reader were heavily influenced by visual forms of storytelling, especially comics by groundbreaking artists like Jack Kirby (to whom Gaiman dedicates an essay in *Cheap Seats*). Likewise, he was also influenced by film and television. He first saw a black-and-white television episode of *The Lion, the Witch and the Wardrobe* when he was six years old, and then begged for the boxed set (32). "I remember what I did on my seventh birthday—I lay on my bed and read the books all through, from the first to the last," Gaiman recalls (32). Reading the works of C. S. Lewis and other members of the Inklings had a profound effect on Gaiman and certainly influenced his later forays in fantasy (33). Gaiman reveals that "the genius of Lewis was that he made a world more real to me than the one I lived in" (35).

Other visually striking—indeed, usually televisual—narratives, including the original *Doctor Who* series, helped shape a prose aesthetic with a strong visual sensibility (Brew). As such, working in visual mediums allowed Gaiman not only to collaborate frequently, but also to see his work translated through others' eyes: "Comics have the joy that you never see in prose: the joy of being able to enjoy your own stuff. I can't enjoy a prose story I wrote, but I can enjoy what Dave McKean or Charles Vess or Jon Muth or P. Craig Russell does to one of my stories," he reveals (243). Gaiman's comics are an obvious starting point for analyzing the visual aspects of his texts. However, analyzing his prose also reveals a great deal about the way Gaiman thinks about and utilizes the visual in his work.

Gaiman frequently blurs the boundaries between visual art and the written word, emphasizing individual perception, both in content and in form. This frequent genre-bending makes classifying and analyzing his work difficult. For example, the "Also by Neil Gaiman" page in *Cheap Seats* uses the term "Illustrated Stories" to describe the texts with pictures that at first glance might seem like "children's books," but which have text-to-image ratios and themes that might indicate older readers.[3] These works are separated from the more obvious "picture books," which are labeled simply "For Younger Readers." The same list in Gaiman's short fiction collection *Trigger Warning* avoids the problem altogether by simply dividing everything Gaiman has written into either "For Adults" or "For all Ages." Whether collaborating with artists and illustrators or placing his text alongside images for his online journaling and blog posts, Gaiman demonstrates a heightened awareness of the visual aspects of his texts and a disregard for the stigma of illustrations marking a text as "less serious" or "for kids."

Gaiman's refusal to replicate the hierarchy that distinguishes adult fiction from children's literature, high culture from low, is evident in his embrace of film and television as well, and they also become ways that he considers point of view. His short essays on films, published in *Cheap Seats*, articulate a commitment to navigating the visual and the linguistic in what might be traditionally regarded as "low" genres, or popular forms of media. "Films deliver their pleasures in different ways," he writes at the start of "The Bride of Frankenstein" (201). He describes the film as "oneiric, a beautiful, formless sequence of silver nitrate shadows," and in this elegant description, deploys the adjectival form of one of the names for Sandman's Morpheus, Oneiros (of or related to dreams). It is a reminder that the root of myths is oral storytelling, but that the language of dreams is mostly visual. The connection between dreams, fiction, and film appears in several of Gaiman's essays; he notes that film "sits in the mind like a dream" (203) and curiously describes film and television as "watched fiction" (*Cheap Seats* 217).

Not surprisingly then, he draws upon conventions of "watched fiction" in the ways his nonfiction presents perspective. Occasionally in the speeches published in *Cheap Seats*, Gaiman addresses the audience in almost screenplay narration fashion. For example, in "Good Comics and Tulips: A Speech," he narrates: "Picture the scene: seventeenth-century Holland. Imagine the screen going all wavy at this point, and a hasty montage of wooden clogs, windmills, dykes with fingers in them, and red-wax-wrapped cheeses that taste more or less like yellow rubber" (230). Playfully using filmic discourse like "picture," "screen," and "montage" to describe the scene, Gaiman draws upon the strengths of one medium while creating in another. This appears again in *Cheap Seats* in another form with the introduction to his edited volume *Best American Comics: 2010*. He bookends the piece with a "script for an undrawn comic" starring himself as editor: "He has the little potbelly of a man who has spent too much of his life behind a desk and the haunted expression of a man one missed deadline away from disaster" (309). The beginning and ending of the introduction are presented in this format, down to the typewriter font.

Gaiman's nonfiction about fiction also mimics conventions of scripts and screenplays, blurring the line between text and visual art. There are several metatextual moments in *Cheap Seats* where Gaiman breaks the fourth wall and addresses the reader, such as the introduction to Douglas Adams's *So Long, and Thanks for All the Fish*, where he asks the reader to skip ahead:

I'll be here when you get back.
No, I mean it.
I'll put down some asterisks. I'll see you after them, when you've read the book.
* * * (367)

This passage echoes Gaiman's advice from his earlier fiction collection *Trigger Warning*: "Welcome to these pages. You can read about the stories you will encounter here, or you can skip this and come back and see what I have to say after you've read the stories. I'm easy" (xvii). These playful moments remind readers of Gaiman's awareness of audience and reader participation. As he writes in *Cheap Seats*, "No two readers can or will ever read the same book, because the reader builds the book in collaboration with the author" (40). In this and many other *Cheap Seats* essays, Gaiman performs the very trick that he commends the subject of the essay for. For example, he honors

Douglas Adams's ability to create prose that breaks "the fourth wall and the author-reader compact" right after doing it himself (371). And, in describing the way that James Branch Cabell uses ironic footnotes to explain references to well-known figures, Gaiman then asks, "after all, who today would bother with an explanatory footnote of John Grisham" and then promptly footnotes John Grisham, John Major, and Howard Stern.

These examples demonstrate Gaiman's playful adoption of conventions from the visual and performing arts within his prose, and the ways he utilizes them to create a social awareness. In terms of music, for example, he wrote twelve vignettes to accompany Tori Amos's self-portraits for her 2001 album, *Strange Little Girls*, as well as introductions to her tour books for *Under the Pink* and *To Venus and Back* (reprinted in *Cheap Seats*).[4] He also wrote text to accompany Amanda Palmer's self-portraits for the book connected to her album *Who Killed Amanda Palmer*. This "collection of photographic evidence," like Amos's self-portraits, is in the style of artist Cindy Sherman—each image contains the artist, in this case Palmer, elaborately costumed as an imagined character. The photographs, done by Kyle Cassidy, Beth Hommel, and others, are presented alongside Palmer's lyrics and Gaiman's text. For example, one black-and-white photo of a dead, naked woman on the floor, with costume jewelry flowing from her gaping mouth, is accompanied by a story about a girl that has diamonds and rubies spilling from her lips (Gaiman's spin on a classic fairy tale by Charles Perrault).

Gaiman was present for many of the photographs, and was inspired by the collaboration he witnessed. "The photographs Kyle took were like stills in lost films, and I would write stories to accompany them," Gaiman notes (*Trigger Warning* xxxiii). He later published the story of the choking girl as "Diamonds and Pearls: A Fairy Tale" in *Trigger Warning*. But *Cheap Seats* returns to the fiction of Palmer's "death" in a new way by including "Who Killed Amanda Palmer," a short piece about where Gaiman was when he "heard Amanda Palmer had been killed"—one of the few essays in *Cheap Seats* that playfully calls the veracity of the nonfiction into question (419). This essay, like many others, points both to an interest in writing about art but also the connection between the visual and the textual in Gaiman's writing, and the fluidity with which he moves between them.

It is clear that the visual arts provide inspiration for Gaiman's work, and that is important because of how perspectival the arts are: he turns to these modes and forms precisely because they let him explore the point of view of the outsider. He also uses visual elements in other ways, including as analogies for writing, imagination, memory, and dreaming. For example, in describing the experience of reading stories by Anthony Martignetti, Amanda Palmer's lifelong friend (and namesake for their baby Ash), Gaiman reveals, "each of the stories shone a light into Anthony's skull and showed the reader the view from his past" (486). Here, Gaiman figures the act of reading as vision, a way to see inside another person's head, to view a person's past from his or her own perspective. In the cinema of the skull, memory transports and connects the maker and the audience. This is a trope that Gaiman returns to multiple times in his nonfiction. For example, he writes that publishing allows "other people [to] look inside your head" (489). This idea even reappears in *Norse Mythology*, Gaiman's retelling of ancient Norse tales: "Look up into the sky: you are looking at the inside of Ymir's skull . . . And the clouds you see by day? These were once Ymir's brains, and who knows what thoughts they are thinking, even now" (33).

Gaiman returns to the analogies of writing as visual and performing art in several places in *Cheap Seats*. He frequently describes writing and imagination in terms of painting, calling his own imagination an "inner landscape" (83), noting that "[b]ehind every Chesterton sentence there was someone painting with words" (37), and that Chesterton "begins almost every story by painting in light" (344). He celebrates the limits of vision: "Technology does nothing to dispel the shadows at the edge of things. The ghost-story world still hovers at the limits of vision, making things stranger, darker, more magical, just as it always has" (50). And in his introduction to H. G. Wells's *The Country of the Blind and Other Stories*, Gaiman notes that the tales "remind us that they are, in some sense, eyewitness reports, with all the limitations and power of such. We are told repeatedly what was seen, and only a little more, and are left to draw our own inferences" (330). These examples demonstrate the ways that visual art informs and inspires Gaiman's nonfiction pieces from *The View from the Cheap Seats*. However, the more important way that vision functions in this collection is in terms of subject matter—in how Gaiman posits that point of view fosters the ability to empathize with others, and, by the end of the collection, to translate empathy into action.

Seeing Through Others' Eyes: Empathy as a Function of Reading

The opening essays in *The View from the Cheap Seats* focus on the importance of literacy, literature, bookstores, and authors in creating an empathetic population. Gaiman analyzes the benefits of reading, particularly reading fiction. He notes that "[i]t is the function of imaginative literature to show us the world we know, but from a different direction" (59) and, later, "[t]he magic and danger of fiction is this: it allows us to see through other eyes" (415). One of the benefits of reading fiction, Gaiman notes, is that it builds empathy:

> When you watch TV or see a film, you are looking at things happening to other people. Prose fiction is something you build up from twenty-six letters and a handful of punctuation marks, and you, and you alone, using your imagination, create a world, and people it and look out through other eyes. You get to feel things, visit places and worlds you would never otherwise know. You learn that everyone else out there is a me, as well. You're being someone else, and when you return to your own world you're going to be slightly changed. (8)

In this passage, Gaiman emphasizes a point that is both deceptively simple and sadly elusive: "everyone else out there is a me." It is a reminder to recognize the humanity of all people, even those "you would never otherwise know." Gaiman's version of this concept has a lot in common with the take on morality by Stephen Pinker, a professor of psychology at Harvard. According to Pinker, "At heart, morality is treating other people the way one would want to be treated oneself; and some version of that, of interchangeability of perspectives. It's the fact that I'm not the only entity in the universe, and I have no grounds for privileging my interests over yours" (Pinker). Pinker is so adamant about fiction's role in empathy, in fact, that he calls it "a kind of moral technology" (Pinker and Goldestein 49). According to Gaiman, the power of this "moral technology" is not just to recognize others, but to be "changed" by the experience.

This may seem like common sense, yet this approach to relations with others is surprisingly difficult. According to Suzanne Keen:

> Experiments in social psychology have already taught us a great deal about the limitations of empathy . . . Whether it is construed as familiarity, similarity, or 'in-group' bias, the reduction of response to those who seem strange, dissimilar, or outside the tribe has been attributed to human evolution [*Empathy and Moral Development* 206]. This phenomenon can be read as prejudice or ethnocentrism or possibly as a practical response to a social world that makes too many demands on our feelings—we have to use some kind of sorting mechanism. (19)

Gaiman's fiction frequently presents characters facing "those who seem strange, dissimilar, or outside the tribe," and perhaps, test the reader's own "limitations of empathy." Gaiman's claims about the power of fiction to promote empathy are part of a much larger historical debate among scholars and researchers, which has resulted in conflicting findings. In summarizing debates about empathy and literature from cognitive literary scholars, Hogan notes:

> The study of literature may train our spontaneous emotional response and inference in everyday life ([Keith] Oatley); it may contribute to our self-conscious adjudication of moral and prudential aspects of emotional reasoning ([Martha] Nussbaum); and it may be part of our developing theoretical comprehension of emotion ([Semir] Zeki and Patrick Colm Hogan]. (287)

Keen is critical of many studies that conclude that students reading fiction become more empathetic, noting that in classrooms the practice of reading does not happen in isolation, and many studies "conflate reading, discussion, role-taking activities, writing tasks, and teaching" with simply "reading fiction" (xiv). She also highlights the chicken-and-egg problem in studying empathy and reading: "Do empathetic people make good readers, or do good readers become empathetic people? Both may be true without guaranteeing that novels routinely do more than entertain, inform, soothe, or excite their readers" (xv). Yet, cognitive literary scholars like Keen who are skeptical of the claims about reading-as-empathy-building still nonetheless note connections. "Readers' cognitive and affective responses do not inevitably lead to empathizing, but fiction does disarm readers of some sense of the protective layers of cautious reasoning that may inhibit empathy in the real world," Keen writes (28).

The importance of visualizing others via reading and empathizing with them is not only to recognize one's own pain and experience in the experience of others (in literary terms, to have the reader identify with a sympathetic narrator), but also to experience something which is physically impossible—what it is to be someone else. Our own perspectives and experiences color everything we perceive, and literature—both nonfiction and fiction—may be the closest we can get to truly seeing from another point of view.

In his fiction, Gaiman's characters are often empathetic, everyday people—children frustrated by their parents (*Coraline*), adolescents trying to understand their identities and place in the world (*The Graveyard Book, The Ocean at the End of the Lane*), adults grappling with loss (*American Gods*), young lovers slowly realizing that they have chosen the wrong romantic partners (*Neverwhere, Stardust*, "How to Talk to Girls at Parties"). In Gaiman's novels, these common, universal challenges and rites of passage often occur in fantastical settings: ghostly graveyards, fairy realms, and parallel worlds.

Gaiman's fiction often offers the protection of fantasy, where the reader is comfortably one step removed from the threats of the story because of unreal elements such as magic. Gaiman's heroes frequently experience the fantastic, and they usually must choose to sacrifice some part of themselves in order to help others. Their choices and experiences may mirror our own world, or help us to make parallels to our experience, but they are not of *our* world. Rather, they are a close version of the world with the magic magnified. We empathize with these characters, and may make connections between their experience and our own, but the onus is on the reader to make those leaps.

Gaiman's nonfiction, however, requires less of a leap—it can be explicitly about the real world in ways that the fiction cannot. The nonfiction, as demonstrated by *Cheap Seats*, is self-consciously and purposely about our world, and the stakes are higher: the protagonists are real, and the fates they face, including death, cannot be undone. Perhaps the strongest example of this is Gaiman's essay, "So Many Ways to Die in Syria Now: May 2014," which was originally published by the *Guardian* and reprinted in *Cheap Seats* in 2016, just as xenophobia and hysteria about refugees fueled Brexit in England and Donald Trump's presidential campaign in the United States, leading to the travel ban in the US against primarily Muslim people in early 2017. Intertextualization, as such, between Gaiman's socially conscious nonfiction and his socially conscious magical fiction is vital because it creates overlapping messages across genres, where each text informs the others, creating major themes across his work.

In reading *Neverwhere*, for example, we are being prepared to consider the very real crisis of homelessness unfolding in our own cities, and by extension, of the refugee crisis occurring in Syria. When protagonist Richard Mayhew stumbles across an injured, confused woman on his way to an important dinner with his fiancée, he chooses to stop and help her, even if it means losing his fiancée (17). Mayhew is an everyday, decent, otherwise unremarkable protagonist—but he chooses to come to a stranger's aid, setting off a chain of events that drive the novel. Mayhew does not know it, but he is following the advice of Gaiman's *Instructions*. In this book, the message, beautifully rendered by Charles Vess, is very clear: "If any creature tells you it hungers, feed it. If it tells you that it is dirty, clean it. If it cries to you that it hurts, if you can, ease its pain." The lesson, explained as the protagonist cat lifts up an injured tabby kitten, is simple and easy for children to follow. The same lesson drawn to its inevitable conclusion in the modern world is far more complex, but calls for a similar action. As Gaiman writes in "So Many Ways to Die in Syria Now: May 2014," the people of Syria are deeply, tragically, inexplicably suffering. And rather than rise to the call of *Instructions*, many industrialized nations are in fact recoiling, doubling down on their efforts to seal their borders and resist rendering aid. As Gaiman writes, "The Jordanian people and government have shown exceptional generosity. There are six million people in Jordan: the Syrian refugees make up 10 percent of the population. If Britain were to do the same proportionally, it would mean accepting six and a half million refugees" (493). What Gaiman does not explicitly state, of course, is that Britain has not accepted anywhere near that number. What counts as a "fair share" of refugees is under debate, but a 2016 Oxfam report showed that "[t]he UK ranks twelfth in the league of the world's 28 wealthiest nations after resettling just 4414 refugees" (Roberts).

As a British citizen living in the United States, Gaiman is acutely aware of the extent to which his native and adopted countries are failing to follow some of the basic principles of *Instructions*, particularly in terms of helping refugees. In 2016, the UK passed the "Dubs amendment" to the Immigration Act (named for former Jewish child refugee Alfred Dubs), pledging to take in 3,000 unaccompanied refugee children. And then they reversed their decision. "I thought it was cowardice," Gaiman stated in an interview. "We help children. That's what human beings do. The idea that we would leave 3,000 children in situations where they are at danger, at risk . . . where terrible things are happening to them. To me, seemed almost inconceivable" (Newman). As a writer of fiction, Gaiman can encourage empathy and illuminate patterns of behavior in the hopes that his audience will take the message to its inevitable conclusion in the modern day. But as a writer of nonfiction, he can cut to the chase: he can explicitly describe what needs to be done. He can combine the strengths of fiction and nonfiction to increase the likelihood of facilitating change.

He does this in "So Many Ways to Die in Syria Now" by situating the story within a specific geographic/visual-spatial scene. He also writes in the present tense, highlighting the immediacy: "We are in a metal shed in Azraq refugee camp, Jordan, sitting on a low mattress, talking to a couple who have been here since the camp opened two weeks ago" (491). The "we" of the opening is unclear—Gaiman is clearly the speaker, but his companions are unnamed. The essay later reveals that Gaiman is traveling with a designer and film producer, but the initial "we" also includes the readers, time-traveling back to May 2014 while also aware of the continuing crisis in their own time, seeing the desperation and uncertainty of growing numbers of refugees. The essay's title comes from the refugee Yalda's explanation of life before fleeing Syria. "We woke up every morning glad we were alive, and went to sleep every night knowing we might not wake in the morning. There are so many ways to die in Syria now," she states matter-of-factly (492).

To focus on the victims rather than the perpetrators, Gaiman uses passive voice and sudden, blunt short sentences: "People were killed" (491). He names some of the people, and faceless, anonymous refugees from newspaper reports become Abu Hani and Yalda—even as Gaiman acknowledges the names are pseudonyms for the refugees' protection. Names are important. They are one step closer to helping readers imagine what it is like to be a refugee. Many Syrians are also parents, and many who are suffering are children. For Gaiman, it was powerful to read about and visit the camps, but the birth of his son sharpened the pain of knowing how many children in particular are cruelly suffering. "Reading about what's happening in Aleppo is soul-numbing," writes Gaiman. "I supported refugees before Ash came along, but having him here makes it feel so real and immediate: I remember the people I saw entering the camps in Jordan who had carried their own babies and small children for hundreds of miles to get them to safety" (Gaiman "Where Do You Run?").

Gaiman notes that "[t]he Jordanian people and government have shown exceptional generosity" before addressing the topic at hand—what can and should industrialized nations in the West do (493)? And, in reading this essay several years after it was originally written, we now know that for many wealthy nations, the response has been to seal their own borders. "Before I came out here, I tried to imagine what a refugee camp would be like," Gaiman writes, reminding us not only of how the privilege of living in the West keeps many people from wondering, much less, seeking out information about people suffering in other parts of the world. Through his nonfiction and the documentary-styled sequences he posts online, Gaiman offers a glimpse, a type of empathetic contact that he hopes will lead to stronger action. This is a view of *these* refugees, in *this* specific camp.

The inverse relationship between the size of a tragedy and our ability to visualize the people who suffer from it, to feel sympathy and empathy for them, is constructed to be especially tragic in effect. The greater the number of refugees, the more difficult it is to conceptualize the crisis. Striking visual images, such as the photograph of three-year-old Alan Kurdi's body washed up on a beach in Turkey that went viral in the summer of 2015, can quickly spark change. But adding another news story into an already saturated social media feed does not change much. What can artists and creators like Gaiman do to boost the signal?

Measuring the efficacy of raising awareness about social issues online is difficult, with some positing that social media activism results in just feel-good "slacktivism," without real change. Nevertheless, Gaiman and Amanda Palmer have taken several actions to draw more attention to these vital issues. In 2017, Palmer released a music video collaboration with choreographer Abel Azcona, "In Harm's Way," inspired by Alan Kurdi and the global refugee crisis. Gaiman posted a link to the NPR post featuring the video on October 30, the day of its release. "Do not watch the video or listen to the song unless you are ready to feel things about humanity," he wrote. In drawing attention to Palmer's work, Gaiman continued his long-established trend of raising awareness about the refugees via social media. It is one of many reasons why the UN Refugee Agency was so drawn to his advocacy. "UNHCR had noticed that when I retweeted their tweets and appeals, more people read them and acted on what they had read," Gaiman reveals (494). And so they invited him to visit the camps and a partnership was born. The UNHCR acknowledged his efforts by appointing Gaiman as a global Goodwill Ambassador in 2017 (UNHCR).

Towards the end of the "So Many Ways to Die in Syria," Gaiman's messages about perception, point of view, empathy, and the need to take action to help others become explicit: "I have stopped thinking about political divides, about freedom fighters or terrorists, about dictators and armies. I am thinking only of the fragility of civilization. The lives the refugees had were *our* lives" (496, emphasis added). Rather than fighting about political sides, his call to action is to be "on the side of people" (497). The gravity of this essay is partially why it is placed under the heading, "The View from the Cheap Seats: Real Things" in the collection. It is another reminder of the view from the lowest structures of society, the most "real" stories within an already "real" collection. This is the view from the people many choose not to see, desperate people who lack the most basic necessities—safety, water, shelter, protection—that the privilege of most Western readers blinds them to. It may also hint at a harder truth: this is a view that entire countries are walling off, refusing to see.

As Elizabeth Law notes, "Gaiman reminds us that the truth of history is the tale the victor tells" and that his "shift[s] in narration [remind] the reader that there is another version, told from someone else's perspective" (190). In his fiction, Gaiman is very invested in characters living at the margins—borders that become heartbreakingly literal in his nonfiction. Because Gaiman's nonfiction both predicts and reflects many of the interests which fuel his fiction, reading the *Cheap Seats* essays and lectures sheds new light on the novels. For example, the setting for the start of *American Gods*, where Shadow Moon prepares to leave prison, takes on greater relevance when reading "Why Our Future Depends on Libraries, Reading, and Daydreaming: The Reading Agency Lecture, 2013," where Gaiman discusses connections between low literacy rates, high rates of incarceration, and the "huge growth industry" of private prisons in America (6). As the penultimate essay in *Cheap Seats,* "So Many Ways to Die in Syria Now" in some ways serves as an endpoint for the trajectory of the essays in the collection: that art and reading are important, that giving people the tools to achieve literacy is essential, and that we are called to do the right thing and use our skills to help others.

Seeing Further by Building Doors Instead of Walls

Gaiman's texts advocate for dissolving boundaries rather than reinforcing them, whether discussing genres, characters, immigrants, or refugees. This preference appears in multiple texts, including Tristan Thorn leaving the village of Wall in *Stardust* and Door, the heroine of *Neverwhere*, creating doors wherever they are needed. Some of the most prominent references to walls in Gaiman's fiction appear in *Norse Mythology*, the 2017 release of which coincided with increasingly heated debates about President Trump's proposed multibillion dollar wall for the US/Mexico border and his promises to make Mexico pay for it.

Norse Mythology briefly mentions how Odin, Vili, and Ve use the eyelashes of the dead giant Ymir to fashion a wall around the world, creating Midgard (33). But a timelier story of wall-building occurs in "The Master Builder," where Odin proposes building an immense wall to keep out the frost giants and other invaders. Loki objects, stating, "Building such a wall . . . would take us many years" (71). When a man arrives offering to do it quickly, Loki has a plan to trick him, so that "they would get their foundations built for nothing" (75). Eventually, when the plan goes south, Loki disingenuously claims: "The apportioning of blame is so difficult. Who remembers exactly who suggested what?" (81). The waste of time and effort, the cruelty in the gods' subversion (and eventual murder) of the builder, and the lack of accountability for these decisions have striking resonances in contemporary politics. In some ways, the brevity of Gaiman's adaptations of these myths makes them more universal, and open for subversive commentary.

Cathy Newman of the BBC asked Gaiman about *Norse Mythology's* modern-day parallels, including Odin's giant wall and the advent of Ragnarok, the end of the world. "It remains to be seen whether Trump will actually remain in office at this point and survive long enough to make a giant wall that nobody really wants to happen," Gaiman states. He continues, "The events of last year, politically, have actually energized me in a fictional way . . . I'm going back to my novel *Neverwhere*. For me, it's taking not only the dispossessed, not only the homeless, not only those who fall through the cracks, but also the refugees, also people who are fleeing war, fleeing intolerable situations, barely getting out with their lives" (Newman). In this statement, Gaiman connects the power of empathy, perhaps most strongly executed in *Neverwhere,* with a reaction to the political events of 2017.

In the stressful, divided political climate of the US, many of Gaiman's fans are taking to the internet, quoting Gaiman's "Make Good Art" speech, which is republished in *Cheap Seats.* Given Gaiman's popularity on Twitter, it was not surprising that technology bloggers noticed the pattern. Rowland Manthorpe of *Wired* writes:

> The day after the United Kingdom voted to leave the European Union, Neil Gaiman's Twitter mentions lit up. "It was strange," he says. "People would quote me: 'At times like this, you do what Neil Gaiman says, you make good art.' Four months later, Donald Trump was elected President of the United States—and the quotes appeared again.'"

Many fans referenced Gaiman's speech as a way of coping with political turmoil. Twitter user Michael Orr wrote, "I am scared, angry, worried for friends and family. How do I turn this into anything good?" Gaiman replied to Orr, "Say what you have to say. Inspire. Remember that change always starts with ideas" (@neilhimself). The power of writing, Gaiman reiterates in *Cheap Seats,* is that it reminds us "THE WORLD DOESN'T HAVE TO BE LIKE THIS. THINGS CAN BE DIFFERENT" (8). The power of the pen (and voice, brush, and keyboard) is vital in Gaiman's work, and he clearly supports "the sacredness of speech" for artists in particular through his work with the Comic Book Legal Defense Fund (*Cheap Seats* 3). But *Cheap Seats* also contains a different kind of defense of free speech, tied to another historical event: the murder of twelve people at the French newspaper *Charlie Hebdo* in response to the publication of satirical drawings of the prophet Muhammad. "Some ideas, some words, some images can be shocking. Being shocked is part of the democratic debate. Being shot is not," writes Gaiman about the tragedy, and his decision to attend the PEN Awards where members of *Charlie Hebdo* were awarded for their courage (76). The inclusion of this essay in *Cheap Seats* is Gaiman's reminder of the power of free speech, but also that free speech must be protected even when it covers points of view that seem reprehensible. This aligns with Nussbaum's research into reading and empathy, which posits "our response to literature involves our concern for the flourishing of other people.

This possibility is particularly important when the targets of our empathy are members of out-groups, particularly groups we think of as disgusting" (Hogan 282). In Gaiman's terms, "I believe that you have the absolute right to think things I find offensive, stupid, preposterous or dangerous, and that you have the right to speak, write, or distribute these things, and that I do not have the right to kill you, maim you, hurt you, or take away your liberty or property because I find your ideas threatening or insulting or downright disgusting" (4). Reading Gaiman's essay after 2017—a year marked by debates over how President Trump uses Twitter, whether or not Milo Yiannopoulous should speak at colleges, and what the media has the duty to report—highlights the continued relevance of Gaiman's nonfiction over time. Some people may find it easier to sympathize with the *Charlie Hebdo* staff and harder in terms of Donald Trump, or vice versa. Yet Gaiman's stance on free speech and the protection of perspectives and the people who voice them is adamantly clear.

Gaiman's nonfiction, like his fiction, frequently focuses on the power of the individual in collective movements, the importance of gathering people together, and the difference that even a regular person can make. But it also can offer funny glimpses into everyday human shortcomings. In *The View from the Cheap Seats'* title essay, Gaiman regales his audience with a humorous take on a single person taking on the status quo, at a very unlikely event: the Oscars. Alone, bored, and prevented from visiting his friends in the better seats, Gaiman jokes he will "persuade the inhabitants of the mezzanines to rise up as one and to storm the stairs, like in *Titanic*" (467). This moment humorously depicts the normally mild-mannered British author inspired to lead a revolt (even if he ultimately heads to the wine bar instead).

The title essay has the feel of a newspaper feature, which makes sense as Gaiman's writing career began with journalism and he has continued to write and perform nonfiction ever since. *The View from the Cheap Seats* in some ways comes full circle to where Gaiman's writing career began, and in other ways, simply makes it more obvious that, regardless of genre, Gaiman's interests and drives have been a steady influence in his work. The genre slippage occurs in a new area with *Cheap Seats*. Readers have seen Gaiman's fantasies that take place in real world settings, and now they are able to encounter creative nonfiction in the "real" world that is still fantastical.

The View from the Cheap Seats is unique among Gaiman's texts to date, and in "finally writing a book with an index," he has offered us a convenient way to read his thoughts that have been scattered across speeches, other people's books, and websites (Holub). It has also reinforced the power of Gaiman's thought processes across genres—and accumulated in one place several important issues that drive him not only as a writer, but also as a global citizen. Although he is most celebrated for his work on comics like *Sandman* and his adult fiction like *American Gods*, in many ways Gaiman's legacy may be the way he uses his skills and power as an author to effect change. Gaiman has long been involved in philanthropy, raising funds for diverse causes including the Comic Book Legal Defense Fund (CBLDF) and the ALS Ice Bucket Challenge (Campbell 210, 213). He started the Gaiman Foundation, whose mission is simply "supporting freedom of speech, the written word, and popular culture, and generally doing good where it can" (www.gaimanfoundation.org). As his extensive philanthropy shows, Gaiman puts his money where his literature is—that is, in support of the voice of the people. But what *The View from the Cheap Seats* highlights is the way that Gaiman uses his writing as a form of social justice activism.

Gaiman recognizes the power of storytelling to change the world, frequently using it to shift the reader into a place of understanding with another's perspective. He is most often recognized for the ways that he impacts readers through his fiction, perhaps because the efforts he does on the behalf of other artists (such as writing introductions and forewords) and causes (the speeches at fundraising events) are less visible. But with the increased visibility of works like *The View from the Cheap Seats*, this may change. They demonstrate the multiple ways Gaiman has been using his craft to better the world and to inspire (and even castigate, where necessary) others to do the same. *The View from the Cheap Seats* highlights a trend that has been consistent throughout Gaiman's career, and collects it in one place where it in many ways continues and reinvigorates the work it started. As Harry Chapin sang, "You can always count on the cheap seats," and Gaiman is counting on his readers to listen, empathize, and make a difference.

NOTES

1. This references Shadow Moon of Gaiman's *American Gods*.

2. To echo Gaiman's "General Apology" for *Trigger Warning*: "I firmly believe that short-story collections should be the same sort of thing all the way through . . . This collection fails the test."

3. These texts include *The Truth is a Cave in the Black Mountains* and *The Sleeper and the Spindle*.

4. *Strange Little Girls* is a 2001 concept album where Tori Amos covers songs that were performed by men. The album's liner notes include thirteen photographs of Amos in character, one for each track on the album and two for "Heart of Gold" (about sisters). Gaiman wrote twelve vignettes for the songs as well, and they are collected on their own as "Strange Little Girls" in *Fragile Things*.

WORKS CITED

@neilhimself. "Say what you have to say. Inspire. Remember that change always starts with ideas." Twitter. 9 November 2016, 8:47 a.m. twitter.com/neilhimself/status/796393794157613057.

Brew, Simon. "Neil Gaiman Interview: All About Writing Doctor Who." *Den of Geek!* 9 May 2011.

Campbell, Hayley. *The Art of Neil Gaiman.* HarperCollins, 2014.

Chapin, Harry. "30,000 Pounds of Bananas." *The Bottom Line Encore Collection.* Bottom Line Records, 1998.

Gaiman, Neil. *American Gods.* William Morrow, 2016.

Gaiman, Neil. "Do not watch the video or listen to the song unless . . ." Facebook, 30 October 2017. https://www.facebook.com/neilgaiman/posts/10154960980156016.

Gaiman, Neil. *Fragile Things.* Harper Collins, 2010.

Gaiman, Neil. *Neverwhere.* Avon, 1997.

Gaiman, Neil. *Norse Mythology.* Norton, 2017.

Gaiman, Neil. *Trigger Warning.* William Morrow, 2015.

Gaiman, Neil. *The View from the Cheap Seats.* Harper Collins, 2016.

Gaiman, Neil. "Where Do You Run?" http://journal.neilgaiman.com. 16 December 2016.

Gaiman, Neil (w), and Charles Vess (i). *Instructions.* Harper, 2010.

Hogan, Patrick Colm. "What Literature Teaches Us About Emotion: Synthesizing Affective Science and Literary Study." *The Oxford Handbook of Cognitive Literary Studies.* Oxford University Press, 2015.

Holub, Christian. "Neil Gaiman Talks *The View from the Cheap Seats, American Gods,* and Nonfiction." *Entertainment Weekly*, 31 May 2016.

Keen, Suzanne. *Empathy and the Novel.* Oxford University Press, 2007.

Law, Elizabeth. "The Fairest of All: Snow White and Gendered Power in 'Snow, Glass, Apples.'" *Feminism in the Worlds of Neil Gaiman.* Tara Prescott and Aaron Drucker, eds. McFarland, 2012.

Malone, Tyler. "Neil Gaiman on Making Art, Mistakes and His *View from the Cheap Seats.*" *Los Angeles Times*, 24 June 2016.

Manthorpe, Rowland. "'It's Going to be Darker. And That's OK': Neil Gaiman on Trump, Brexit and the Death of Social Media." *Wired*, 7 February 2017. http://www.wired.co.uk/article/neil-gaiman-norse-american-gods.

Newman, Cathy. "Neil Gaiman Interview." BBC 4, 15 February 2017. www.channel4.com/news/neil-gaiman-interview.

Palmer, Amanda (lyrics), with Neil Gaiman (stories), Kyle Cassidy (photography), and Beth Hommel (photography). *Who Killed Amanda Palmer: A Collection of Photographic Evidence.* Eight Foot Books, 2008.

Pinker, Steven. "Steven Pinker Defines Morality." *Big Think.* http://bigthink.com/videos/steven-pinker-defines-morality.

Pinker, Steven, and Rebecca Goldstein. "Steven Pinker and Rebecca Goldstein." *Seed Magazine*, 19 May 2004. http://stevenpinker.com/files/pinker/files/2004_08_salon.pdf.

Roberts, Rachel. "The UK Has Taken Just 18% of its 'Fair Share' of Syrian Refugees, Report Shows." *Independent*, 16 December 2016. http://www.independent.co.uk/news/uk/home-news/syrian-refugees-uk-fair-share- report-a7478891.html.

UNHCR. "Neil Gaiman Appointed UNHCR Goodwill Ambassador." 20 February 2017. http://www.unhcr.org/en-us/news/press/2017/2/58aa8bee4/neil-gaiman- appointed-unhcr-goodwill-ambassador.html.

COMICS GRAMMAR IN NEIL GAIMAN AND DAVE MCKEAN'S PICTURE BOOK COLLABORATIONS

KRYSTAL HOWARD

While Neil Gaiman and Dave McKean have worked together on a variety of comics projects for adults since the late 1980s,[1] they have also collaborated on, as of this writing, three picture books for young readers: *The Day I Swapped My Dad for Two Goldfish* (1997), *The Wolves in the Walls* (2003), and *Crazy Hair* (2009).[2] Notably, within Gaiman and McKean's picture book collaborations, the medium and grammar of comics contribute significantly to the visual meaning of the texts and the complex ways in which readers engage with these works. In this chapter, I argue that Gaiman and McKean's picture books utilize formal features of comics including the speech balloon, the panel, and gutter, and the visual echoing or braiding of specific images—all of which require significant reader interaction—in order to emphasize how their works straddle the line between both the darkness and the light in traditional children's narratives.

While Gaiman's playful revision of well-known fairy-tale narratives introduces darkness typically reserved for adults into their picture books for children, it is McKean's unique hybrid collages that enhance the eerie features conveyed in their collaborations.

McKean's collage illustration techniques include a variety of visual media (painted images, photographs, and ink drawings), and as Petros Panaou and Frixos Michaelides point out, "mixed media and innovative employment of comic book codes are further elements that empower McKean's work to break away from comic book clichés and transcend limitations of the graphic novel genre" (64). Each of Gaiman and McKean's picture books employ the darkness of traditional fairy-tale and gothic-style narratives, while simultaneously infusing their narratives with absurdity, playfulness, and humor.

21

Comics, Picture Books, and Participatory Reading

Scholars working at the intersection of children's literature and comics have emphasized the formal connections between picture books and comics, as well as the unique ways their shared features call upon readers as active participants. In "On Comics-Style Picture Books and Picture-Bookish Comics," Nathalie op de Beeck remarks, "picture books engage the comics medium to differing degrees" (472), noting that "like comic books and graphic novels and so on, picture books have complex meanings that emerge from the interaction of their verbal/visual form and content along with the material signification of their trim sizes, typical page counts, and fabrication" (469). Philip Nel further explains in "Same Genus, Different Species?: Comics and Picture Books" the relationship between the two thusly: "Picture books and comics are kin: adjacent branches of the same literary-artistic family tree, cousins with slightly different expectations of their readers" (445).

Comics and picture books often rely on similar elements of visual form, but assume different competencies of their readers. Picture books, such as those by Gaiman and McKean, which engage the comics medium to a larger degree, have added expectations of their readers. McKean's use of the "visual grammar" of both picture books and comics is clear throughout his collaborations with Gaiman, where many times full-page images are placed adjacent to a page that includes two or four panels in a comics-style grid layout. Moreover, Scott McCloud has argued that the reader is the "silent accomplice" and "an equal partner in crime" in a comics work (68), and he goes on to state that "participation" and "allowing viewers to use their imaginations" creates a great deal of intimacy between the reader and the comics creator (69).

Picture books also reflect reader participation, but to varying degrees. Often, reader participation is supervised and facilitated by an adult mediator. In "Chaperoning Words: Meaning-Making in Comics and Picture Books," Joe Sutliff Sanders submits that a picture book, as opposed to a comic, "anticipates a reader who chaperones the words as they are communicated to a listening reader" (61). Sanders notes that "comics . . . anticipate a skilled reader who can absorb the content on first reading, [while] . . . picture books . . . anticipate a readership that will return to the book again and again as the listening reader learns the patterns of fixing meaning chaperoned by the speaking reader" (64). While the degree and level of reader participation in picture books and comics differs, the use of the features of comics throughout Gaiman and McKean's picture books highlights the ways in which their works anticipate a sophisticated reader who can recognize and interpret formal approaches from both styles of visual/verbal narrative.

Further, their use of comics grammar—the speech balloons, panels, and gutters, and visual echoing or braiding—speaks to the degree to which McKean and Gaiman expect their readers to interact with their text, as a viewer and listener and as a meaning-maker and silent accomplice who understands the significance of form.[3] These genre bending elements mirror a blurring in approach to content that juxtaposes terror and darkness with humor and silliness.

Speech Balloons in *The Day I Swapped My Dad for Two Goldfish*

The use of the speech balloon as a complex element of comics grammar is evident in Gaiman and McKean's earliest picture book collaboration, *The Day I Swapped My Dad for Two Goldfish*. Will Eisner explains that the speech balloon "contribute[s] to the measurement of time" and "attempts to capture and make visible an ethereal element: sound" (26). Perry Nodelman identifies speech balloons as "comics-like visitors in [many] picture books" (436–37) in his essay on the structural and formal similarities between comics and picture books. In addition to McKean's collage style, one of the defining features of *The Day I Swapped My Dad for Two Goldfish* is the use of speech balloons, which appear on almost every page of the text, as well as the comics-style panels, which appear frequently throughout the narrative placed adjacent to full-page illustrations.

Robert C. Harvey argues that speech balloons, as a technical hallmark of comics, "breathe into comic strips their peculiar life," and once a speech balloon points its "tail" to its speaker, that character seems more alive. Partly this is because the words spoken begin to shape the character's personality; but it is also the simultaneity and proximity of words and picture—and their single mode of presentation—that animate the characters for me (8).

In *The Day I Swapped My Dad for Two Goldfish*, the speech balloons do just that—bringing the adult and child characters of the narrative to life and infusing the narrative with humor in stark juxtaposition to the shadowed and complexly layered collage illustrations. For instance, on pages 13 through 17 of the work, after having just swapped his dad for two goldfish named Swaney and Beaney, the young speaker of the narrative and his mother engage in a discussion about his new goldfish and the whereabouts of his father, all while he has his little sister bound and gagged in the corner of his room. This sequence of

pages features thirteen speech balloons, at least one on each page, in addition
to four panels in the traditional comics-style grid layout on three of the five
pages. The speech balloons and panels on these pages work to focus the reader's
attention on particular verbal and visual elements of the narrative. The features
of comics grammar also set the pacing of the narrative by directing the eye of
the reader, as well as reading time through narrative expectation. On page 13,
the top half of the page depicts the image of the speaker's mother outlined in
the upper left-hand corner of the page, with the sky, the mother's figure, and
the hint of background smudged in watercolor against an all-white background.
The first bit of text on the page appears just to the right of the image and reads:
"When my mother came home I said, 'Mom, can we buy some goldfish food?'"
This is the only dialogue that does not appear in a speech balloon within the
five-page sequence. The bottom half of the page signals a shift into the comics-
style mode: a panel appears that contains an exchange between mother and
son, illustrating the middle of the mother's body (from the shoulders to the
knees) and the speaker's figure from the head to the knees and demonstrating
the narrative's focus on the child character.

Throughout these pages, the mother's face is almost always obscured: either
the edge of a panel cuts off her head, her figure is viewed from a distance or distorted through the glass of a fishbowl, or her back is turned. Despite her partial
figural representation, the mother's speech is always clearly represented in the
speech balloons. Her language, and the fact that it is directed at her children, is
emphasized by this visual representation. The focus of the narrative images and
dialogue centers directly on the child characters in the picture book, always allowing the eye of the viewer to land on the faces, eyes, and bodies of the speaker
and his younger sister; the comics panel directly reflects this emphasis on the
child. The narrative continues on page 13 as the mother asks, "Where's your
father?" and the child responds, "Come and see my goldfish," while on the next
page the mother responds, "Very pretty dear." The spread on pages 15 and 16
underscores the elements of darkness and playfulness that distinguish Gaiman
and McKean's picture book collaborations. While the images on page 16 portray
an alarming representation of the speaker's younger sister bound and gagged,
the text portrays an indifferent (and laughable) reaction from the mother. The
full-page illustration on page 15 is an amalgamation of visual media in McKean's
signature collage style: the figure of the mother with her back turned, scratching
her head, is centered on the page and surrounded by scraps of postage stamps,
photographs, as well as envelope, letter, and newspaper fragments. This image
is contrasted to the facing page, which includes two panels that span the width
of the picture book page. The collage from the previous page spills into the

gutters of the comics-style page. The collage illustration suggests a myriad of possibilities of meaning for the young reader and his/her chaperone. The collage reflects the maternal figure's scattered thoughts: her body as seen from behind is surrounded by postage stamps, a partially obscured photograph of a child, and a variety of textual documents containing numbers and text.

From this collage emerges a bizarre illustration indicating the results of the young speaker's play. The first panel on page 16 depicts the speaker's sister from the nose up with her speech balloon dialogue, "mumf, mumf, mumf." The speaker and his bowl of goldfish appear to her right where he directs his mother and the reader, "Don't pay any attention to her," and "Come and look at my goldfish." The panel below this one depicts the little sister, her mouth and body wrapped with twine, and narrates the following: "But my mother untied my little sister and took the sock out of her mouth." A speech balloon appears in the center of the panel, its tail leading to the arms of the mother as she pulls the twine away from the body of the little sister: "Do you know where your father is?" The panels on page 16 depict—in a wicked, fantastical way—an antagonistic relationship between siblings in which, upon threat of tattling, a child might tie up and stopper the mouth his sister. Emphasizing seemingly harmless yet mischievous play, the mother calmly unties her daughter without reproaching her son. And, once free from the twine, the little sister does in fact tattle on her brother by shouting the answer to her mother's question, "He swapped him to his friend Nathan for those two goldfish" (17).

In this sequence, the panels and the speech balloons within them highlight the ability of the anticipated audience for *The Day I Swapped My Dad for Two Goldfish* to recognize the formal features' meaning-making capacities. Although their picture book uses techniques commonly associated with comics, it still assumes a "*different reading situation*" (59), as Sanders terms it, one in which words are chaperoned by a speaker, for a listener. As Sanders points out, "we know that comics and picture books are different. With the exception of some provocative instances of overlap between the two, it is actually quite easy to point to a book and say with confidence that it belongs in one group and not the other" (58). This is certainly true for Gaiman and McKean's picture book collaborations, which are all clearly picture books (as indicated by their content and material design—i.e., abbreviated page length and book size); it is their use of comics grammar throughout the pages of the text that complicates the chaperoning of their picture book. Panaou and Michaelides rightly point out, "while these 'hybrids' certainly do imply an experienced reader—one who is familiar with the conventions of each of the enlisted genres—they also imply a reader who, being a child of the postmodern era, accepts and celebrates flexibility, fluidity, and transmutation" (66). Gaiman and McKean's choice to employ hybridity demonstrates that they anticipate a reader who straddles the line between independent reader and guided listener. Furthermore, their picture books infer a reader who through repetition will eventually become (or is already becoming) a sophisticated analyst of complex visual signifiers. The acumen expected by Gaiman and McKean of their reader is further apparent in their use of other formal elements of comics that measure time beyond the speech balloon.

Panels and Gutters in *The Day I Swapped My Dad for Two Goldfish*, *The Wolves in the Walls*, and *Crazy Hair*

While the speech balloon is a significant formal element of comics, the panel and gutter may be an even more recognizable, and certainly more richly theorized, aspect of comics. Each of Gaiman and McKean's picture book collaborations make use of the panel and the gutter to varying degrees. While *Crazy Hair* includes only one spread that can be read as including a series of nontraditional panels and gutters, *The Day I Swapped My Dad for Two Goldfish* contains eighteen pages that include one or two framed panels, and *The Wolves in the Walls* has eleven pages that are comprised of either two or four panels per page. Because of its appropriation of the four-panel-comics-style grid, *The Wolves in the Walls*'s use of the panel and the gutter stands out as most akin to traditional comics systems. As McCloud explains, the panel and the gutter, and the formal work they achieve through their arrangement, uncover the central drive of the comics medium: closure (65–67). Underscoring the participatory aspects of the medium, McCloud explains, "Closure in comics fosters an intimacy surpassed only by the written word, a silent, secret contract between creator and audience" (69). McCloud breaks this process of closure down into the formal pieces of comics: the panel and the gutter. "Comics panels," observes McCloud, "fracture both time and space, offering a jagged, staccato rhythm of unconnected moments" (67); in "that space between the panels . . . the gutter . . . human imagination takes two separate images and transforms them into a single idea" (66); and, thus, comics is "a medium where the audience is a willing and conscious collaborator and closure is the agent of change, time and motion" (65). In picture books, the panel and gutter work likewise to slow time and to invite the reader to create links among the fractured moments depicted in a spread and across the text. As formal features, they require the reader to work harder toward closure.

Several picture book theorists, such as Nathalie op de Beeck, have noted that one difference between comics and picture books is that comics tend to rely on panel-to-panel closure, while picture books utilize page-to-page closure (469), but as Nel points out, "many picture books have gutters that are *not* places where the pages join. Panels, both with and without borders, have long been a feature of the picture book. . . . [in] Neil Gaiman and Dave McKean's *The Wolves in the Walls*, panels have formed part of the visual grammar of picture book narrative" (446). On eleven of the fifty-three pages of the text of *The Wolves in the Walls*, a full-page illustration is placed adjacent to a page that includes panels in a comics-style layout. This repeated layout complicates the traditional page-to-page closure of the picture book by asking the reader to consider scenes and moments further broken. The first time a page of multiple panels appears is on page six of the picture book, when Lucy is having a conversation with her mother. Lucy explains to her mother that "there are wolves in the walls . . . I can hear them" (5). Lucy's mother responds in the first panel, "No. . . . There are no wolves in the walls. You must be hearing mice, I suppose" (5). The second panel depicts Lucy insisting that she hears wolves, while her mother responds, "I'm sure it's not wolves. . . . For you know what they say . . . If the wolves come out of the walls, then it's all over." The final two panels depict Lucy asking, "what's all over?" with her face occupying almost the entire panel and her eyes wide with shock. Her mother's response, "It. . . . Everybody knows that" (5), as she focuses on jarring her jam, emphasizes her ironic resignation. Nine of the eleven comics-style panel pages in the picture book depict a similar back-and-forth discussion between Lucy and her family members, while two of them depict the action of either Lucy or the wolves moving throughout the house. The use of multi-paneled pages in order to depict conversations and movement within a text further evokes McCloud's discussion of the significance of panel-to-panel transitions. McKean and Gaiman's use of "action-to-action" and "subject-to-subject" panel transitions within their picture book speak to the high level of reader interaction required.

One particularly striking spread in *The Wolves in the Walls* occurs just after the family is driven from their home by the wolves in the walls. Pages 19 and 20 depict the family in the garden outside their home discussing their options and Lucy's thoughts about what might be happening to her beloved, left-behind pig puppet. The dark colors and shadows that dominate this spread are above all telling of the various dark, terror-driven literary forms the work draws upon—the gothic and fairy-tale traditions—in order to communicate the experiences of its young female protagonist, and the use of comics grammar further underscores elements of formal emphasis upon which the reader is intended to focus. In fairy tales, wolves devour pigs and young girls, and in gothic tales, young women are driven from their homes and terrorized by villains. The implications of referencing these genres will not be lost on the child reader (who is quite familiar with fairy tales) or even the adult chaperone (who is more likely to draw connections between the terror depicted in both the gothic and fairy-tale traditions). Page 19 utilizes a four-panel grid. Each of the four panels depicts the family home at the center, while the only changing features in the four panels are the characters who appear flanking the house and the white text that runs horizontally parallel above and below the house. Lucy is figured in each panel, her face and body gradually becoming more visible and moving into the foreground to eventually obscure some of the house. These slight shifts in focus would not be possible without the use of panel transitions, which although seemingly simple, provide the reader with a complex body of knowledge about the characters and the mindset of the protagonist. Lucy's gradual transition from a peripheral to a central figure in these panels underscores her developing boldness, and the fact that she will eventually take matters into her own hands. The use of the panels and gutters on this page emphasize and foreground the gaps left on the page and implicate the reader as decoder.

Echoing McCloud's discussion of the gutter, Barbara Postema points out in her *Narrative Structure in Comics: Making Sense of Fragments*, the gutters or "the gaps—the lapses of time between the different moments of the sequence—are what produce the continuity of the sequence, as two panels work to imply what happened in between," and she goes on to further observe that "one of the differences between comics and textual literature is that in comics these gaps are visible in a literal way, putting the narrative processes of comics on display. This makes comics a self-conscious form and also one that involves its readers very directly" (xiv). The subject-to-subject panel transitions show Lucy in conversation with first her father, then her mother, then her brother, and finally her mother again. The choice by Gaiman and McKean to utilize this type of panel transition accentuates the type of visual decoding they expect from their reader—a reader who is able to understand and extract meaning from a complex visual transition.

On page 19, each panel stays within the same scene, focused on the repeated image of the house—a looming, shadowed, gothic structure—while all the while depicting Lucy in conversation with her oblivious family members as they discuss relocating to the "Arctic Circle," the "Sahara Desert," and "outer space" in response to the wolves' invasion of their home. Once again, Gaiman and McKean expertly strike a balance between darkness, in their depiction of the gothic landscape, and lightness, in their representation of absurdity and playfulness in the dialogue between the characters in *The Wolves in the Walls*. The safety of the domestic space is disrupted through the house's dark figural representation in the repeated image central to each panel in the grid. The image of the dark, looming house is countered by the family members' outlandish suggestions that living in extreme climates (the arctic, the desert, outer space) would be preferable to returning to their wolf-inhabited house, and Lucy's verbal reactions ("Hmmph!" and "Bleah") emphasize the ridiculous nature of their proposals.

This juxtaposition between gloomy and playful is further emphasized on the facing page, which is a full-page illustration of Lucy sleeping next to her family in the garden, while her imaginings of what her pig puppet might be experiencing at the hands of the wolves is made manifest on the page above her head. The full-page image on page 20 is dominated by the inked-in figure of an abstract wolf hovering above Lucy's head and dropping her pig puppet into his mouth. It is clear to the reader that the figure of the wolf is a fantasy because of the sketched-in quality of its rendering, as well as its similarity to the mess of gnarled tree branches in the background. Significantly, the use of the four-panel comics grid layout on the previous page encourages the reader to view the facing page not as a traditionally illustrated picture book page, but instead as a single comics panel that takes up the entire page.

In the comics mode, a single-panel page encourages the reader to spend much more time focusing on the details of the images and text included because of its spatial dominance in comparison to multi-panel pages. Much like the repetition of the house in all four panels on the previous page, the use of a single, large panel on page 20 highlights the significance of what is depicted on the page. As this spread indicates, the most noteworthy aspects of the narrative at this point are the house and the wolf, as well as what each of these symbols represent to the young protagonist. The wolf and the house are staples of traditional children's literature, and both are emblems of the dueling senses of terror and lightheartedness that are often infused in the genre. The wolf is representative both of a very real predator, particularly for young girls, as well as a tangible yet fantastical antagonistic figure of didactic lessons; the house likewise is characterized as a space of tranquility and safety, but also as a space that can quickly turn against young, unassuming characters.

Visual Echoes and Braiding in *The Wolves in the Walls* and *Crazy Hair*

The use of panels is not the only feature of comics that appears in *The Wolves in the Walls*. McKean also employs what Thierry Groensteen calls "braiding" throughout his illustrations in order to provide visual echoes of particular images—specifically of the wolf—for the viewer. Just as the use of the artistic practice of collage communicates an aesthetic of assemblage, so too does the use of braiding within comics. As Groensteen suggests, "comics is not only an art of fragments, of scattering, of distribution; it is also an art of conjunction, of repetition, of linking together" (22). McKean's use of dual visual forms (elements from both comics and picture book) and his deployment of braiding and sophisticated panel transitions mark his illustrative work—in not only *The Wolves in the Walls*, but also in *Crazy Hair*—as demanding significant reader/viewer involvement.

Braiding within *The Wolves in the Walls* occurs through the recurrence of Lucy's own drawings and imaginings of the wolves which appear again and again throughout the picture book. These drawings first appear on the front and back covers of the book; then again as the subtle background for the dedication page; on page 2, framed on the wall leading up the stairs in Lucy's home; on page 3, providing a type of "accent wall" in the family room; on page 21, leading up the stairs; and on page 23, as the wallpaper in Lucy's bedroom.

Lucy's conception of the wolves is not only figured in her drawings, but also in her thoughts, as evidenced by the image on page 20. As Groensteen emphasizes, braiding "carries out this sort of bridging," or as Jan Baetens and Pascal LeFèvre remark, "comics demands a reading capable of searching, beyond linear relations, to the aspects or fragments of panels susceptible to being networked with certain aspects or fragments of other panels" (qtd. in Groensteen 146). Silke Horstkotte further highlights "a roaming, non-linear reading pattern" inferred by comics (41). The technique of braiding within the picture book underscores the significance of Lucy's own renderings of the wolves, calling attention to the way in which readers are asked to link together fragments across the entire work.

In addition to the figural representation of wolves throughout the narrative in McKean's inked-in, sketched style, Lucy's drawings and imaginings of wolves throughout the text invoke the reader's work as an investigator and active agent in the narrative. From the very first images depicted on the front and back cover of Gaiman and McKean's *The Wolves in the Walls*, in which Lucy is shown drawing her wolves, readers are asked to search for Lucy's sketches of wolves. Likewise, even the realistic eyes that peer through the cutouts in Lucy's sketch contribute to the call to the reader to uncover the mysteries of the wolves in the walls. Thus, the braiding of this particular image throughout the picture book holds significance not only in terms of illustrative complexity and play, but also in relation to how Gaiman and McKean expect their audience to engage with their text.

In Gaiman and McKean's most recent picture book collaboration, *Crazy Hair*, the complex visual features of comics are once again on display. While *Crazy Hair* does not use speech balloons or traditionally figured panels and gutters, the work does include one spread that employs Groensteen's concepts of braiding and arthrology. Arthrology, as Groensteen conceives of it, involves the way in which panels in comics relate to one another, whether linear though a sequence or distant within a network (146). Noting the visual echoing that occurs in comics, Groesnteen indicates that, "within the paged multiframe that constitutes a complete comic, every panel exists, potentially if not actually, in relation with each of the others" (146). As Bart Beaty and Nick Nguyen note in their introduction to Groensteen's *System of Comics*, "It is within these explications of arthrology that Groensteen raises the idea of braiding within comics: the way panels (more specifically, the images in the panels) can be linked in a series (continuous or discontinuous) through non-narrative correspondences, be it iconic or other means" (ix). Groensteen's description and theories of arthrology and braiding, and his approach in general, "provide important and useful tools for analyzing the specific formal functioning of comics as a system that speaks by and through images" (ix). Drawing a connection between Groensteen's arthrology and picture book theory, Nodelman points out that "[i]t is possible, of course, to see picture books in that way, too: we can and do reread some or all of the pages, even while in the process of first reading the story they form part of. We can and do make nonchronological connections between the individual segments, remembering an earlier appearance of a visual object" (439). In other words, both comics and picture books call to the reader to revisit the images within panels, pages, and spreads, and to recognize links across an entire work.

Braiding and general arthrology are indeed what occur formally in the spread on pages 31 and 32 of *Crazy Hair*. This spread includes a series of, what I read as, eight nontraditional and occasionally overlapping panels; each of these eight panels is colored and semitransparent, while the background or the gutter of the spread feature swirls of the "crazy hair" shown weaving through each page in the picture book. These images can be read as panels not only because the colored backgrounds delineate them as separate, but also because they each depict Bonnie at a different time and in a different place. This spread asks the reader to engage in complex visual analysis of the illustrations on the page and to decipher the movements and actions of Bonnie across time and space.

While this representational style is quite different from that of traditionally arranged comics, the sheer colored boxes formally allude to the panel as a visual signifier. Occurring in the text immediately following a scene in which "there came a rumbling" (27–28) from the narrator/protagonist's crazy hair and Bonnie is pulled into the crazy hair by "one huge arm" (30), the spread sketches each of the many activities Bonnie engages in while "safe inside [the] crazy hair" (32). The spread on pages 31 and 32 is unique in that it portrays a single subject multiple times in different times and places; there is no other page quite like it in the rest of the narrative. These pages are also marked by a significantly different illustration style; previous pages feature McKean's signature collage-style images, where characters' features are marked by shadows that create a sense of depth and a rounded quality, and the hair weaving through the text appears realistically rendered. By contrast, the spread on pages 31 and 32 includes images sketched in black ink, with colors used sparingly to highlight and separate different scenes. Furthermore, each of the images depicted in the spread is previously illustrated for the reader on various preceding pages. For example, the first panel that appears in the spread features a lion perched atop a circus platform; this figure calls back to the text and images on pages 7 and 8: "Prides of lions / Make their lair / Somewhere in my crazy hair." The fourth, sixth, and seventh panels that appear on pages 31 and 32 feature a hot-air balloon, a pair of hunters deciphering the contents of a map, and a group of parrots balanced on the length of Bonnie's arm, respectively; these images likewise echo previous illustrations on pages 13–14, 10, and 6 of *Crazy Hair*.

The intricacy and layered nature of this particular spread in *Crazy Hair* marks Gaiman and McKean's endeavor as one that is highly invested in using comics grammar within the picture book form to demonstrate the sophistication of their text and to underscore the level of reader interaction necessary to render meaning. The fact that these complex images can be found in the penultimate spread of the picture book further highlights the fact that McKean and Gaiman expect their young readers and their chaperones to recognize the braiding and visual echoes that this spread alludes to in its multilayered illustrations.

From a visual theory standpoint, the use of arthrology, braiding, and visual echoes across their picture book collaborations is a complex formal choice for Gaiman and McKean. Not only does this decision speak to the high level of artistry they commit to their picture book as writers and illustrators, but also the credit they give their young readers in piecing together the fragments of their text in order to make meaning. *The Day I Swapped My Dad for Two Goldfish*, *The Wolves in the Walls*, and *Crazy Hair* are picture books, but they also push beyond the traditional picture book form to combine comics grammar and a variety of other mediums as well (including poetry in *Crazy Hair* and collage art in all three works). In fact, on his author website, Gaiman refers to *The Wolves in the Walls* not as a picture book but as a "graphic novel for all ages." Gaiman further notes that McKean's collage style, including paintings, photographs, and "funny-scary line drawings of wolves," combines to create something completely unexpected as well as hauntingly beautiful and powerful.

Each of McKean and Gaiman's picture book collaborations strikes a balance between both lightness and darkness. Whether depicting playful violence between siblings, gothic humor, or the playful devouring of a child by crazy hair, Gaiman and McKean invite readers to explore "funny-scary" content through a hybrid form that requires them to decode complex visual signifiers and remain active in their reading practice. While McKean's unique illustrative style in each of his collaborations with Gaiman inspires both a lightness and darkness in these works, Gaiman and McKean's use of comics grammar within their picture book collaborations work invites a sophisticated reader and implies a high level of interface between reader and text. *The Day I Swapped My Dad for Two Goldfish*, *The Wolves in the Walls*, and *Crazy Hair* are marked by their hybridity, and the use of speech balloons, panels, and gutters, and braiding contribute to their blended distinction. It is clear that Gaiman and McKean see their picture book collaborations as breaking the boundaries of form, genre, audience, and content.

NOTES

1. See, for instance, works such as *Violent Cases* (1987), *Black Orchid* (1988), and *Hellblazer* (1990).

2. In addition to their picture book collaborations, Gaiman and McKean have also worked together on a variety of middle grade and young adult projects from *Coraline* (2002) and *The Graveyard Book* (2008) to *MirrorMask* (2005).

3. Silke Horstkotte argues that comics scholars should move away from the idea that comics narrative has a grammar that requires a linear reading (34–36). I argue instead that comics grammar (the formal features that direct reading practices and time in a work), whether employed in graphic narratives or picture books, already imply a nonlinear reading of images. This is particularly true of braiding which asks the reader to recall and piece together visual echoes. It is also true of the gutter and speech balloon requiring the reader to infer meaning and make connections among narrative fragments.

WORKS CITED

Eisner, Will. *Comics and Sequential Art.* Poorhouse Press, 1990.

Gaiman, Neil. *Crazy Hair*, illus. Dave McKean. HarperCollins, 2009.

Gaiman, Neil. "Neil Gaiman on Dave McKean." Neil Gaiman: Author Website. HarperCollins Publishers. http://www.neilgaiman.com/Cool_Stuff/Essays/Essays_By_Neil/Neil_Gaiman_on _Dave _McKean. Accessed 19 December 2016.

Gaiman, Neil. *The Day I Swapped My Dad for Two Goldfish.* HarperCollins, 1997.

Gaiman, Neil. *The Wolves in the Walls*, illus. Dave McKean. HarperCollins, 2003.

Groensteen, Thierry. *System of Comics.* Bart Beaty and Nick Nguyen, trans. University Press of Mississippi, 2007.

Harvey, Robert C. *The Art of the Funnies: An Aesthetic History.* University Press of Mississippi, 1994.

Horstkotte, Silke. "Zooming In and Out: Panels, Frames, Sequences, and the Building of Graphic Storyworlds." *From Comic Strips to Graphic Novels: Contributions of the Theory and History of Graphic Narrative.* Jan-Noël Thon and Daniel Stein, eds. De Gruyter, 2013, pp. 27–48.

McCloud, Scott. *Understanding Comics: The Invisible Art.* Harper Perennial, 1993.

Nel, Philip. "Same Genus, Different Species?: Comics and Picture Books." *Children's Literature Association Quarterly* vol. 37, no. 4, 2012, pp. 445–53.

Nodelman, Perry. "Picture Book Guy Looks at Comics: Structural Differences in Two Kings of Visual Narrative." *Children's Literature Association Quarterly* vol. 37, no. 4, 2012, pp. 436–44.

Op de Beeck, Nathalie. "On Comics-Style Picture Books and Picture-Bookish Comics." *Children's Literature Association Quarterly* vol. 37, no. 4, 2012, pp. 468–76.

Panaou, Petros, and Frixos Michaelides. "Dave McKean's Art: Transcending Limitations of the Graphic Novel Genre." *Bookbird: A Journal of International Children's Literature* vol. 49, no. 4, 2011, pp. 62–67.

Postema, Barbara. *Narrative Structure in Comics: Making Sense of Fragments.* RIT Press, 2013.

Sanders, Joe Sutliff. "Chaperoning Words: Meaning-Making in Comics and Picture Books." *Children's Literature* vol. 41, 2013, pp. 57–90.

DREAMING THE UNIVERSE
The Sandman: Overture, Creation Myths, and the Ultimate Observer

KRISTINE LARSEN

Overture: A Matter of Time

In *The Sandman: Overture* no. 2, Dream (in his Daniel aspect), rebukes the protests of his loyal servant Lucien that he must not leave his guests waiting in the Dreaming.

Dream explains that "even I cannot argue with time. And it is definitely to-day" (41). The task had been determined by his sister, Desire, a century prior, to recover Time's, his father, time-bending saeculum from Mad Hettie. The device had been left in Mad Hettie's care after Desire had borrowed the device in order to aid Dream (in his Morpheus aspect) in his grand mythological journey to right a cosmic wrong he had perpetrated millennia before. But Gaiman is, as always, ahead of his reader, as Desire's appointing of Dream-Daniel's task is not revealed until the tale's epilogue. In the universe of *The Sandman*, time indeed "goes in so many ways" (Ibid.), an appropriate, if not understated, metaphor for the sometimes bewildering predictions of twentieth-century physics.

The Sandman: Overture is set in a critical time in the history of science, and, as I will argue, important aspects of the underlying mythos of the entire Sandman series flag it as a distinctively modern creation myth. In particular, this is achieved through its reliance on perhaps the most controversial aspect of the scientific syncretism of "quantum cosmology" developed in the 1980s—the role of the observer in not only shaping but perhaps even giving reality to the universe. I will demonstrate that Death's, Dream's sister, central role in Dream's journey (a fact of *The Sandman* series that is hopefully apparent to even the most casual reader) is, from a physics perspective, a necessary condition, in that she plays the critical role of the Ultimate Observer who gives order, unambiguity, and meaning to Gaiman's fictive quantum cosmology.

Dream and Death: Black Holes and Many Worlds

Regardless of the fractured and dizzying nature of time in universe of *The Sandman* (perhaps no better illustrated than in the hallucinogenic, technicolor depiction of Time's realm in *Overture* no. 4), the patient reader of Gaiman's opus comes to realize that, as is the case in our primary world reality, every event in the series occurs precisely at the time and in the order that it is meant to. Some larger, overarching figure organizes without undermining the plurality of times, places, and time-places onto which *The Sandman* is mapped, setting into place the various flows, contraflows, and excursions that simultaneously fracture and unify *The Sandman*'s multiple temporalities.

A case in point occurs at the very beginning of *Preludes & Nocturnes*, set very specifically in June 1916. The resulting imprisonment of Dream by an English spiritualist results in an epidemic of sleeping sickness, a mythic explanation for the real world epidemic of encephalitis lethargica (von Economo disease) that crossed the globe for a decade beginning in 1916 (Koch 22). While the timing of the "present day" of *Overture*—September 1915—is, of necessity, set prior to Dream's capture in June 1916, this choice strikes me as particularly symbolic. Late 1915 also marked Albert Einstein's historic publication of four papers establishing the foundation of his General Theory of Relativity, while the final review paper presenting his completed groundbreaking formulation of gravity as the warping of an interwoven space-time burst upon the world the next year (Sauer 17). In a very real sense, 1915–16 forever changed humanity's understanding of the universe, marking both the destruction of the Newtonian view of gravity as a mysterious action at a distance and the birth of a new conception of reality. One universe was destroyed, in a sense, as another was given birth, parallel to the main storyline in *Overture*. It is therefore appropriate that when Morpheus is taken out of his 1915 timeline the Mad Star imprisons him "inside the event horizon of a dark star" from which "nothing ever gets out"—a black hole (Gaiman et al., *The Sandman: Overture* 108). The scientific paper that predicted the existence of black holes was published by Karl Schwarzschild in, not coincidentally, 1916. These two discoveries would, eventually, lead to more nuanced human understandings of existence, and nonexistence, not only through the mathematical and scientific breakthroughs they would enable but also through the ramifications of those discoveries: the wholesale destruction afforded by the atomic bomb and the specter of a black hole's inescapable, irresistible, annihilating pull.

The first two decades of the twentieth century also saw the development of the other reality-shattering pillar of so-called modern physics in which Einstein played a critical role (and which Gaiman has creatively referenced in a number of his works):quantum mechanics. Governing the behavior of microscopic systems such as atoms and molecules, quantum mechanics also demonstrated that the comfortable, deterministic Newtonian view of reality as a simple "if/then" statement needed to be replaced with a dizzying, Zen-like web of potentiality, where the seemingly obvious distinction between a wave and a particle breaks down and it is impossible to simultaneously know how something is moving and where it is located. Perhaps the most disconcerting feature of quantum mechanics is the realization that any system is not in an unambiguous state of existence until it is observed or measured. Instead, it is "an undefined superposition of states and it takes an act of measurement or observation to force the system into a particular one" (Carr 158). Before the intervention of the observer, an electron can be said to have neither gone through door number 1 nor door number 2, but instead its so-called "wave function" is described by a mixed state of existence where it has gone through *both* door 1 and door 2. It takes the act of actively observing the quantum game show to break the tie and decide whether the electron has won a new car or is going home with a lovely consolation prize. As sardonically (and most famously) discussed by Erwin Schrödinger, the outside observer often dictates *through observation* the mere fact of existence or nonexistence, life or death.

In the standard Copenhagen interpretation of quantum mechanics, the observation "collapses" the wave function, a process by which the unrealized potentiality disappears (e.g., the electron goes through door 1, so the potentiality of it having gone through door 2 disappears); in the more radical Many Worlds Interpretation (MWI), both potentialities are given reality—there is a copy of the observer and electron in which s/he observes it to have gone through door 1, and another, equally "real" set of observer and observed in which the electron traveled through door 2. Scaled up to our everyday level, the MWI suggests that, as Gaiman and co-author Reaves note in *InterWorld*, important decisions by an individual "can cause worlds to splinter off into divergent space-time continua" (72–73), the sum of all such possible realities often termed the Multiverse. However, these myriad copies of "you"—what physicist Frank Tipler terms "different aspects" of the observer—have independent existences and do not interact, thus explaining Dream's confusion at finding himself surrounded by "a hundred hundred aspects of me from across the universe" (Gaiman et al., *The Sandman: Overture* 46), an event the likes of which has never before occurred in the history of the universe. When a wave collapses, all extant copies of it are apparently deleted from existence, but in *The Sandman*, they form a cohesive multiplicity, engaging with one another on the page. Thus, we see

Gaiman drawing upon the mind-blowing aspects of twentieth-century physics while simultaneously engaging in a masterful speculative game of "what if," morphing reality to his wishes within the world of Sandman. But quantum physics is not the sole domain of Dream and dreams. Rather, all of the Endless alternately find themselves occupying the roles of both observer and experiment within this fictional quantum mythology.

Morphing Morpheus: The Anthropic Principle(s) and the Quantum Mythology of Sandman

In a famous passage from *American Gods*, Gaiman offers (through the character of Samantha Black Crow) that "I can believe that light is a particle and a wave, that there's a cat in a box somewhere that's alive and dead at the same time" (394). The second piece of this statement refers to perhaps the best-known conflict between quantum mechanics and our everyday experience of reality, the so-called Schrödinger's Cat thought experiment alluded to above. Included in a 1935 trio of papers published in German, physicist Edwin Schrödinger (whose view of cats was apparently rather diametrically opposed to that of Gaiman's) used the example of a particularly unfortunate feline to illustrate how the role of the observer predicted by quantum mechanics leads to seemingly nonsensical situations when scaled up from the microscopic level of atoms to the macroscopic level of our experiences. Schrödinger came up with the idea of a "diabolical device"—a steel box in which there is a cat and a radioactive atom whose decay would trigger a hammer to shatter "a small flask of hydrocyanic acid" (Trimmer 328). At the end of an hour, the atom will have decayed, in which case the cat will have been visited by Death, or it will not have, in which case the cat is alive (if not rather annoyed at having been trapped in a box for that long). The problem lies in the outcome of the experiment having not yet been observed.

According to the predictions of quantum mechanics, until Gaiman opens the box and observes the state of the cat, the wave function exists in a "mixed state"—in Schrödinger's words, the wave function of the system would have "the living and the dead cat (pardon the expression) mixed or smeared out in equal parts" (Trimmer 328). Clearly, having the cat both alive and dead at the same time makes no sense at our level of reality. We see something similar in *The Kindly Ones*, as reality is affected by the uncertainty of the outcome of the Fates' pursuit of Morpheus. Destiny meets a copy of himself, Desire closes off his/her realm, and Delirium transforms into a school of tiny fish. As the walls between the parallel realities begin to break down, the multiple Destinies note:

> As events happen, the conflicting destinies will merge into a whole. . . .
> As the events take place, the conflicting destinies will cease to exist. . . .
> Events that never did happen and now never shall, will cast their conclusions and occurrences out into the world. (Gaiman et al., *The Sandman: The Kindly Ones*, Part 11, 14–15)

In the Copenhagen interpretation, Gaiman's act of observation upon opening the box collapses the wave function, and the possibility that the cat has died disappears from reality, leaving him free to console the very much living cat. However, in the MWI, Gaiman and the cat split into two very real aspects, one in which the cat is alive, and another in which Gaiman is writing a rather depressing blog post concerning the demise of this innocent creature (and the guilt he feels concerning his apparent role in it).

So, if the observer plays a central role in the ultimate reality of the universe, does this mean that the universe has a vested interest in making sure that consciousness (and hence life) exists within it? At least in the universe of *The Sandman*, the answer appears to be a resounding *yes*. But as the Schrödinger's Cat thought experiment suggests, the possibility that actively participating observers is a universal necessity derives from the laws of physics rather than fiction. Motivated by seeming coincidences in the values of important constants in our universe (such as the strength of gravity), as early as the 1950s physicists began suggesting that the universe, while not designed in a theological or supernatural sense, appears to be unusually friendly to the existence of life. The so-called Weak Anthropic Principle, often considered as nothing more than a tautology, simply claims that if the universe was significantly different from how we observe it, we could not exist *to* observe it. However, the Strong Anthropic Principle states that the universe had no choice in the issue—it had to possess the exact properties such that intelligent life (consciousness) would eventually arise. More controversial still is the Participatory Anthropic Principle, which states that, due to the role of the observer in quantum mechanics, "observers are necessary to bring the Universe into being" (Barrow and Tipler 22). This is the viewpoint reflected, again, in *InterWorld*, when Jay explains to Joey Harker (another aspect of himself from another quantum reality in the Multiverse) "consciousness is a factor in every aspect of the Multiverse. Quantum math needs a viewpoint, or it doesn't work" (Gaiman and Reaves 72–73).

The anthropic principle burst into the public consciousness in 1986 with the publication of physicists John D. Barrow and Frank J. Tipler's exhaustive, bestselling, and controversial examination of the scientific, philosophical, and historical implications of the concept. Although the book, like the concept itself, was the subject of sometimes-open derision (e.g., Gardner), in spite of this backlash (or, perhaps, because of it), *The Anthropic Cosmological Principle* was not only a commercial success but became an influential work touching myriad disciplines, including postmodern criticism, theology, and the arts (Packer 165). It is worthy to note that Gaiman began work on *The Sandman* the following year. There appears to also be a Gaiman Anthropic Principle at work here, reflecting an intimate connection between the reality of *The Sandman* and twentieth-century physics and establishing the centrality of Death to the series in her role as the ultimate observer. However, there is an additional force at work in the universe of Sandman, one that has a common genesis with science and, at least in the real world, has become estranged—rather like Delirium—from its more rational siblings. This is, of course, the uniquely human power to create myths and connect them to dreams.

Recreating the Universe: The Power of Myths and Dreams

David and Margaret Leeming explain that "[a] myth is a projection of an aspect of a culture's soul. In its complex but revealing symbolism, a myth is to a culture what a dream is to an individual" (vii). It is therefore not surprising that, in his essay "Reflections on Myth," Gaiman offers:

> When I was writing Sandman . . . I experimented with myth continually. It was the ink that the series was written in. Sandman was, in many ways, an attempt to create a new mythology—or rather, to find what it was that I responded to in ancient pantheons and then to try and creative a fictive structure in which I could believe as I wrote it. (77)

While there is obviously much of classical myth that resonates with Gaiman (as seen in *American Gods, Odd and the Frost Giants, Norse Mythology,* and numerous other works), there is perhaps one overarching aspect of myth that played a particularly important role in the Sandman series. *The Sandman: Overture* begins with the definition of the word *overture,* including, "The first part of an event. The very beginning of something" (Gaiman et al., *The Sandman: Overture* no. 1). The specific beginning that is being referenced here is nothing less than the creation of a new version of the universe of *The Sandman* itself, through the death of a version that has gone very wrong. Thus *The Sandman: Overture* fulfills the classical role of a creation myth.

Barbara Sproul explains that "[t]he most profound human questions are the ones that give rise to creation myths: Who are we? Why are we here? What is the purpose of our lives and our deaths? How are we to understand our place in the world, in time and space?" (1). R. J. Stewart argues that creation myths are more than simply prescientific descriptions of the origin of the universe; they emerge "from certain states of consciousness, from apprehensions of the universe communicated through visual symbols, poetry, and, in the earliest forms of sacred tales, chants, or epics, through music. The myths are not 'explanations' but resonant re-creations that echo the original creation" (2). Although each creation myth is unique, there is an archetypical structure common to the vast majority of them. Most importantly, a creation myth explains the origin of the universe and various objects in it (including the sun, moon, and stars, as well as humans and other forms of life) and identifies the creative process at work (e.g., creation through spoken word or song, war, death of a deity, or separation of parts). More detailed myths can also address the origin of a culture's worldview (such as gender roles), the source of evil and death, and the end of the world (Larsen 199). This is certainly the case in the grand mythos of *The Sandman*.

The fourth movement of *Overture* begins in the form of a story, a creation myth, a narration to set the stage for Morpheus's reunion with his father, Time, and mother, Night:

> Before the beginning was the night. And the night was without boundaries and the night was without end. In the beginning was *time*. The relentless beat in which things could happen, in which everything could *become*, dust could coalesce, matter could *exist*. In that coming together, the universe was possible, all versions of it. In it, people could dream and die. (85)

Note the importance of dreaming and dying in defining both the lives of people and the universe. As in many real world counterparts, the creation myth of *Overture* provides answers for both the beginning and ending of a particular universe. Indeed, beginnings and endings are so entangled as to be synonymous in *Overture*. The work begins with the dream of a sentient, carnivorous plant, Quorian, and the violent, fiery death of a similarly vegetative aspect of Dream, identifiable as such through his trademark black-and-white hues. Morpheus is interrupted in his task to uncreate (an interesting euphemism for destroying) the Corinthian and is drawn back to the Dreaming before being "pulled halfway across the universe in one fraction of forever, with a pain that feels like birth" (Ibid., 28).

According to Charles Long, this tension between birth and death, creation and destruction, is necessary, as "creation must be understood as creation 'over against' something. In the most general sense this 'something' is often referred to as chaos or the void. . . . There must be destruction of the old before a new creation can take place" (30). Indeed, Destruction explains to Dream that their existence is like that of a two-sided coin: destruction is necessary because "[n]othing new can exist without destroying the old" (Gaiman et al., *The Sandman: Brief Lives,* Chapter 8, 16). Perhaps the most significant (albeit strictly hypothetical) example is the possible destruction of the real-world universe through a future reversal of its well-known expansion, collapsing back down to the quantum point-like state from which it derived in what has colloquially been termed the "Big Crunch." In the 1920s, physicists explored the possibility that such an event could result in the birth of a new universe (through what would be a second Big Bang), leading perhaps to an infinite series of such cyclical or oscillating universes. However, a decade later, Richard Tolman demonstrated that the laws of nature (specifically of entropy) put serious restrictions on such phoenix-like rebirths (Heller and Szydlowski 327).

Nevertheless, the laws of fictional universes are not constrained by the often inconvenient and limiting rules of our primary cosmos. As Morpheus, the Dream of Cats (actually Desire in disguise) and an orphan named Hope Beautiful Lost Nebula journey to the City of the Stars, a swarm of metal beetles tries to prevent their passage, prophetically noting that the "universe must die, that a newer, more perfect one can take its place" (Gaiman et al., *The Sandman: Overture* 64). Despite the dangers, Morpheus must undertake this task to set things right. It is his fault that

> [a] star has gone mad, and the madness is spreading, like a cancer. . . . The galaxies themselves will shake and vanish. The other realms in their turn will fade and be destroyed. Soon enough, the mind that is the universe will cease to think and all things will cease to be. (Ibid., 47)

In the past, Morpheus had hesitated in killing a vortex; perhaps in recognition of his role as Ultimate Observer, he realizes the inherent centrality of chaos to the universe, as chaos is considered a force of creation rather than destruction in some mythologies. However, in this particular case the resulting madness had infected her entire world, and while he had reluctantly destroyed the planet, Morpheus had failed to follow Death's admonition to destroy the planet's star as well.

But how can a dream destroy a universe, let alone recreate another one? In some Hindu traditions, it is said that we are living within the god Vishnu's dream, and this universe will dissolve when Vishnu awakens. Dream's realm, the Dreaming, borrows its name from another real-world creation myth, that of Australian Aborigines. Their Dreaming refers to

> a "Dreamtime" of the distant past when deities performed "walk-abouts," creating people and sacred places and establishing clans, their totems (spiritual relationships with particular animals), and their socio-religious systems, including taboos. The Dreaming, then, is the given tribe's spiritual and original history, the process by which it and the world around it was created. (Leeming and Leeming 76–77)

In the *Dream Country* tale "A Dream of a Thousand Cats," a cat version of Morpheus recounts how in the distant past humans were the prey and play things of much larger felines, until one of the humans encouraged his brethren to "[d]ream a world in which we are the dominant species. . . . If enough of us dream it, then it will happen. Dreams shape the world" (17). And so their group dream eventually did change reality, from a cat-centric world to the reality we experience today, and in doing so "dreamed the world so it ALWAYS WAS the way it is now. . . . They changed the universe from the beginning of all things, until the end of time" (19). According to Gaiman, the humans have created a new universe with an internally consistent timeline stretching back to the beginning of time; however, an alternate but equally consistent interpretation is that the characters have instead transitioned to a different reality in the multiverse in which humans, not cats, have always been the dominant species.

The beginning of the end comes about in *Overture* after Morpheus is rescued from the black hole by Destiny, who summons his brother in order to explain the appearance of a ship in Destiny's realm. Aboard is the Dream of Cats/Desire, who has managed to save a thousand different representatives from different worlds in this small part of the Dreaming. She reminds Morpheus that "once the world belonged to the cats" and he had "allowed it to change." As she explains to him, "it is the nature of Dreams, and ONLY of Dreams, to define Reality. Destiny is bound to existence. Death is limited by what she will or will not accept" (143). Hope remains, but as the representative of the dead. In that role only she can tell the survivors of the plan to "dream the UNIVERSE. Dream it the way it has to be" (Ibid., 149). In doing so, they will reset everything, for

"There will be nothing TO remember. The universe will always have been the way it was" (Ibid., 150). Dream alone, however, will remember.

It is indeed ironic that Lord Shaper (as Morpheus is sometimes called), the shaper of dreams and nightmares, cannot shape this new universe—only the dreamers themselves can, through their collective dream, when he forces the ship, and their dream, into reality. In his words, "I take everything I have and weave their dreams into something whole" (Ibid., 153). As the image of the heartbeat of the universe flatlines across the page, a nude Morpheus shrinks and blinks out of existence to the words "[a]nd then . . . there is nothing in the universe" (Ibid., 155). Several pages of blank ink then explode into another Big Bang, as the heartbeat restarts across the page. Morpheus notes, "I hold on to the dream . . . I feel it ripping through me: the pain of a universe coming into existence . . . For a fraction of a moment, the Ship exists in a universe in which it cannot be, the final remnant of something doomed and lost. And then it flares . . . And ceases ever to have existed" (Ibid., 160–62). Weakened, Morpheus journeys back to his own realm to heal and regain his strength before being waylaid by the invocation of an English spiritualist in 1916 and the original tale of *The Sandman* begins. Destruction begets creation, and it begins with a dream—a dream directed by Hope, in the form of a dead girl. Once more, we return to the creative power of chaos, and perhaps come to understand Morpheus's reason for not destroying the vortex when initially faced with the decision. The mind may be omnipotent, in some sense, but it is certainly not omniscient. According to the Many Worlds Interpretation, its decisions have the power to split the universe (or, in this fictional case, create one anew), but when the decision is made to do so, there is no guarantee of the result. Morpheus's journey demonstrates why metaphors of childbirth are so ubiquitous in creation myths. It is also no accident that physicists commonly use the term "child universe" to describe the theoretical process predicted by inflationary cosmologies in which a self-contained bubble of space-time could branch off of our main universe. An observer in the main or mother universe would not be able to directly view the evolution of the child, as the umbilical cord of space-time would lead to an event horizon rather than a uterus—the unseen evolution of the child universe would occur in what would appear to the mother as a black hole (Holcomb, Park, and Vishniac 1058).

Like a newborn baby, a nascent universe is ripe with potentiality, but no parent can ever be certain as to how their progeny will turn out in the end.

Overture Redux: The Mind of the Universe

I must now return to the beginning of *Overture*, and Glory's call to action to Morpheus. If he does not correct his past mistake, "[t]he other realms in their turn will be destroyed.

Soon enough, the mind that is the universe will cease to think and all things will cease to be" (47). This seems distinctly at odds with the explanation given fewer than thirty pages earlier that Destiny is the keeper of book of the universe:

> Imagine a book that contains everything that is happening, everything that has happened, everything that will happen. There is nothing that exists that is not written in this book. . . . The book is the universe, and only blind Destiny sees how the universe shapes itself into stories. (Ibid., 15)

Of course, in *The Sandman: Endless Nights,* Gaiman muddies the waters even further by stating that "inside the book is the Universe" (152). Specifically: "Everything is in there, from the beginning of time to the end. He did not create the path you walk. But the movements of atoms and galaxies are in his book, and he sees little difference between them" (Ibid., 150–51). Note that time is said to have an end.

Gaiman's seemingly paradoxical statement intimately connects to what has previously been referred to as a Gaiman Anthropic Principle, although it requires further analysis to unpack its meaning. How can the universe be both a book (or in a book) and a mind? How can cessation of thought destroy the universe? Perhaps the answer is largely in the same way that an electron can be both a particle and a wave. It has aspects of both, and in any particular situation, its book-like or mind-like aspects will be more evident (and relevant). A book requires an author, who writes the stories in his/her mind and translates them into words on a page. But the book of the universe "shapes itself into stories." Is the book its own author? Is the universe, then, to be seen as utterly self-contained, bringing itself into being without outside influence or control? This metaphor for the universe resonates quite deeply with Alexander Vilenkin's model of our infant universe (at the time of subatomic size and hence susceptible to the laws of quantum mechanics) "tunneling" from a literal state of nothingness into somethingness before expanding into the full-fledged space-time we now observe. A similar creation *ex nihilo* is featured in the creation myth of the Uitoto people of Colombia:

First there was only a vision, an illusion that affected Nainema, who was himself the illusion. Nothing else existed. Nainema took the illusion to himself and fell into thought. He held the vision by the thread of a dream and searched it, but he found nothing. Then he searched it again, and he tied the emptiness to the dream thread with magical glue. Then he took the bottom of the phantasm and stamped on it until he could sit down upon this earth of which he had dreamed. . . . Gazing as himself, the One who was the story created his story for us to hear. (Leeming and Leeming 281)

A central question in *The Sandman* series is the ultimate role of the Endless. They are not gods, in a traditional sense, but rather appear to represent great cosmic ideas.

Destruction tells Dream that "[t]he Endless are wave functions" (Gaiman et al., *The Sandman: Brief Lives*, Chapter 8, 16). Perhaps they represent nothing less than the wave function of the universe itself. As James Hartle explains, in a quantum cosmology there is a wave function that describes the evolution of the universe from beginning to end (45). But like Destiny's book, it does not lay out a single path, but must take into account all the myriad possible trajectories—all the possible futures, as Delirium describes them, "Like wiggly worms, millions and billions and squillions of wiggly worms, all wiggling in different ways trying to get to the same place . . . a nothing place"—the end of the universe (Gaiman et al., *The Sandman: Endless Nights* 136). Does the wave function of the universe ultimately exist in a mixed state of all these possible trajectories until it is observed by a mind? Barrow and Tipler suggest that such a "Participatory Universe" probably requires a supreme consciousness, a so-called "Ultimate Observer who is in the end responsible for coordinating the separate observations of the lesser observers, and is thus responsible for bringing the entire Universe into existence" (470). From a location in the distant future, at the time when there are no further observations by individual minds, s/he achieves the final collapse of the wave function of the quantum universe into one possibility. It is not until this end of the universe that it is actualized, through the mind of this Final Observer (who, in the formalism of Barrow and Tipler, of necessity must be considered as being able to exist outside of our Universe). This gives credence to the so-called Final Anthropic Principle: once consciousness arises in the universe, it must persist until the end. Or, rather, perhaps it is the end of consciousness that truly defines the end of the universe.

While the universe of *Overture* is remade by the united vision of a thousand dreamers, with Morpheus acting the role of facilitator, this is a remaking of the universe, rather than the creation of the universe from nothing. Morpheus is confined to the universe and, one can argue, in paying for his previous sins with his own pain and suffering is remade himself along with it (although he alone remembers that it has changed). But there is a nice parallel with the Final Anthropic Principle: "consciousness is essential to bring the entire Cosmos into existence" (Barrow and Tipler 471).

So who, then, is the Ultimate Observer in the universe of *The Sandman*? As Desire (in her cat guise) reminds Morpheus, "it is the nature of Dreams, and ONLY of Dreams, to define Reality. Destiny is bound to existence. Death is limited by what she will or will not accept" (Gaiman et al., *The Sandman: Overture* 143). But Dream is bound to the universe, although he has the ability to remake it (just as our dreams remake our lives, if we listen to them). Destiny indeed came into being with the universe, but appears to cease with its end, as the universe will have no more stories to weave. Destruction is also doomed in the end; as the star Mizar explains, Destruction is "the process that fuels all the stars. Without him, all would be lifeless and dark" (Gaiman et al., *The Sandman: Endless Nights* 69). But a thousand trillion years in the future the last stars will burn out, as the universe runs out of the hydrogen that fuels Destruction's nuclear fusion, and in 10^{100} years, the very atoms that compose matter, along with all stellar corpses including black holes, will also be destroyed (Adams and Laughlin xxvi).

With no further disintegration possible, Destruction will have no place in the cosmos. If nothing changes—if nothing can be born and there is nothing left to be destroyed—how can one measure Time? Time was there in the beginning, but does it retain meaning in the end? The end of the universe is, then, the ultimate Night, who was there before it all began and will apparently be there beyond the end. But how does one measure an Endless Night without the promise of a day to come? Recall that the coming together of Time and Night made all versions of the universe "possible"—producing a potentiality, a probability. But, without the consciousness to interact with it, does the universe truly come into being, in a quantum mechanical sense? Time complains that all of his children, save Destiny, bother him with requests, while Night has the opposite grievance. Each remains in his or her separate realm, apart from both each other, and the rest of the universe; how, then, can they give meaning to a universe that they merely provided the *possibility* of existing?

The Ultimate Observer, who directs the minds of every consciousness in this reality and all other possible ones, is someone we can never escape, who intrudes upon our minds more often more than we care to admit. Someone who can influence dreams, and the actions of her little brother, Dream. She is Death. Destruction says of her "[a]s this universe came into being, Destiny came with it, alone in the darkness. Before the first living thing came into existence, our sister was there, waiting" (Gaiman et al., *The Sandman: Brief Lives,* Chapter 8, 11). Destruction also notes "our existences are brief and bounded. None of us will last longer than this version of the universe." "Except our sister," Delirium interjects (Ibid., 16). In *The Doll's House,* Dream reminds Desire that humans are not pawns to be toyed with; rather, it is the Endless who are the toys of humanity, and "[w]hen the last living thing has left this universe, then our task will be done" (Part 7, 23). In the words of Delirium, "my sister will take my brother's book and say goodbye . . . and then it's all done. And that's it for this time round" (Gaiman et al., *The Sandman: Endless Nights* 136). In *The Dream Country* tale "Façade," Death explains to Urania Blackwell that, "[w]hen the first living thing existed, I was there, waiting. When the last living thing dies, my job will be finished. I'll put the chairs on the tables, turn out the lights and lock the universe behind me when I leave" (20). She has the power to accept the end of the universe, and, it seems, to ultimately define it. Destruction spoke the truth when he explains to Morpheus that Death "defines life" just as Dream defines reality (Gaiman et al., *The Sandman: Brief Lives,* Chapter 8, 16). When the last living being has breathed its last breath, there will be no one left to despair, fall into delirium, desire, or dream.

Death truly is the Ultimate Observer.

◆ ◆ ◆

This chapter began with a reflection upon how *The Sandman: Overture* was keenly affected by, and reflects, not only the time in which it was written, but the time in which it is set. The same is certainly true of Gaiman scholarship. In a 2012 work, I argued that Gaiman masterfully utilized quantum physics in his creation of what I termed Quantum Cosmological Goddesses, like *Neverwhere*'s Door and *MirrorMask*'s Helena, who had the ability to pass between parallel dimensions and realities. A year later, the first issue of *Overture* was released, and the world of Gaiman scholarship not only discovered that the wave function of the Sandman universe exists in a far more mixed and intricate quantum state than we had imagined, but that it would take the collective work of myriad observers—dreamers and visionaries each in his/her own right—to bring sense to the dizzying complexity of this fantastical creation. As Gaiman wrote in Destiny's tale in *Endless Nights,* "It is all in his book. One day he will lay it down, when the book is done, and what comes after that is still unwritten" (151). A rather prophetic statement regarding Gaiman scholarship, in my mind. I hope that the author will kindly view the participatory contributions of the minds who crafted this particular book as but one step in continuing the stories of his universe.

WORKS CITED

Adams, Fred C., and Greg Laughlin. *The Five Ages of the Universe*. Touchstone, 2000.

Barrow, John D., and Frank J. Tipler. *The Anthropic Cosmological Principle*. Oxford University Press, 1988.

Carr, Brandon J. "On the Origin, Evolution, and Purpose of the Physical Universe." *Modern Cosmology & Philosophy*. John Leslie, ed. Prometheus Books, 1998, pp. 140–59.

Gaiman, Neil. *American Gods*. HarperTorch, 2002.

Gaiman, Neil. "Reflections on Myth." *Columbia: A Journal of Literature and Art*, no. 31, 1999, pp. 75–84. *JSTOR*, www.jstor.org/stable/41807920. Accessed 6 November 2016.

Gaiman, Neil, and Michael Reeves. *InterWorld*. Eos, 2008.

Gaiman, Neil, et al. *The Sandman: Brief Lives*. DC Comics, 1994.

Gaiman, Neil. *The Sandman: The Doll's House*. DC Comics, 2010.

Gaiman, Neil. *The Sandman: Dream Country*. DC Comics, 2010.

Gaiman, Neil. *The Sandman: Endless Nights*. DC Comics, 2003.

Gaiman, Neil. *The Sandman: The Kindly Ones*. DC Comics, 1996.

Gaiman, Neil. *The Sandman: Overture, The Deluxe Edition*. DC Comics, 2015.

Gaiman, Neil. *The Sandman: Preludes & Nocturnes*. DC Comics, 2010.

Gardner, Martin. "WAP, SAP, PAP, & FAP." *New York Review of Books*, 8 May 1986. http://www.nybooks.com/articles/1986/05/08/wap-sap-pap-fap/. Accessed 1 November 2016.

Hartle, James. "Theories of Everything and Hawking's Wave Function of the Universe." *The Future of Theoretical Physics and Cosmology*. G. W. Gibbons et al., eds. Cambridge University Press, 2003, pp. 38–50.

Heller, Michael, and Marek Szydlowski. "Tolman's Cosmological Models." *Astrophysics and Space Science* vol. 90, 1983, pp. 327–35.

Holcomb, Katherine A., Seok Jae Park, and Ethan T. Vishniac. "Formation of a 'Child' Universe in an Inflationary Cosmological Model." *Physical Review D* vol. 39, no. 4, 1989, pp. 1058–66.

Koch, Christof. "Sleep Without End." *Scientific American Mind* vol. 27, no. 2, 2016, pp. 22–25.

Larsen, Kristine. "Doors, Vortices, and the In-Between: Quantum Cosmological Goddesses in the Gaiman Multiverse." *Feminism in the Worlds of Neil Gaiman*. Tara Prescott and Aaron Drucker, eds. McFarland, 2012, pp. 261–79.

Larsen, Kristine. "In the Beginning: Using Creation Myths in the Astronomy Classroom." *Cosmos in the Classroom 2010*. Andrew Fraknoi, ed. Astronomical Society of the Pacific Press, 2011, pp. 199–201.

Leeming, David Adams, and Margaret Leeming. *A Dictionary of Creation Myths*. Oxford University Press, 1994.

Long, Charles H. *Alpha: The Myths of Creation*. George Braziller, 1963.

Packer, Joseph. *Alien Life and Human Purpose: A Rhetorical Examination through History*. Lexington Books, 2015.

Planck Collaboration. "Planck 2015 Results. XI. CMB Power Spectra, Likelihoods, and Robustness of Parameters." *ArXiv*, 30 June 2016, arxiv.org/pdf/1507.02704.pdf.

Sauer, Tilman. "Albert Einstein's 1916 Review Article on General Relativity." *ArXiv*, 13 May 2004, arxiv.org/pdf/physics/0405066v1.pdf.

Sproul, Barbara C. *Primal Myths*. Harper San Francisco, 1991.

Stewart, R. J. *The Elements of Creation Myth.* Element Books, 1989.

Tipler, Frank J. "The FAP Flap." *New York Review of Books,* 4 December 1986, www.nybooks .com/articles/1986/12/04/the-fap-flop/. Accessed 1 November 2016.

Trimmer, John D. "The Present Situation in Quantum Mechanics: A Translation of Schrödinger's 'Cat Paradox' Paper." *Proceedings of the American Philosophical Society* vol. 124, no. 5, pp. 323–38.

Vilenkin, Alexander. "Creation of Universes from Nothing." *Physics Letters B* vol. 117, no. 1–2, pp. 25–28.

NEIL GAIMAN AND THE MULTIFARIOUS APPROACH TO THE SUPERHERO

DARREN HARRIS-FAIN

Superheroes have been a staple of comic books since the late 1930s, long before Neil Gaiman fell in love with them in the 1960s. Unlike his contemporaries Frank Miller and Alan Moore, whose best-known work draws on conventions of superhero comics while revising and challenging them, Gaiman is known less as a writer of superhero comics and more as an author of mythological and fantastic fiction, particularly in regards to *The Sandman* (1989–96). Yet *The Sandman* emerged from superhero titles published by DC Comics, with Gaiman adopting the shared name of two different DC superheroes as one of the many names for his godlike Morpheus. Both the Golden Age and Silver Age Sandman appear in Gaiman's *The Sandman*, as do other DC superheroes. Gaiman has also written about other established characters from DC and Marvel, as well as Image Comics' Spawn and the British superhero Miracleman. This chapter surveys, as much as it possibly can, Gaiman's comics work within the genre of the superhero.[1]

Gaiman's early superhero work evinces traits for which he would become well known—particularly a strong mythic element and interest in the nature and function of stories, especially about ordinary people juxtaposed with supernatural or godlike beings. At the same time, many of Gaiman's superhero stories are straightforward and traditional, while elsewhere he engages in humor, sometimes mixed with postmodern self-reflexivity. Finally, like he often did with the title character in *Sandman*, frequently Gaiman's treatment of superheroes is oblique rather than direct, focusing on ordinary characters while superheroes are on the margins, rather than the other way around as in most superhero comics. Gaiman's superhero stories, considered chronologically, do not reveal a clear development from one stage to another; instead, they use a variety of techniques from the start—means of approach that fall into five categories:

1) the straightforward/direct; 2) the oblique/indirect; 3) the revisionist; 4) the comic; and 5) the mythic. These categories are not mutually exclusive, but they are sufficiently distinct to allow for a clear taxonomy of his writing in this genre, and considering them this way allows for clearer connections to his other comics work and to other aspects of his diverse career.

The Straightforward/Direct Approach

As a genre, superhero comics established their narrative conventions early in their history. Either through natural gifts or extraordinary effort, superheroes possess abilities that they choose to use in the service of fighting crime, doing so usually as costumed vigilantes who hide their real identities rather than as properly authorized extensions of the police or the military. Traditional superhero stories thus focus primarily on the actions and adventures of the superhero in pursuing these self-appointed duties, though they also often explore how their lives as superheroes complicate their "civilian" identities. In such traditionally straightforward stories, the superhero is not just the protagonist but also, as the name implies, a hero, a character readers are led to admire or identify with.

One of Gaiman's most straightforward superhero stories, which is "more entrenched in existing continuity than anything else Gaiman has written" (Wagner et al. 263), is also one of his earliest. In "Green Lantern/Superman: Legend of the Green Flame," a lonely Hal Jordan seeks his purpose after the dismantling of the Green Lantern Corps and turns to his fellow galactic superhero in Metropolis. Reporter Clark Kent is sent to cover a museum event, and Hal joins him. There they encounter the lantern used by the Golden Age Green Lantern, and when Hal tries to connect it to his ring, the lantern's magical green flame plunges him and Clark into a supernatural realm where they seem to be dead. Aided by Deadman and the Phantom Stranger, Superman and Green Lantern go through hell itself before returning to the real world.

"Green Lantern/Superman: Legend of the Green Flame" focuses almost entirely on the title superheroes, and the parts that don't serve to establish the old lantern's discovery by the Blackhawks and the Phantom Stranger's role. Even when Clark is at the *Daily Planet*, his thoughts reveal his powers as he hears Hal before seeing him and speculates, based on his tread, that he's lost weight. Hal and Clark are mugged as they walk through a park, and Hal cages the muggers with his ring. At the museum, Hal and Clark are transformed into their superheroic identities, and for the remainder of the story, the focus is on these characters' actions as Green Lantern and Superman, battling a series of supernatural threats. Throughout, readers receive what decades of superhero comics have led them to expect: a world of costumed superheroes hiding their identities from the public dealing with problems despite their great powers; the use of these powers in action-packed scenes; the defeat of evil through suffering and courage; and the restoration of order.

Another traditional superhero story written by Gaiman is his contribution to Todd McFarlane's *Spawn*, launched in 1992. McFarlane was widely acclaimed as an artist, but his writing for *Spawn* drew criticism, so he commissioned other comics writers—including Gaiman, Miller, Moore, and Dave Sim—to write for the series, developing stories in collaboration with McFarlane. Gaiman's issue, *Spawn* no. 9 (March 1993), introduces Angela, an angel who for centuries has hunted and slain hellspawn, humans transformed into superpowered demonic creatures like Al Simmons/Spawn, the title character. In Angela's medieval backstory, her "hunter's manual" says, "The young hellspawn are often confused and emotional, and respond to 'good' or 'noble' impulses as easily—or more easily—than they do to 'evil.'" Indeed, the medieval Spawn she encounters is literally like a knight in shining armor who offers her his services, thinking her a damsel in distress. When Angela attacks him, Al Simmons's Spawn says he doesn't want to hurt her. Gaiman's depiction of Spawn thus contributes to a traditional superhero trope: the monstrous being who, though initially depicted as a cold-blooded antihero, possesses the capacity for goodness.

Angela, a fearsome, scantily clad warrior, was so popular that Gaiman was asked to continue her story in a mini-series (1994–95), which he introduced with an uncredited sequence in *Spawn* no. 26 (Wagner et al. 240). Angela is framed by a fellow angel who hates her. She is put on trial, and her friends enlist Spawn as a witness to support her story. He and Angela briefly become allies and lovers. Although she's presented as an angel, in reality she's a superheroic figure who hunts alien monsters for pleasure and works as a bounty hunter. The abundant action mostly occurs in the angels' Elysium and a portion of Hell, but it is not unusual for traditional superhero comics to be set in unearthly realms and to include supernatural beings. In the end, Angela decides not to return to her "angelic" role and to go freelance.

Oblique/Indirect Approaches

Gaiman's treatment of superheroes is usually straightforward and tradition-al when dealing with them indirectly as minor characters rather than major ones—that is, when he treats them obliquely. Such an approach, despite Gaiman's typical traditionalism when employing this technique, is nonetheless somewhat unconventional. While there are examples of superhero comics that focus on characters who aren't superheroes before Gaiman—one thinks of DC's Lois Lane (1958–74) and Jimmy Olsen (1954–74) comics—such an approach was rare before Gaiman made use of it.

One example is "Brothers," published in *Swamp Thing Annual* no. 5 (1990) and collected in *Neil Gaiman's Midnight Days* (1999). Brother Power the Geek—introduced in 1968 as an animated mannequin that becomes a counterculture hero—returns to Earth in the 1980s after being exiled in space in the 1960s, innocently wreaking havoc. When the satellite descends to Earth, it is observed by Firestorm, who calls Sarge Steel at the Pentagon. Firestorm is curious about it but otherwise seems unconcerned about it crashing into Tampa, and when he hangs up on Steel, Steel calls him a "crazy bastard" and a "damn super geek" (Gaiman, *Neil Gaiman's Midnight Days* 24–25). Later, Steel calls Batman, who asks about Brother Power's similarities to the Swamp Thing. He directs Steel to Abigail Cable and says, "Ms. Cable is to be treated with *respect*" (33). He too hangs up on Steel and continues about his business in the Batcave. In the end, it is an aging hippie, rather than the superheroes, who saves the day by talking some sense into the naïve Dollman.

Batman is also used as a marginal character in two Gaiman stories about Batman villains. "Pavane," a Poison Ivy origin story, appeared in *Secret Origins* no. 36 (January 1989) and presents her as obsessed with Batman. Having mastered control of plants, she devises a costume and goes to Gotham City hoping to seduce him, only to be frustrated. Gaiman also wrote about the Riddler for a one-shot *Secret Origins Special* in 1989.

While Batman appears in the framing story "Original Sins," warning a television producer against interviewing his enemies, he doesn't appear at all in "When Is a Door." Here the Riddler, evoking both Silver Age Batman stories and the 1960s show, waxes nostalgic for the good old days of colorful capers, gaudy costumes, and oversized props. Now, he says, evoking the darker, grittier superhero stories of the 1980s, the game has changed. Back then, he says, "No one ever hurt anybody. Not really. Nobody died" (Gaiman, "When Is a Door" 53). Now, he says, "The Joker's *killing* people, for God's sake!" (53).

Superheroes appear as marginal characters in *The Sandman*, whose title character, known as Dream, Morpheus, and other names, is a godlike embodiment of dreams and is himself a secondary character in several of the stories in the series. In the second issue, Dream, recently freed from bondage, asks the Hecate about his missing talismans and is told that the "League of Justice" may know about his dreamstone, with the panel showing Batman taking it from a figure bound by Green Lantern (*The Sandman, Volume 1: Preludes and Nocturnes* 75). Three issues later, Dream appears in the Justice League headquarters, waking Scott Free (Mister Miracle). Scott doesn't know where the stone is and wonders if Batman might, then says, "Nope, it's 3:30 AM. He'll be at work" (143). He wakes J'onn J'onzz, the Martian Manhunter. He sees Dream as a Martian god and bows down to him, supplying Dream with the information he seeks, after which he and Scott retreat to the kitchen.

And while superheroes are relatively scarce in *The Sandman*, they do make occasional appearances in its seventy-five-issue run. The original crime-fighting Sandman from the Golden Age, Wesley Dodds, appears briefly, both near the series' beginning and at the end. Also at the end, Clark Kent, Batman, and the Martian Manhunter are present (through their dreams) at Morpheus's wake, and the dreams they share reflect on their various comic book and media incarnations:

> CLARK KENT: "*Odd?* As odd as the dreams where I'm a newsreader, or the one where I've got an ant's head, or where I'm a *gorilla*. Once I dreamed I had this weird virus and I had to keep going forward in time until the end of the universe . . . The one I hate is where I'm just an actor on a strange television version of my life. Have *you* ever had that dream?"
>
> BATMAN: "Doesn't *everyone?*" (ellipses in original)

The prequel *The Sandman: Overture* (2013–15), likewise, briefly alludes to the Green Lantern Corps and the Space Canine Patrol Corps. Although the series extends far beyond the traditional DC universe, it nonetheless incorporates superheroes as a part of its world, usually obliquely.

Perhaps Gaiman's most indirect references to DC superheroes occur in the story "The Heart of a Star" in *The Sandman: Endless Nights* (2003). Dream brings his lover, the alien Killalla of the Glow from Oa, to a parliament of embodied stars, only to lose her to Oa's star. Her ability to summon a green-lit power through her imagination anticipates the Guardians, who later oversee the Green Lantern Corps. Likewise, Dream's sister Despair's conversation with Rao, Krypton's star, anticipates another familiar story:

> *Think* about it, Rao. Wouldn't bringing life onto a planet that is inherently unstable add to the beauty of life? It at any moment it could explode . . . Truly, it would only be *perfectly* beautiful, a perfect piece of art, if one single life-form escaped. To remember, to mourn, to despair. (76)

In this story, set when Earth's sun, Sol, is young and does not yet support life, neither Green Lantern nor Superman appears, and yet their future stories are obliquely suggested here. Indeed, so indirect are the references to the superheroes who would eventually emerge as champions of these suns' planets that only a reader already versed in their respective origin stories will understand the oblique allusions. In this respect, Gaiman's oblique approach takes the casual allusions that knowledgeable readers will catch to an extreme degree: suggesting the presence of superheroes who appear nowhere in the narrative.

Gaiman's oblique treatment of superheroes is not limited to DC's characters, as is shown in his mini-series *Eternals* (2006–2007). Here characters such as Iron Man and Hank Pym's Yellowjacket are given small roles to play, but the focus is on the title characters, godlike aliens who, while denying they're superheroes, wear colorful costumes. In the case of *The Eternals*, however, Gaiman's indirect treatment of conventional superheroes has less to do with realistically marginalizing them to focus on ordinary characters than with updating characters he'd loved in their earlier comics and more fully integrating them into the Marvel universe. Thus *The Eternals*, in spite of its oblique treatment of superheroes, is closer to a traditional comic book story than other examples in which he employs this approach.

Revisionist Approaches

Yet despite these straightforward or oblique superhero stories, Gaiman's superhero comics are not always traditional, as they often engage in revisionism similar to Miller's and Moore's early work. Nor has Gaiman opposed superhero revisionism, apparent in his admiring 1992 introduction to Rick Veitch's *Bratpack*, a dark, disturbing deconstruction of superhero comics. But he has expressed reservations about the direction superhero comics took after Miller's and Moore's breakthrough works: "The problem with the mid-eighties revival of interesting superheroes was that the wrong riffs were the easiest to steal. *Watchmen* and *The Dark Knight Returns* spawned too many bad comics: humorless, gray, violent and dull" ("Confessions" 258). Instead, Gaiman's attraction to revisionist superhero stories stems from the possibility that they can say something important and do so in an original way. Writing in 1999, he said he was burned out on superheroes but grew excited when discussing the project that became "Whatever Happened to the Caped Crusader?" because it was envisioned as "the coolest, strangest Batman story you can imagine, in which every relationship in the world of Batman was turned inside out and upside down" ("Confessions" 260). Gaiman seems more interested in using revision as a tool to examine the superhero genre's connective tissues and how they reflect the role superhero stories play in culture, rather than to make a statement about their ability to depict dark narratives.

An example of Gaiman's superhero work that falls halfway between traditionalism and revisionism is *Marvel 1602*, which, while revisionist, nonetheless is rooted in Gaiman's fannish enthusiasm, seen in his interview with John Rhett Thomas in *Eternals*:

> What I was doing with *1602*, was I thought . . . it would be really fun to write something that feels like I am doing something in the Marvel Universe for the first time, I want to take all of the Marvel characters that I loved when I was seven or eight and I want to put them all in the story and have complete control over everything, including all continuity, and I'm going to set it four hundred years ago and it's going to be mine!

In *1602*, Gaiman transposes classic characters such as Daredevil, Thor, the X-Men, and the Fantastic Four to seventeenth-century England, where they deal with political intrigues of the day and the possible end of the world. The miniseries is traditional in its storytelling and characterization, conforming to the norms of traditional superhero comics, and revisionist in its deviation from the "normal" Marvel universe and imaginative recastings of familiar figures in Elizabethan/Jacobean garb. However, as Renata Dalmaso ponders, does it present significant changes extending beyond the story's time and place?

One significant way *1602* is revisionist, according to Dalmaso, is in its depiction of female characters, particularly those with enhanced abilities or powers, such as Jean Gray's psychic powers or the extraordinary physical skills of Natasha, *1602*'s rendition of the Black Widow. While realistically depicting the limitations women in England and the American colonies would have faced in the early seventeenth century—including Susan Storm, the counterpart to the Fantastic Four's Invisible Woman, whose invisibility symbolizes the condition of women under patriarchy, or Jean Gray, who must masquerade as John Gray to fit in with her male counterparts—*1602* subverts notions of women's powerlessness in both the seventeenth century and in the 1960s comics that provide the basis for the book's characters (123–26, 128–29).

Working on *1602* in the aftermath of 9/11, Gaiman said he wanted to distance the story from a world with bombs and guns: "I didn't want to write a story in which might made right—or in which might made anything" (Afterword). A similar critique of conventional superhero violence is present in Gaiman's more revisionist early graphic novel *Black Orchid* (1988–89). Along with using experiments with paneling and interior monologue practiced by Miller and Moore, *Black Orchid* was "[t]he first comic to incorporate a first-person narrative style into a female superhero title" (Cantrell 104)—a technique pioneered by Moore in *Swamp Thing* and *Watchmen*. The book *begins* with the capture of the title character, an obscure DC superhero introduced in 1973. As Mikel Gilmore writes in the introduction, this is a passé opening in superhero comics ("Introduction," *Black Orchid* 5). What is surprising, however, is that mere moments later, Black Orchid's captor "kills her—the woman who is the namesake of this book—in a brutal and unflinching manner" (5). The captor monologues metanarratively about his own undermining of the expectations of the superhero genre. Yet, despite her own (temporary) demise, Black Orchid opposes crime not with violence but peacefully whenever possible. Gilmore explains that *Black Orchid* "is the first major work of comic book literature that uses violence as a critique of the uses of violence—that is, a critique of not only how violence figures into our actions and our psychology, but also how it figures into our myths and our art" (7). As in *Marvel 1602*, Gaiman uses the tools of revision to critique the genre of the superhero from within.[2]

Gaiman's writing about the British superhero, Miracleman, retains the revisionist bent of Moore's earlier revamping of the character. Moore had realistically extrapolated how the world would be radically altered if superheroes actually existed and concluded with a utopian world that would seemingly preclude the viability of superhero stories.

Gaiman liked that he could be as strange and experimental as he wished in *Miracleman* (Campbell 142). As Gaiman observed, he was actually relieved he did not have to write stories like the earlier ones and could instead explore the ramifications of normal people living in a superhuman utopia (Khoury 118)—especially given his belief that imperfect people could still do interesting things even in a utopia.

The stories collected as *Miracleman: The Golden Age* depict Miracleman's earthly paradise as a world where the title superhero is a godlike figure atop a terrestrial Olympus looking down on human affairs and intervening only from afar, unlike his conventional comic book counterparts. In fact, he is barely present at all; instead, following Gaiman's oblique approach, the book focuses on ordinary people. Not counting covers, depictions in paintings and statues, memories, and the windmill keeper's fantasies in the Miraclewoman story "Skin Deep," Miracleman only appears on eight pages out of 160.

Miracleman's female counterpart, Miraclewoman, is more prominent in "Skin Deep," but also presented through Gaiman's revisionist lens. The story, patterned on the myth of Cupid and Psyche (Khoury 120), concerns a windmill keeper whose relationships with "normal" women have failed because he always faults them for their flaws. One night he sees Miraclewoman in the sky. He says, "I love you," and in his captioned interior monologue he says, "I said it, to myself, but to her, in the lightning, the words whipped from my lips by the wind even as I whispered them. . . . Nobody could have heard me, not in that wind, not over that noise. Nobody human." But she is not human, and she hears him and descends, saying, "Do you? That's very nice of you." They become lovers, but she eventually mentions his past relationships and chides his superficiality in admiring her superhuman state. She shows him her human form, asks him to make love to her as a real, imperfect woman, and then leaves him, as he returns to his former wife—hardly the stuff of traditional superhero fare.[3]

Here and elsewhere in Gaiman's superhero stories, one of the key features of a revisionist approach to the genre is a combination of greater realism and an accompanying deflation of the appeal of the superhero fantasy. Another example, yet again drawing on Gaiman's interest in obscure DC characters, is "Sandman Midnight Theatre" (1995, collected in *Neil Gaiman's Midnight Days*), featuring Wesley Dodds, the original Sandman. As in his stories from the 1930s and 1940s, he wears a gas mask with a suit, a trench coat, and a fedora and uses a sleep gun to subdue criminals while sleuthing. Unlike his Golden Age depiction, but like revisionist superheroes decades later, he has a complex psyche rather than simply being an uncomplicated do-gooder, and he has a sex life. His girlfriend also challenges superhero conventions. When, for instance, he says, "the Sandman is not without certain avenues to follow," she responds, "*Why* do you do this? Why do you *do* these things? Why do you talk about yourself in the third person? I don't understand it, Wesley." Later, he approaches her as the Sandman and says, "Miss Belmont . . . this is no place for you . . . you must leave. . . ." Unperturbed by his expressionless mask, she says, "Wesley, take that off *right* now. I'm not going to talk to you with that face on."

Comic Approaches

Comic books, which have been superheroes' primary venues for most of their history, are so named because they began as magazine collections of newspaper comic strips, which in turn were called this because, prior to the advent of serialized adventure strips, they featured humorous characters doing and saying humorous things. Yet, like the adventure strips in the newspapers, superhero comics have tended to be not only straightforward but also serious.

Despite occasionally humorous superhero stories, such as those featuring Plastic Man or the original Red Tornado, superhero stories from the start have tended not to be comic. This tendency became even more pronounced during the revisionist boom that started in the 1980s, whose superheroes were not only serious, they were dead serious. Thus, for Gaiman to embrace the comic mode in some of the superhero stories was a push against the tide of treating superheroes more realistically and seriously, and it too could be considered a kind of revisionism, challenging the more dramatic tone of most other titles.

In "Carnival," for instance, a couple dressed as Nightwing and Starfire are depicted as an obese young woman and a scrawny old man, introducing a light moment into an otherwise serious scene in *Miracleman: The Golden Age*. Other examples of Gaiman's comic mode can be found in *Eternals*. The Wasp is part of a reality television show called *America's Next Super Hero*, and she shows the contestants (all young superpowered beings, whom she encourages to register as superheroes in connection with Marvel's Civil War storyline) a public-service announcement with Mr. Fantastic holding up a copy of *Gulliver's Travels* to encourage reading. A similarly lighthearted approach to the superhero is the appearance of Mister Miracle and the Martian Manhunter in *The Sandman*. When they encounter Dream in the Justice League International headquarters, they're wearing bathrobes with a JLI logo, and after Dream departs, J'onn places his hand on Scott's back and says, "Come, Scott Free; let us hit the kitchen. I have a secret stash of Oreos of which you are welcome to partake" (*The Sandman, Volume 1: Preludes and Nocturnes* 143).

As Orion Ussner Kidder has argued, Gaiman makes occasional use of metafiction in *The Sandman*, both in characters realizing they are part of a created narrative and in how the concluding book in the series breaks the fourth wall by including the reader among those present for Morpheus's wake (151–53, 154–59). A metafictional approach that combines elements of both kinds of metafiction can be found in one of Gaiman's most humorous stories to date, "A Black and White World," which Gaiman wrote for *Batman: Black and White*. Batman and the Joker are presented as actors self-consciously fulfilling their roles within the pages of a comic book, chatting with each other in the green room while running their lines before being called into action (directed by Lobo). Along with Simon Bisley's art, which shows a dark, brooding Batman and his maniacal arch-nemesis as friendly colleagues who only fight each other as part of their job, the story also indulges in occasional in-jokes, as when Batman asks someone at the studio for a copy of *Newsweek* and she says, "Only *Time*, I'm afraid, Batman. Company policy" (76)—a reference to Time Warner's ownership of DC.

"Metamorpho: The Element Man" is also metafictional and comic in nature, extending even to action scenes, as when the ancient Element Man tries to kill Stagg's French chefs—"Daddy always makes sure his expeditions are well-catered, Rexikins" (71)—with chlorine gas. Metamorpho and Element Girl transform the chlorine into sodium chloride by adding sodium, but when Sapphire exclaims, "My hero!" (71), one chef says, "Element Man, a hero? My omelettes, zey are all burnt, and *ptui* salt everywhere. He is no hero" (71). In addition, Stagg's Neanderthal servant has several comic asides. Hoping his romantic rival Rex will meet his doom, he says, "Miss Sapphire, as we watch Mr. Mason head to his certain death, may we discuss Java's excessive masculine attributes? Are you perhaps interested in male bodily hair? Java has a superfluity of it, all down his back. Java does not mind if you touch it" (74). Even when it appears that Rex and Element Girl are defeated, and Stagg's butler (actually an alien) says the recovered Star of Atlantis will help recover a spaceship that "will make all dreams come true" (76), Java interjects: "Will there be giant vegetables? . . . Java dreams of giant vegetables. Chiefly rutabaga and unusually knobbly turnips. But not ever broccoli" (76). When the alien explains that the spaceship's activation will destroy Earth, Java whispers, "Okay. Sometimes maybe Java dreams of broccoli" (76). All this, along with the kids' commentary, infuses a purportedly serious story with a comic undercurrent. As a result, the story reads like both an affectionate homage to Silver Age superheroes and a contemporary revisionist work—revisionist both in technique and in its use of humor.

Mythic Approaches

It is often said that superheroes are akin to characters from ancient myth; for instance, Richard Reynolds's groundbreaking 1992 study on superheroes was subtitled "A Modern Mythology." It is easy to understand why people would make this connection. The powers of many superheroes—super speed, super strength, invisibility, and the like—have their counterparts in the gods and demigods of classical mythology. Moreover, some superheroes, such as Marvel's Thor and Hercules, are drawn directly from the world of mythology. However, most superhero narratives, as fantastic as they might be, employ the conventions of realistic fiction. That is to say, superhero writers and artists have tended to treat their unbelievable characters in a believable fashion, as real figures who act within a real world. Such characters may have parallels in mythology, but they themselves are not treated in a mythic fashion. In contrast, a myth is a story that, while touching on reality, is specifically about origins and about the doings of gods and heroes—it is specifically a story, and in fact the Greek word μῦθος (mythos) simply means "story." A myth is a kind of narrative crafted to get at a deeper reality rather than one describing a narrative set in the real world.

Therefore, in addition to being comic and metafictional, "A Black and White World" is also mythic in a sense, with Batman and the Joker aware of their status as hero and villain in a story created for an audience. The same is ultimately true in Gaiman's "Whatever Happened to the Caped Crusader?" Readers are presented with alternate, competing, and contradictory versions of Batman's death and funeral, complete with different visual styles from panel to panel that reference different periods in the character's history. This is observed by a dead Batman talking to his murdered mother, and the message is that there have been, and will continue to be, different Batman stories over time. In other words, Batman stories are not simply stories, but they are myths; they are not simply one more or less realistic Batman story after another, but they are stories about a character who transcends the real to become an idea functioning over time within a culture, even if the stories about this idea do not cohere into a consistent canonical continuity. As Gaiman explained in his introduction to *Batman: Cover to Cover* (2005), "One of the greatest joys to the concept of Batman is that he isn't one thing, that he contains all the Batmans that have walked the streets of Gotham City in the last sixty-five years. . . . None of them more real, more valid, more true than any other" (266). Thus "Whatever Happened to the Caped Crusader?" exemplifies Gaiman working in what might be called his most characteristic mode, that of the mythic.

In *Miracleman: Apocrypha* (1991–92), Gaiman again presents the title character as a mythic figure, along with the superhero stories he encounters. Gaiman wrote the framing stories, in which Miracleman, unsatisfied with reality, thinks, "I crave the unreal," and turns to the library of his utopian Olympus—specifically, "the library of the apocrypha": "This is what I need. I desire lies. The precious lies that bind . . . Give me your fictions" (7–8). He chooses comic books about his fictional adventures, and the series itself consists primarily of these Miracleman stories "that never were." Reflecting on comic books, he thinks:

I regret that one branch of the art-form is almost dead, burnt out. Superman and Batman. Spiderman [*sic*] and the X-Men: all of them have returned to comic-book limbo, the silent abode of the no-longer-published; remembered only by collectors and historians. . . . Briefly I mourn the four-color heroes: overtaken by events, homeless metaphors for the revenge of the powerless. (36)

Superhero comics, he reflects, are like myths: stories about godlike beings, but clearly *stories*, designed for specific purposes. Although in his utopia reality has matched the impulses behind superhero comics, they are still being published about him and others in the Miracleman universe. Even though he is real within the context of his comics, he has become a mythic figure.

This mythic approach to the superhero is most specifically Gaimanesque. As he has said, "As a writer, and, more specifically, as a writer of fiction, I deal with myth a great deal. Always have. Probably always will" ("Some Reflections on Myth" 54).

Moreover, he has explicitly connected comics to myth, and superhero comics in particular: "comics have always dealt in myths: four-color fantasies, which include men in brightly colored costumes fighting endless soap opera battles with each other (predigested power fantasies for adolescent males)" (57–58). Much of his career has been devoted not only to the exploration of various myths and the creation of new ones, but also to a reflection on the nature of stories and how they function in our lives. In Gaiman's most characteristic work, stories are not simply entertainments but ways of engaging with and understanding ourselves, our relationships with others, and our place in the world. In this way, Gaiman is perhaps even more of a pioneer than his peers, taking superheroes from the realm of fantasy into that of myth.

✦ ✦ ✦

Although the five general categories into which Neil Gaiman's superhero stories fall do not correspond directly to the chronological arc of his work in the genre, there is a sense of development from his early superhero stories to his latest efforts. His traditional superhero stories tend to be imitative in nature, while his more radical stories are transformative, changing the shape of the superhero genre. Yet this is not a simple parallel. For instance, "Metamorpho" imitates the conventions of Silver Age comics while simultaneously transforming them through his comic and revisionist innovations. "Whatever Happened to the Caped Crusader?" is mythic in nature, while paying tribute, through imitation, to generations of earlier Batman stories.

Gaiman's superhero stories thus exhibit not only a great deal of diversity but also a degree of intertextuality and complexity, even at their most commercial or imitative. Gaiman himself has distinguished between "the workaday, more or less pulp fictions which are turned out by the yard by people who are trying their hardest, or not" and the other kind, the "precious few" that "move beyond the literal" and have something to say ("Confessions" 259). While Gaiman's own superhero stories have run the gamut from the workaday to the inspired, his best work in this genre reveals its artistic potential as well as its tonal and technical diversity—a range that parallels Gaiman's work as a whole. It is hoped that this chapter, with its taxonomy of Gaiman's superhero stories and its corresponding overview of his work in this field, will enable readers to make fruitful connections between Gaiman's better-known work and his lesser-known contributions to superhero comics.

NOTES

1. Having written that, it would be best noted that this chapter points to examples, not coverage.

2. For more on the radical revision presented by *Black Orchid*, see Sarah Cantrell, "Feminist Subjectivity in Neil Gaiman's *Black Orchid*," *Feminism in the Worlds of Neil Gaiman: Essays on the Comics, Poetry and Prose*, edited by Tara Prescott and Aaron Drucker (McFarland, 2012, pp. 102–115).

3. Similar mundane marital and domestic concerns characterize former-Sandman Hector Hall's (now married to Fury, aka Hippolyta Hall) appearance in *The Sandman* no. 11.

WORKS CITED

Campbell, Hayley. *The Art of Neil Gaiman*. Harper Design, 2014.

Dalmaso, Renata. "When Superheroes Awaken: The Revisionist Trope in Neil Gaiman's *Marvel 1602*." *Feminism in the Worlds of Neil Gaiman: Essays on the Comics, Poetry and Prose*. Tara Prescott and Aaron Drucker, eds. McFarland, 2012, pp. 116–30.

Gaiman, Neil. Afterword. *Marvel 1602*, by Gaiman, art by Andy Kubert, colors by Richard Isanove, lettering by Todd Klein. Marvel Comics, 2004, n.p.

Gaiman, Neil. "Angela," art by Todd McFarlane. *Spawn*, no. 9, March 1993, Image Comics.

Gaiman, Neil. *Angela*, art by Greg Capullo and Mark Pennington. Image Comics, 1995.

Gaiman, Neil. "*Batman: Cover to Cover*." *The View from the Cheap Seats: Selected Nonfiction*. William Morrow, 2016, pp. 263–66.

Gaiman, Neil. "A Black and White World," art by Simon Bisley, lettering by John Costanza. *The DC Universe by Neil Gaiman: The Deluxe Edition*. DC Comics, 2016, pp. 78–85.

Gaiman, Neil. *Black Orchid*, art by Dave McKean, lettering by Todd Klein. DC Comics, 1991.

Gaiman, Neil. *The Books of Magic*, art by John Bolton et al., lettering by Todd Klein. DC Comics, 1993.

Gaiman, Neil. "Confessions: On *Astro City* and Kurt Busiek." *The View from the Cheap Seats: Selected Nonfiction*. William Morrow, 2016, pp. 257–62.

Gaiman, Neil. *Eternals*, art by John Romita Jr. et al., colors by Matt Hollingsworth, lettering by Todd Klein. Marvel Comics, 2007.

Gaiman, Neil. "Green Lantern/Superman: Legend of the Green Flame," art by Eddie Campbell et al., colors by Matt Hollingsworth, lettering by Todd Klein. *The DC Universe by Neil Gaiman: The Deluxe Edition*. DC Comics, 2016, pp. 86–124.

Gaiman, Neil. "The Heart of a Star," art by Miguelanxo Prado, lettering by Todd Klein. *The Sandman: Endless Nights.* DC Comics, 2003, pp. 57–78.

Gaiman, Neil. Introduction. *Bratpack,* by Rick Veitch. King Hell Press, 2003, n.p.

Gaiman, Neil. "Jack Kirby: King of Comics." *The View from the Cheap Seats: Selected Nonfiction.* William Morrow, 2016, pp. 274–77.

Gaiman, Neil. *Marvel 1602,* art by Andy Kubert, colors by Richard Isanove, lettering by Todd Klein. Marvel Comics, 2004.

Gaiman, Neil. "Metamorpho: The Element Man," art by Michael Allred, colors by Laura Allred, lettering by Nate Piekos. *Wednesday Comics.* DC Comics, 2010, pp. 67–78.

Gaiman, Neil. *Miracleman: The Golden Age,* art by Mark Buckingham, colors by D'Israeli, lettering by Todd Klein. Marvel Comics, 2016.

Gaiman, Neil. *Neil Gaiman's Midnight Days,* art by Richard Piers Rayner et al., colors by Tatjana Wood et al., lettering by Todd Klein et al. DC Comics, 1999.

Gaiman, Neil. "On the Stairs," art by Teddy Kristiansen, lettering by Rob Leigh. *Solo: The Deluxe Edition.* DC Comics, 2013, pp. 341–46.

Gaiman, Neil. "Original Sins," art by Mike Hoffman and Kevin Nowlin, colors by Tom McCraw, lettering by Todd Klein. *The DC Universe by Neil Gaiman: The Deluxe Edition.* DC Comics, 2016, pp. 23–29, 48, 75–77.

Gaiman, Neil. "Pavane," art by Mark Buckingham, colors by Nansi Hoolahan, lettering by Augustin Mas. *The DC Universe by Neil Gaiman: The Deluxe Edition.* DC Comics, 2016, pp. 7–21.

Gaiman, Neil. *The Sandman, Volume 1: Preludes and Nocturnes,* art by Sam Kieth et al., colors by Robbie Busch, lettering by Todd Klein. DC Comics, 1995.

Gaiman, Neil. *The Sandman, Volume 10: The Wake,* art by Michael Zulli et al., colors by Daniel Vozzo and Jon J. Muth, lettering by Todd Klein. DC Comics, 1997.

Gaiman, Neil. *The Sandman: Overture,* art by J. H. Williams III, colors by Dave Stewart, lettering by Todd Klein. New York: DC Comics, 2015.

Gaiman, Neil. "Some Reflections on Myth (With Several Digressions onto Gardening, Comics and Fairy Tales)." *The View from the Cheap Seats: Selected Nonfiction.* William Morrow, 2016, pp. 54–63.

Gaiman, Neil. "Whatever Happened to the Caped Crusader?" art by Andy Kubert and Scott Williams, colors by Alex Sinclair, lettering by Jared K. Fletcher. *The DC Universe by Neil Gaiman: The Deluxe Edition.* DC Comics, 2016, pp. 145–208.

Gaiman, Neil. "When Is a Door," art by Bernie Mireault and Matt Wagner, colors by Joe Matt, lettering by Bernie Mireault. *The DC Universe by Neil Gaiman: The Deluxe Edition.* DC Comics, 2016, pp. 49–58.

Gaiman, Neil. "You Never Forget Your First Time." *Batman Cover to Cover: The Greatest Comic Books Covers of the Dark Knight.* DC Comics, 2005. 34–35.

Gaiman, Neil, et al. *Miracleman: Apocrypha,* art by Mark Buckingham et al. Eclipse Books, 1992.

Gilmore, Mikal. Introduction. *Black Orchid,* by Neil Gaiman, art by Dave McKean, lettering by Todd Klein. DC Comics, 1991, n.p.

Harris-Fain, Darren. "Revisionism in Graphic Genre Fiction." *The Cambridge Companion to the Graphic Novel.* Stephen E. Tabachnick, ed. Cambridge University Press, 2017.

Khoury, George. *Kimota! The Miracleman Companion.* TwoMorrows, 2001.

Kidder, Orion Ussner. "'Everybody's Here': Radical Reflexivity in the Metafiction of *The Sandman*." *Critical Insights: Neil Gaiman*. Joseph Michael Sommers, ed. Salem Press, 2016, pp. 146–60.

Round, Julia. "Transforming Shakespeare: Neil Gaiman and *The Sandman*." *Beyond Adaptation: Essays on Radical Transformations of Original Works*. Phyllis Frus and Christy Williams, eds. McFarland, 2010, pp. 95–110.

Thomas, John Rhett. "The *Spotlight* Interview with Neil Gaiman." *Eternals*, by Neil Gaiman, art by John Romita Jr. et al., colors by Matt Hollingsworth, lettering by Todd Klein. Marvel Comics, 2007, n.p.

Wagner, Hank, et al. *Prince of Stories: The Many Worlds of Neil Gaiman*. St. Martin's, 2008.

"No Light, but Rather Darkness Visible"

Illuminating Gaiman's Murkier Pages

AT THE EDGE OF THE BARELY PERCEPTIBLE
Temporality and Masculinity in *Mr. Punch* and *Violent Cases*

CHRISTOPHER D. KILGORE

Neil Gaiman's comics work has received considerable critical attention as a new episode in fantastic literature, a postmodern bricolage of genres, historical eras, ideas, and perspectives. He and his collaborating artists are renowned for their ability to conjure other realms—the Dreaming of *The Sandman,* the alternate London of *Neverwhere,* the mythic terrains of *The Graveyard Book* and *Ocean at the End of the Lane*—and show us protagonists crossing the boundaries between Earth and its others. Alongside these predominantly fantasy-oriented works, however, Gaiman's collaborations with artist Dave McKean, in particular, tend toward even more complex story structures, characters, and story-worlds. Whereas his mainstream work tends to plunge readers and characters into fantastic spaces, three of the stand-alone McKean collaborations, *Violent Cases* (1987), *Signal to Noise* (1989, 2000), and *The Comical Tragedy or Tragical Comedy of Mr. Punch* (1995, hereafter *Mr. Punch*) inhabit altogether more liminal spaces. Perhaps as a result of their uncomfortable genre-defying narrative and style, but also because of their murky, hermetic attitude, the available scholarly work tends to emphasize their murkiness. As I have suggested elsewhere, *Signal to Noise* creates an imaginary space, a film fully envisioned (but never realized) by a dying auteur (Kilgore 25–26), but *Violent Cases* and *Mr. Punch* develop in a different direction. They use a memoirist's autobiographical narration, shrouded in failed memory, to synchronize and then collapse seemingly separate times and places. That is, they articulate what Brian Richardson and others have in the past decade taken to calling *unnatural narratives,* in that their words, images, and graphics ask readers to create an impossible temporality, where violent events from different epochs seem to coincide (in *Violent Cases*) and where an old children's puppet-play both gives shape to *and* discloses a hidden family history of male family members' violence against women (in *Mr. Punch*). This chapter argues that the strange temporalities in these two books portray and critique a hereditary culture of domestic and public masculine violence, putting Gaiman and McKean in line with other critical work of the 1980s and '90s graphic narrative renaissance (particularly *Watchmen* and *Maus*), and at odds with the traditional masculinities prevalent in mainstream comics.

Temporality in Graphic Narrative

I will use, here, a critical framework based on media-specific theoretical models of narrative reading and reading in comics, combined with Richardson's notion of "unnatural" narrative, so a little background and terminology are necessary. Like verbal narrative, graphic narrative functions by way of a system of differences: the "word" of conventional narrative becomes the convention of the "panel" in graphic narrative, the lines or spaces that segment page-space into meaningful components. In general, conventional comics invite readers to follow the panels in the reading-order of text (for comics in English, left to right and top to bottom), and the sequencing generally aligns with the temporal flow of events in the story-world. However, as ably illustrated by Scott McCloud in *Understanding Comics* and Thierry Groensteen in *The System of Comics*, the sequence of panels has a complex relationship to the story being told, and there is no concrete or set relationship between the panels' organizing activity and the reader's reconstruction of temporality (McCloud 94–117; Groensteen 26–30). Large, small, horizontal, vertical, inset over full-bleed (when a panel's images run straight to the edge of the page), or distorted—what determines how readers rebuild the story-world is the relationships among the panels themselves, and with the material they segment. That is, the panel's dividing line and the intervening gutter (the blank space between panels) operate very much like what Jacques Derrida calls the *trait* (7) and *passepartout* (12): these boundaries divide but also conjoin.

Conventional graphic narration uses specific formats, styles, and cues, which serve to advance a seamless story, drawing the audience into the narrative world. Furthermore, although even early comics frequently defied consensus reality in flights of fancy, the conventions of graphic narration also followed those of science fiction and fantasy prose, in adopting a realism of style, if not of content (particularly in "golden age" and "silver age" comic books, as well as their descendants). As much in graphic narrative as in prose narrative, however, there has always been a strong undercurrent of what Richardson calls "antimimetic" or "unnatural" narration, narratives that defy the norms of realist poetics (4). Characters in Dan O'Neill's *Odd Bodkins* strip climb up other characters' voice balloons, for instance, and Art Spiegelman's mouse-people in *Maus* famously debate their own status as animal figures. The field of "unnatural narratology" attempts to collect all of these instances under one conceptual umbrella, and to re-analyze our theoretical assumptions about how narrative works by avoiding what Richardson calls "mimetic bias" (xvii).

The field of unnatural narrative is broad, and there is still considerable disagreement about which texts fit its conceptual frame—some would include any deviation from scientific reality, while others focus more closely on meta-narrative moments. But among the most central examples are texts that occupy what Farah Mendlesohn has called "liminal fantasy," a category she adapts from Tzvetan Todorov's "fantastic" proper. These narratives present strange events, but refuse to let the reader decide, once and for all, whether fantastic or supernatural forces are really at work, or even whether the events were "real." Graphic narratives in this category use the conventions of narration to dislodge the reader from comfortable absorption of story material, creating ambiguities about spatiality, subjectivity, and the ontological status of characters and events. For example, as I have demonstrated elsewhere, Gaiman and McKean's *Signal to Noise* makes a screenwriter seem to appear inside the story-world of his own draft narrative at the moment of his death, and his imaginary characters seem to persist after his death (Kilgore 34, 36). That the screenwriter character is dead is not up for dispute, but that one moment lingers, squirming about even after the completion of the reading process.

Violent Cases and *Mr. Punch* generate an altogether different kind of ambiguity, one that creates a problem with time. Both books use "unnatural" or antimimetic techniques to collapse seemingly disparate events into a single impossible moment. In presenting a trans-generational "moment" of male violence, both books assert the hereditary cycle of violence, but also reject a deterministic acceptance. That is, in an ironic mode endorsed by temporal theorists Paul Ricoeur (208) and Ned Lukacher (120), the compression into a single trans-generational moment is precisely what emphasizes that moment's contingency—the sense that it might not have to work this way. Finally, whereas Gaiman's other work—from the *Sandman* series to *American Gods*—would fit securely into the fantasy or new-wave fantastic genre, *Violent Cases* and *Mr. Punch* (like *Signal to Noise*) do their serious work in the liminal zone of the antimimetic or "unnatural," the indeterminacy that Todorov calls the "fantastic" proper (qtd. in Isaac Cates 149; see also Sandor Klapcsik 193, and David

Goldweber 166 for further discussion). That is, if a work like *The Sandman* series posits a "night and day" of our world and its others, these books usher us into twilight: our world—but somehow not quite our world.

Temporal Compression: *Violent Cases*

First published in 1987 as, to use Paul Gravett's words, "a radical departure, a leap of faith," because it was "creator driven and originated, experimental, non-genre 'graphic novel/fiction' by two unknowns" (*Violent Cases* iii), *Violent Cases* received popular critical acclaim and achieved considerable financial success. Enclosed in lavish collage-style frontispieces and covers, McKean's artwork unfolds in ambitious layouts that, by and large, follow graphic narrative conventions. The artwork itself, however, departs from the classic clearline style, alternating between sketchy pencil or charcoal work, multimedia collages, gouache or watercolor, and deep-black or blue-solid tones. The resultant effect parallels and augments a noir style, which McKean highlights by occasionally importing newsprint-style halftone reproductions from noir cinema classics like *The Maltese Falcon* (see, for example, Figures 5.1 and 5.2).

Scholarly criticism available as of this writing has tended to view *Violent Cases* as either an enigmatic piece of postmodernist play, or an opaque text that requires psychoanalytic interrogation. Joe Sanders (19), Klapcsik (193), and Cates (144) see the text as rejecting the basic premises of memoir, asserting that the fog of memory makes adequate recall impossible—a classically postmodernist concern with metanarrative. Klapcsik makes this basic thesis more concrete, directly calling both *Violent Cases* and *Mr. Punch* "liminal fantasies" engaged with a critique of cognition (204) in classic postmodernist fashion. These ambiguities lead Hannah Means-Shannon to assume that the text's opaqueness presents the narrator's traumatized, evolving psyche, amenable to a Jungian psychoanalytic reading, and concluding that, rather than cognition, the text's subject is the evolving differentiation between the self and the other (370–71). Along a similar vein, David Goldweber envisions some of the book's chief emissaries of violence as seductive characters whose influence offers vitality and energy to an otherwise drab childhood (157). To my eye, however, *Violent Cases* offers a clearer vision than the postmodernists suggest, but along a different, less reductive interpretive path than the existing psychoanalytic approaches to the text.

Like *Maus* and other ambitious graphic narratives of its time, *Violent Cases* unfolds as a first-person narration of the narrator's past experiences, beginning with a single page divided up into thirty-five panels, each barely an inch by two inches, establishing a framing narrative before embarking on the story being told. In the framing narrative, the narrator, a visual representation of Gaiman added by McKean, lights a cigarette and addresses the reader directly, breaking the proverbial fourth wall. This pattern continues throughout: as he struggles to tell a convoluted story about events he may or may not have fully witnessed, his narrating situation remains undisclosed—if the book's past or memory is hazy, then its present is nearly blind. Little in the way of furniture can be seen around him: he might be alone in a modern apartment, or, as the tiny panels segment his image, casting bars across the depicted room, he might be in prison. His initial comments script-tease the reader with half-truths and innuendo: "I would not want you to think that I was a battered child," he claims, before adding, "However . . . // I wouldn't want to gloss over the true facts" (1).[1] Here, rather than beginning with simple declaratives, he piles on two negations, a negating conjunction, and a question, all in the name of deriving the truth.

The narrator's account winds across multiple occasions during a period in his childhood, around age four, in the 1950s—a time period when, as he puts it, men wore hats. The basic time sequence seems clear: The narrator's father attempts to tug him up the stairs to bed, thereby breaking a bone in the boy's arm. The father then takes the boy to "an osteopath he had heard about" (4), a much older man who claims to have done chiropractic work on none other than Al Capone. Later, the boy meets the osteopath again, at a birthday party for the daughter of his parents' wealthy friends, and at that very party the past catches up to the osteopath, and sinister figures abduct him. Thus far, the story seems clearer than some accounts would have it. As may be apparent in this thumbnail sketch, however, unlikely details trouble the plot, and some material seems to have migrated out of the osteopath's gangster memories and into the impressionable boy's life.

The telling of the story—the text, as related by the minimally depicted frame narrator, and rendered in McKean's images—problematizes the story's reconstruction in several key ways. First, the narrator proclaims that he cannot remember the osteopath well. He recalls having to ask his father, and as the narrator's father attempts to recount his impressions, the images on the page shift, portraying representations of the images he recalls: "an eagle's nose," he says, and an eagle appears, in nearly scientific detail, overlaid with ambiguous printed text and a map of Europe as the father adds hair and an accent, "middle European," but then folds on top of that the idea that "he looked like a *red Indian chief,—/ a Polish* red Indian chief" (6)—and the image adds a sketch

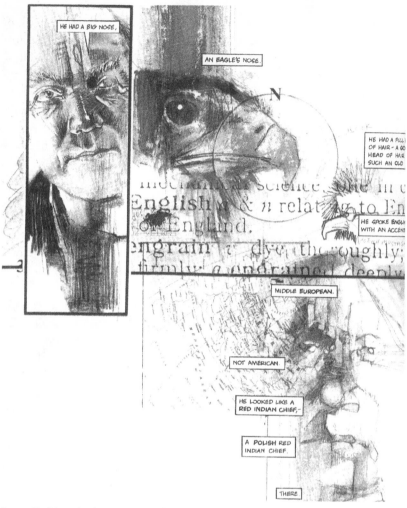

Figure 5.1. The father and son's reconstruction (*Violent Cases* 6).

of a face whose features appear vaguely Native American (Figure 5.1). After all of this careful reconstruction, the narrator abandons this effort and returns to his tale with his own description of "an owl-like man, chubby and friendly / peering at me over thick spectacles" and—in contrast to what the images on the page portray—"not the gaunt grey chief of my father's description" (7; Figure 5.2). He then acknowledges that this might be another "doctor perhaps,—/ or no-one at all" (7), although the vaguely Einstein-like figure is how the osteopath appears throughout much of the book, following the standard conventions for comic book realism.

Figure 5.2. The son's reconstruction (7).

At this point, the combination of words and images has already suggested a clear pair of alternatives in terms of story: readers may accept that the story represents reality to the best of memory's ability to recall; or readers may suspect that the story represents either a child's fantasy or an adult's prevarication. Had Gaiman and McKean left the matter here, it would work much as other nonfiction autographic narratives work (and as Sanders [19, 20] and Cates [145] suggest), as a portrayal of the vagaries of memory, yet presenting those vagaries *realistically*. This is not what happens, however.

When the narrator, still between ages four and five, meets the osteopath again, the latter at first appears exactly as he did before, with wildly wavy white hair, thick glasses, prominent nose, and mustache. He again regales the young boy with tales of Al Capone's violence, and as the story comes to a close, and the huge, round man who serves as a children's magician enters the hotel bar, a series of small panels intrudes over the action. The framing narrator interrupts: "I suppose I should intrude here, in the interests of strict accuracy,—// and

Figure 5.3. The young osteopath (29).

point out that the picture I have of [the osteopath] at this point is neither the grey haired Indian—// nor the tubby doctor,—// nor the amalgam of the two I remembered earlier in this narrative" (29). Instead he proposes a younger man altogether, "like Humphrey Bogart's partner in *The Maltese Falcon*" (29)—and the images obligingly insert a pointillist rendering of that figure, evoking a film still. The narrative continues, at first blending the glasses and blue-tint of the original osteopath with the film still (Figure 5.3), but then later rendering the osteopath younger still, a slender man in thinner glasses (Figure 5.4).

These later images, appearing just before gangsters haul the osteopath away, do not seem only intended to reaffirm the uncertainty of memory (Sanders's understanding [19]), or just to portray the narrator's shifting relationship with his subject (as Cates might say [147]), and it seems a stretch to say that they directly tag the *entire* sequence as imaginary (see Means-Shannon [362]). Rather, they create an *impossible* temporal sequence. Earlier, the osteopath recounts his arrival in America and apprenticeship to another osteopath at eighteen, in 1917, and his emigration to Portsmouth in England "after the second world war" where he appears to have settled (9). This timeline makes him, as he says, an

Figure 5.4. The even younger osteopath (36).

"old" man of fifty-six if the encounter occurs in 1955, and older if it happens later. But the Einstein-esque visual images make him look older still, while the later images make him appear in his late twenties or early thirties, the same age as he would have been during his work on Al Capone's back.

This specific temporal shift coincides with an equally important temporal alignment. While games of musical chairs continue outside at the children's party, the now-youthful osteopath describes a different party, where Capone gathered people on his payroll, tied them up in a basement, and beat them to death with a baseball bat. In its portrayal of the narrative, *Violent Cases* juxtaposes images to align Capone's event with the children's party. As children run around the chairs, Capone stalks around his victims, and, as blood flies, the children squabble and struggle for seats. Just as the osteopath's change in age and appearance draws the eras closer together, the interleaved panels integrate the osteopath's story with the childhood experience and the framing narrative (the narrator's "now"). Perhaps most remarkable of all is the child narrator's reaction: "In my head I saw a party, green rabbit-shaped jellies and fairy cakes on a crisp white check table cloth/ A bat hitting. // Blood and brains spatter grey and red on the white. / Al helps himself to some jelly" (32). Rather than being frightened, the narrator completes the transposition: "I thought of the other children, / their heads bloody caved-in lumps," and then over the broken-open last panels, "I felt fine about it. / I felt happy" (34). Before departing the party, the child witnesses the osteopath suffering an apparent abduction by Mafioso figures wielding baseball bats. The present-day narrator admits that this event is among "those bits of one's memory that simply do not work" (37), but it links chronologically with a later moment, when he seems to remember seeing the Mafiosi driving a hearse, possibly with a silver coffin inside, possibly containing the osteopath's body.

The key scenes fold together several eras, and also several distinct events, binding the three occasions together directly, and suggesting that they form, somehow, literally the same moment. The final segment of the book cements this point in a tour de force of "unnatural" narration, a page of panels bracketed at both ends by statements by the narrator, who describes the hearse's passing. In between, however, appear sixteen equal-sized panels that do not connect easily with anything the narrator says (Figure 5.5): the car's wheel snaps a branch, and juxtaposed panels link the snapping with a breaking party-popper and the child narrator's broken arm, and then the wheel splashes through a puddle, and an adjacent panel portrays a splash of blood from Capone's "party."[2] In the final row of panels at the end of the book, the passing hearse merges into the wallpaper behind a hat rack that appeared in the first panels, in the narrator's family home, a stand-in for the narrator's (hat-wearing) father. In this final segment the conventions of narration itself break down—it is unclear whether the page should be read as an expression of the narrator's childhood consciousness as he experienced the car's passing; a portrayal of the narrator's present consciousness as though from the outside; or an amalgamation from multiple sources.

It is tempting to say that what happens is merely indeterminate, whether as a result of memoir's failings or psychological trauma, but I do not follow Richardson's suggestion (20–21), which Klapcsik (204) also tacitly endorses, that indeterminacies subvert interpretation, nor Sanders's (19) suggestion that readers alone get to decide. Indeed, recent readings of nonfiction narration through the perspective of the unnatural have suggested that these kinds of indeterminacies

Figure 5.5. Combined events (44).

in fact enhance our ability to understand the intricacies of traumatic events (see Stefan Iversen 93). Following this line of thought, rather than attempting to resolve which parts of the narrative are "real," I would argue that it is more productive to understand the impossible moment as creating a single event. That event is an act of violence, where a man exacts physical and emotional injury

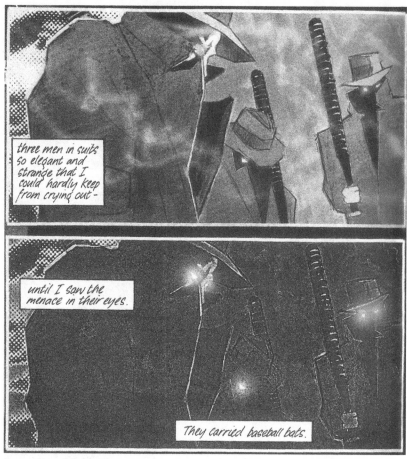

Figure 5.6. Men with bats (40).

upon another weaker male: the father, through impatience and an imbalance of strength, breaks his son's arm; the osteopath inflicts his past upon his child patient; Capone beats his fellow gangsters to death; the child narrator imagines beating the squabbling children to death; and then the osteopath himself suffers the same fate. The sequence of narration carries the event toward its abstraction, conjuring finally the bat-wielding Mafiosi as embodiment of violence itself, men with bats, in coats and hats—themselves rendered in exaggerated menace, cartoon figures summoned off the page (Figure 5.6).

This is not a mere symbolic or metaphoric rendering; it is an inheritance of violent behavior, passed from one generation to the next. The suffering of violence becomes, through the glamorized image of the gangster, a desire to inflict violence, paying it forward in an ugly karmic inversion. It implicates the narrator himself, in his ambiguous, evasive present—as Cates seems to recognize when he suggests that the narrator's father is himself a gangster (145). It is, however, also no accident that the male figures appear alternately as figures of weakness (the child) and of strength (the gangsters) and sometimes both (the osteopath is a hard-edged tale spinner and then a weeping abductee), and that figures of absolute power are rendered with specific anti-realist graphical distortions. The Mafiosi loom in outsized, excessively inked darkness, their bats and grins adopting a mainstream-comics sheen, and their apparent mob boss, the corpulent magician, always has clothing that trails chalked or penciled stars off of his body and even out of the panel (Figure 5.7).

That is, the violence that *Violent Cases* exposes and critiques is simultaneously a violence of masculine self-assertion, and the violence of male figures in conventional comics narratives. Its portrayal here opens itself to numerous socio-historical readings: on these pages we might find a transatlantic perspective on the Bonnie-and-Clyde glamorization of the gangster figure, or on the rags-to-riches stories of bootleggers made wealthy by Prohibition. We might find also, in this portrayal of the rise and fall of Prohibition itself, a broader socio-historical masculine reaction against a constitutional amendment perceived as driven by women's temperance leagues.

Violence Avoided: *Mr. Punch*

In *Violent Cases*, men aim their violence at weaker men who pass it on in their turn, and women play nearly no role; in *Mr. Punch*, Gaiman and McKean return to consider that other probability: that violent men also take their toll on the women in their lives. Gaiman and McKean's version of *The Comical Tragedy or Tragical Comedy of Mr. Punch* features a similar narrative framing mechanism, with a nameless narrator recounting and struggling to understand a childhood event. As in *Violent Cases*, the narrator's present-day circumstances are indeterminate, but readers cannot even see him. Instead, those elements of the narrative where he mentions his narrating "present" appear against a visual backdrop of a work desk strewn with objects related to his story—timepieces, a mask, random gears and other mechanical elements, and a few vines. As in *Violent Cases*, this narrator is haunted by opaque memories of childhood events: he recounts a visit with his grandparents during the labor and delivery of his younger sister, a visit that ultimately reveals a shocking act of violence against a woman. The narrative unfolds in zigzag fashion, leaping forward and backward in time in ways that might threaten the story's

Figure 5. 7. The conjuror (28).

coherence—were it not for the puppet show whose scenes are interlaced with the narrative: the titular *Punch and Judy* show. Integrating the show with the narrative presents a challenge for readers attempting to construct a clear chronology of the story events—and critics have read it in the same way as they have read *Violent Cases*, usually in the same article: they emphasize the story's indeterminacy (Klapcsik 204; Cates 145) or psychoanalyze the narrator and the authors (Means-Shannon 360; Goldweber 157; Sanders 20). As in *Violent Cases*, however, the narrative system of *Mr. Punch* does something rather more complex and definite. Gaiman and McKean use the puppet show to collapse multiple generations, people, and events into a single *moment* of male violence—this time presented as a male reaction against specific events and concepts coded female—thereby endorsing a specific reading of the Punch and Judy show.

Widely supposed to have arrived in England in the 1660s via Italian productions of marionette shows featuring a character called Pulcinella, the Punch puppet show came into its own in the mid-1700s, and may constitute an amalgam of the Italian character and unnamed English antecedent (e.g., George Speaight). It features a central character, Mr. Punch, who inherits from his Italian source a hunched back and exaggerated nose and chin. The transformation from the Italian marionettes to cheaper, sturdier hand puppets somewhere in the early 1700s gave Punch and his cohorts the ability to get into physical altercations, which the puppeteers—called Professors, supposedly by royal decree (see Susan Brookes-Morris 74)—exploited to comic effect. The exact script varies, but nearly always begins with a scene of domestic strife, where Punch cannot manage his infant child, and throws the baby off of the puppet stage. Confronted by his wife Judy, he at first feigns innocence, but ultimately the two beat one another with sticks, and Judy, too, succumbs. The scenes that follow repeat the same pattern: other puppets, often including a doctor, a policeman, a beadle, a hangman, and the devil himself, attempt to impose social order and meet the same fate. These grisly affairs were played for laughs, and the play has remained popular with shifting audiences, who have grown older and more nostalgic as the years have passed.

Scholarly critics differ sharply over potential readings: some have called Punch a working man's hero, a rebellious, childlike character who escapes all attempts to confine him (e.g., Leslie Katz and Kenneth Gross). By contrast, some see him as a kind of trickster figure, whose comic antics let him put the lie to English propriety: Punch shows us the truth about domestic violence happening behind closed doors (F. Scott Regan and Bradford Clark 366). Finally, following the obvious gendered coding, Rosalind Crone understands Punch's later iterations as a byproduct of Victorian nervousness about masculinity, and about the ideological assertion of "separate spheres" for men and women. Under Crone's reading, it becomes significant that Judy initiates most of the violence between the two, primarily by imposing childcare on Punch, and goading him into physical conflict—she becomes a stock "shrew" character. That is, Punch's violence and his portrayal as rebel constitute an antifeminist reaction, a reassertion of masculinity in the face of emasculating social conditions.

Based on how the story unfolds, Gaiman and McKean seem to lean more strongly toward this kind of reading. Rather than simply present the show's scenes as segue material between the narration, Gaiman and McKean do something rather more "unnatural." Each of the *Punch and Judy* intrusions occur as *part of* the story. The narrator begins by describing a shore-side fishing trip with his maternal grandfather, and during that trip, he finds a seemingly haunted *Punch and Judy* booth. The booth is empty, but when he goes around in front, the show begins, and Mr. Punch and his wife Judy appear—hand puppets animated, apparently, by no actual human hands (Figure 5.8). Their play supplants the narrator's story of his childhood, and the organization of the panels on the page changes, becoming more regular and less beset with full-bleed individual panels or other intrusions. When Mr. Punch throws his baby out the window, the child narrator flees, and the adult narrator picks up the tale. More or less the same pattern obtains throughout the book: intrusions by the *Punch and Judy* show are motivated within the narrative, and yet pick up the play more or less where the previous episode left off. If the narrator or Gaiman and McKean had merely interrupted the flow of narration to show us more of *Punch and Judy* every so often, we could dismiss the intrusions as a mere stylistic device. But, as part of the story-world, the puppet show gives shape to the narrator's experiences and memories as they occur.

It is no accident that *Punch and Judy* makes the narrator seize up and flee every time he sees the show. Key details link all three of the story's primary adult male figures—the paternal grandfather (not named), Great-Uncle Morton, and a mysterious Punch professor named Swatchell—with the Punch narrative. Swatchell is an actual professor, of course, and played a mentor role to the grandfather long ago. He returns now to claim a place in the grandfather's failing arcade—and perhaps to help him deal with a new entanglement. Morton has physical features that parallel Punch's own, including a hunchback and prominent nose (Figure 5.9). The narrator's family offers many possible explanations of Morton's spinal deformity, including being thrown downstairs as a child, and tellingly, falling out a window. His childhood, then, mirrors that of Punch's baby, and his adult body mirrors that of Punch. Finally, all three,

Figure 5.8. Punch and Judy (*Mr. Punch* 5).

but most especially the grandfather, are implicated in a brutal assault on a fe-male employee, whom the grandfather had seduced and impregnated. Casual statements suggest that this is not the first time, either. But the grandfather's parallels run deeper: the grandfather served as Swatchell's assistant after the spectacular failure of a soap-selling con in Wales, and in all visually depicted accounts of his earlier endeavors, he appears in the text as a puppet-like crea-ture (Figure 5.10). In early life, his face is a distorted photograph, and later, when he loses his reason, the visual images portray that same photographic face, but mask-like, with punched-out eyes. These cues encourage the reader to recognize the three men as Punch, as men who will not countenance social responsibility.

Just as in *Violent Cases*, these parallels enmesh the present-day narrator. In a key digression from his story, he begins to ruminate over his tale, declaring, "In a perfect world, it occurs to me now, I would write this in blood, not ink," because it compels truth (13). He then gently remonstrates with himself, adding, "There, now. And already I'm speaking of blood; and it's the past I meant to speak of" (13). The reference to blood points in two directions. First, it impli-cates the narrator in the kind of violence he has witnessed, suggesting he too may have something to regret. Secondly, in "speaking of blood" the narrator suggests the old metaphor for heredity: what was *in his grandfather's blood*, so to speak, might run in his own—a thought reiterated in McKean's visuals. As the narrator describes the grandfather's eventual madness, the panels track ever closer to the photograph's punched-out eyes, until, in a sudden shift in perspec-tive, the reader appears to be looking out of a mask rather than into the empty eye-holes (Figure 5.11). And, indeed, past the page-turn, the images reverse, and a mask retreats from the panel's point of view. The narrator's view—of the desk

Figure 5.9. Uncle Morton (30).

and its mechanical bits, of the mask—is linked to the reader's view, through the eyes of his grandfather's face.

These connections also point toward a narrative element common across all of the material, including interviews with the narrator's present-day family. The characters all turn away from uncomfortable topics—from the violence implicit in most of the grandfather's and Morton's experiences, but also from matters of childbirth and sexuality more generally. One key, difficult scene helps

Figure 5.10. The puppet grandfather (15).

concretize what the men in this book refuse to face: the narrator describes a dream in which a doctor is "cutting open" Punch's erstwhile girlfriend Polly. The lurid visuals, soaked in red, show a sequence in which "a / huge hand // came out" (48) of Polly's body, rendered in pale, overexposed photographic form. In response, the doctor attacks it with a scalpel, while "Punch laughed, / and [the narrator] wondered / who the third hand belonged to" (48; Figure 5.12). This is certainly bizarre, as Goldweber (167) observes, but it does not appear meaninglessly so, as he implies. Likewise, to read the white hand as solely a metaphor for the narrator's childish psyche, as Sanders (30) suggests, ignores the suggestive parallels between what is happening to Polly, and what happens to the woman who plays the mermaid. The white hand is what the narrator as a small boy knows but cannot fully identify, and also what Punch flees: the threatening hand of sexual and social responsibility, in the form of paternity.

As in *Violent Cases*, the motif of the puppet show renders the field of possible events legible as a singular *moment*, a violent moment that both is and occasions a turning-away, a relinquishing of *responsiveness*, or the ability to acknowledge the claim of others upon the self. This is what Morton and the

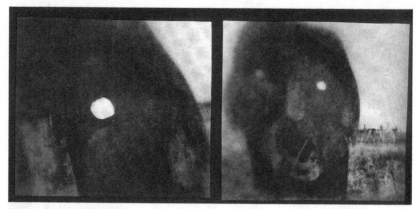

Figure 5.11. The grandfather mask (15).

grandfather—and Mr. Punch himself—embody, and it commits Gaiman and McKean to Crone's interpretation of Punch and Judy. Rather than endorsing a view of Mr. Punch as a trickster-hero, an insouciant avatar of social rebellion, they appear to identify that notion of rebellion with Crone's post-Victorian reinterpretation. The vision of Punch as a hero is an antifeminist vision, and specifically an expression of Victorian nervousness about a masculinity diminished by changing socioeconomic conditions and cultural mores. Crone suggests (and, thus far, Regan and Clark [366] agree) that Punch and Judy was in some ways merely honest: For all that late-Regency and Victorian ideologies of marriage might prate about domestic tranquility, women were and went on being battered (Crone 1058–1059).

But, particularly as bowdlerized by the Victorians, Punch framed this violence safely as slapstick comedy (and we get the term, as Ray Sparks points out, from Punch's own stick, specially designed to make a louder noise), letting audiences transfer the blame to Judy the shrew and her baby.

At the end of the book, the narrator himself performs the same move, deciding, "I don't know what the truth was. I am not even sure that I care" (80). He then briefly considers becoming a professor himself (84), before abjuring the whole business: he "went about [his] life" (89). There is a certain coy self-contradiction here: regardless of this decision, the narrator has nonetheless committed his story to the page, though the context remains ambiguous. By retelling his own story, with its embedded Punch and Judy show, he has actually retold the "oldest, wisest" play (35) yet again, serving as ventriloquist for Punch, and performing the compounded act of revealing uncomfortable truths while also hiding them from himself.

◆ ◆ ◆

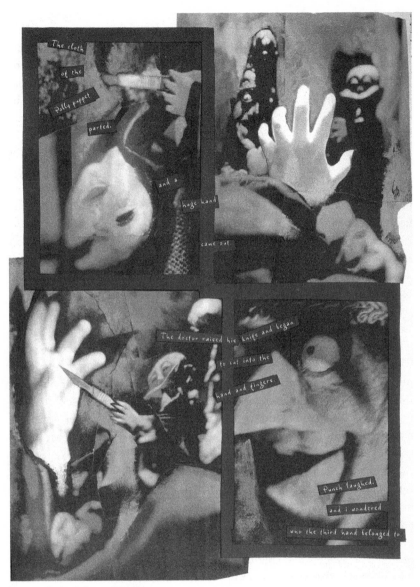

Figure 5.12. The hand of responsibility (48).

Gaiman and McKean use temporal anomalies to turn the reader's attention to how time itself is—somehow, paradoxically—both determined and open to chance or decision, as outlined in detail by Ricoeur and Lukacher. The people in both of these books mark out the process of aging, for each book features central male characters in childhood, adolescence, adulthood, advanced middle age, and senescence. These phases tend to carry each from fantasies of power, through actual power (with limitations, revealed in the action) and into a diminishment of power. The narratives catch these men in their vulnerable moments—in age, and in the contexts of family life, rather than business or social acumen. Both books use their temporal compressions to throw this image of vulnerability in stark relief against the violent exercises of power by which these men try to make the world fit their will. *Mr. Punch*, in particular, does so in ways that suit the recommendations of Lukacher (120) more than those of Ricoeur (208). These paradoxical stories and impossible temporal progressions present the ironic temporality that Lukacher envisions by compressing events into signal *moments*, even as they clearly signal their own inadequacy, by rendering those moments' connection to lived duration (to narrative progression) difficult to maintain. Where Ricoeur might say that these irruptions can be re-assimilated, or humanized (xi, 3), Lukacher would recommend that we understand their winking movement toward and away from meaning as a signal of a deeper problem with the event they present to readers.

In adopting the medium of the graphic novel, the books highlight both the hereditary power of the gesture of masculine violence, but also the sense that it need not unfold in this way. Both books contravene most of the narrative conventions of the genre as they stood in the late 1980s and early '90s. They prefer the framed narrative of the autobiographical memoirist to the objective third-person view. They favor process-based visuals—the sketchy, half-finished images in *Violent Cases* and the multimedia collages in *Mr. Punch*—over the cinematic polish of mainstream comics. And when they do make use of the vocabulary of traditional comics—in the shiny Mafiosi bats in *Violent Cases* or the swift action sequences in *Mr. Punch*—these elements undermine conventional action-adventure-oriented narrative processes, the kind of stories where muscular men resolve conflicts in dynamically rendered combat. As in Crone's reading of the Punch and Judy shows, Gaiman and McKean implicate readers in the truth that male violence is more often domestic than public; that it more often afflicts women and children than "worthy" villains; and that, too often, those who see it turn away rather than bear witness. At the same time—along the ironic lines sketched out by Lukacher—the narrators *do* bear witness, by relating their failures to relate.

NOTES

1. Single slashes (/) indicate a transition across speech-balloons or narration-boxes, while double slashes (//) indicate also a transition across panels.

2. There is also an event involving a star, which I lack space to consider here.

WORKS CITED

Brookes-Morris, Susan. "Britain Meets . . . Mr. Punch!" *Britain* vol. 80, no. 5, 2012, pp. 74–76.

Cates, Isaac. "Memory, Signal, and Noise in the Collaborations of Neil Gaiman and Dave McKean." *Drawing from Life: Memory and Subjectivity in Comic Art*. Jane Tolmie, ed. University Press of Mississippi, 2013, pp. 144–62.

Crone, Rosalind. "Mr and Mrs Punch in Nineteenth-Century England." *Historical Journal* vol. 49, no. 4, 2006, pp. 1055–82. Doi: 10.1017/S0018246X06005735.

Derrida, Jacques. *The Truth in Painting*, 1978. Geoff Bennington and Ian McLeod, trans. University of Chicago Press, 1987.

Gaiman, Neil, writer, and Dave McKean, illustrator and designer. *The Comical Tragedy or Tragical Comedy of Mr. Punch*. Vertigo/DC Comics, 1995.

Gaiman, Neil. *Violent Cases*, 1987. 3rd ed. Kitchen Sink, 1997.

Goldweber, David E. "Mr. Punch, Dangerous Savior." *International Journal of Comic Art* vol. 1, no. 1, 1999, pp. 157–70.

Groensteen, Thierry. *The System of Comics*, 1999. Bart Beaty and Nick Nguyen, trans. University Press of Mississippi, 2007.

Iversen, Stefan. "'In Flaming Flames': Crises of Experientiality in Non-Fictional Narratives." *Unnatural Narratives—Unnatural Narratology*. Jan Alber and Rüdiger Heinze, eds. Berlin: De Gruyter, 2011, pp. 89–103.

Katz, Leslie, and Kenneth Gross. "The Puppet's Calling." *Raritan* vol. 15, no. 1, 1995, 1–28.

Kilgore, Christopher D. "Unnatural Graphic Narrative: The Panel and the Sublime." *JNT: Journal of Narrative Theory* vol. 45, no. 1, 2015, pp. 18–45.

Klapcsik, Sandor. "The Double-Edged Nature of Neil Gaiman's Ironical Perspectives and Liminal Fantasies." *Journal of the Fantastic in the Arts* vol. 20, no. 2, 2009, pp. 193–209.

Lukacher, Ned. *Time-Fetishes: The Secret History of Eternal Recurrence*. Duke University Press, 1998.

McCloud, Scott. *Understanding Comics: The Invisible Art*. HarperPerennial, 1993.

Means-Shannon, Hannah. "*Violent Cases* and *Mr. Punch*: Neil Gaiman and Dave McKean Reflect Darkly on the Imagery of Individuation." *Studies in Comics* vol. 2, no. 2, 2011, pp. 357–73.

Mendlesohn, Farah. *Rhetorics of Fantasy*. Wesleyan University Press, 2008.

O'Neill, Dan. *The Collective Unconscience of Odd Bodkins*. Glide, 1973.

Regan, F. Scott, and Bradford Clark. "Punch and Judy: (England: 1682-Present)." *Fools and Jesters in Literature, Art, and History: A Bio-bibliographical Sourcebook*. Vicki Janik, ed. Greenwood, 1998.

Richardson, Brian. *Unnatural Narrative: Theory, History, and Practice*. Ohio State University Press, 2015.

Ricoeur, Paul. *Time and Narrative*. 3 vols. Kathleen McLaughlin and David Pellauer, trans. University of Chicago Press, 1984.

Sanders, Joe. "Of Parents and Children and Dreams in Neil Gaiman's *Mr. Punch* and *The Sandman.*" *Foundation* vol. 71, 1997, pp. 18–32.

Sparks, Ray. "Packing a Punch." *Britain* vol. 10, no. 8, 2000, pp. 32–34.

Speaight, George. "The Origin of Punch and Judy: A New Clue?" *Theatre Research International* vol. 20, no. 3, 1995, doi.org/10.1017/S0307883300008658.

Spiegelman, Art. *Maus II.* Pantheon, 1991.

"EVIL WITCH! I'M NOT SCARED!"
Monstrous Visualizations of the Other Mother in Multimodal Adaptations of Neil Gaiman's *Coraline*

JUSTIN WIGARD

Since its first publication in 2002, Neil Gaiman's *Coraline* has captured the imagination of readers of all ages through Dave McKean's surreal illustrations. It has spawned numerous adaptations with perhaps the most popular forms being P. Craig Russell's graphic novelization of Gaiman's original novella and Henry Selick's stop-motion film adaptation. Within these narratives, arguably the most discussed figure, next to Coraline herself, is the Other Mother, a character who offers Coraline both an invitation to a magical world and eternal imprisonment at the same time. However, in looking at the phenomenon of *Coraline* itself, a curious trend emerges over time: each successive adaptation places a stronger prominence on visuals than the one prior, seen most clearly in the different ways that each of these adaptations render the Other Mother by using visualization techniques unique to their specific medium. These illustrations do more than just construct the Other Mother in visual mediums; they embody the monstrous qualities of the Other Mother as she moves from surreal hag to realistic simulacra to a hybridized arachnid monster.

In this chapter, I will attempt to bridge a crucial gap in research on *Coraline* by focusing on the visual semiotics of the narrative across its adaptations, specifically by examining the intertextual connections between McKean's surreal and monochromatic illustrations in Gaiman's novel, Russell's comic book adaptation grounded both in realism and a muted pastel color palette, and Selick's garishly, brightly colored film version. The dominant discourse surrounding the canonical children's text has keyed in to the novella's psychoanalytic underpinnings, Gothic conventions, and postfeminist ideology while largely leaving out discussion of the visual aspects of Gaiman's novella, namely, McKean's illustrations. When examined intertextually, the illustrative styles used to depict the Other Mother (surrealism, realism, and a hybridized blend of the two) give insight into what monstrous traits are emphasized through medium-specific visualization techniques, ultimately revealing the fears that the Other Mother embodies through visual semiotics.

Of Psychoanalysis and the Gothic

Upon its first publication, *Coraline* garnered critical attention almost immediately, prompting several foundational investigations into the psychological underpinnings of Coraline's expeditions into the Other World and resultant conflicts with the Other Mother. David Rudd looks to key images in Gaiman's novel (the Other Mother's dismembered hand, Coraline walking off into the mist, the animation of various inanimate objects through the implementation of button eyes) as representative of Freud's notion of the Uncanny. By examining fictional embodiments of the Uncanny, "that class of the frightening which leads back to what is known of old and long familiar," Rudd offers a means of understanding the novel's intertextual relationship with earlier children's narratives and fairy tales (Freud 340). Elizabeth Parsons, Naarah Sawers, and Kate McInally build on this by suggesting that Gaiman's *Coraline* is a postfeminist fairy tale itself, in that the Other Mother here represents "real power, agency, authority, and autonomy," traits that ultimately lead the Other Mother to being overthrown and replaced with Coraline's real mother, who only "'masquerades' as empowered" (387). Further extending this connection, Rudd focuses on how the novel situates Coraline's position within her world, showing that the novel's psychoanalytic underpinnings allow one to see the ending of *Coraline* imbued with emotional growth when Coraline recognizes the burden she puts on those around her as "*she* is the one being overly demanding of her parents and neighbors," culminating in Coraline putting an end to the Other World and taking responsibility for her actions (167). In a similar vein, Richard Gooding argues that "the uncanny offers clues to the psychological costs of Coraline's renegotiation with her parents," effectively keying into the anxieties tied to Coraline's relationship between the Other World and reality, between her Other Parents and her real parents (391). These seminal conversations fail to account for McKean's imagery, which provides rich insight into the uncanny.

There is no question that Gaiman's *Coraline* is indebted to and entrenched within the Gothic, seen in its plucky young female heroine, looming yet mysterious manor-like house, and ghastly figures. Karen Coats looks to these conventions within Gaiman's *Coraline* as endemic to cultural anxieties about desires that the characters have (Coraline's desire to not be bored, the Other Mother's "regressive desire to consume Coraline," and a desire to exert their personal desire over the other) and how they address these desires in the narrative (88). More specifically, Coats taps into how Gothic desires are depicted visually through McKean's artistry, arguing that "the images are attempts to capture mental states and meanings that require interpretation rather than unthinking absorption" in several projects with Gaiman: *The Wolves in the Walls*, *Coraline*, and *Mirrormask* (82). Coats's insight into the Gothic conventions at work in three of Gaiman's texts for children are invaluable (the mother/daughter plots, sinister mysteries, and clearly defined villains chief among them), yet she only focuses on McKean's imagery in *The Wolves in the Walls* and *Mirrormask*, eschewing his surreal illustrations in Gaiman's *Coraline* in lieu of dissecting the Gothic anxieties within the novella's narrative. As a result, this investigation intends to build upon Coats's work by examining McKean's illustrations in conversation with other visual adaptations of Gaiman's *Coraline* as a means of understanding the anxieties entrenched in the Other Mother illustrations.

Whereas Coats highlights the connections between Gaiman's Coraline and Lucy Clifford's "The New Mother," Jax Goss's extended investigation into the adaptive changes between the two narratives provides the closest corollary to the current study. In Clifford's short story, a pair of children disregard their mother's wishes and warnings, until one day they find that she has been replaced by a New Mother, one with bony arms and two glass eyes. Here, Goss notes that "they look more or less alike" by highlighting similarities uniting the two figures, since both have too-long arms and eyes replaced with material objects: glass eyes for the New Mother, large black buttons for the Other Mother (70). Drawing on the work of Coats and Rudd for this investigation, Goss focuses on the humanistic stakes of these conceptions, showing that "the lack of real eyes in these characters shows a lack of humanity, which reveals their monstrousness in a way that [typical] fangs and claws could never do. They do not have real eyes, and this makes them somehow soulless" (72). Thus, the Other Mother's bodily construction is monstrous from the outset in its inhumanity. What is missing in Goss's intertextual analysis, however, is an exploration of the parallels between the visual adaptations of the Other Mother, particularly concerning how the Other Mother is represented across adaptations. By focusing exclusively on Gaiman's antecedents, particularly in their textual construction, Goss's research leaves a critical gap in scholarship surrounding *Coraline* that the ensuing exploration into the visual construction of the Other Mother is intended to bridge.

Much like Goss, I look to Linda Hutcheon's theory of adaptation as a means of understanding the intertextual connections between these three versions of the Other Mother. For these adaptations of *Coraline*, the visual styles act as one such mode of intertextuality, putting each of the Other Mother's iterations into conversation with one another. Hutcheon sees these adaptations not as contingent on faithful translation, but on "both (re-)interpretation and then (re-)creation" (8). In a span of seven years, the novella was adapted into both a graphic novel and a stop-motion animated film, which Hutcheon attributes to the desire to see the same narrative in new forms or interpretations. This is not to say that the adaptation need be wholly unrecognizable, as the points of recognition and repetition are just as important to consumers. For the *Coraline* narrative, then, one of these main points of recognition (beyond the titular protagonist) and reinterpretation is the figure of the Other Mother. To expand on the extant conversation, then, is to analyze the Other Mother in her varied adaptations, particularly for her visual similarities and points of departure as a monstrous character trying to capture the protagonist.

Jeffrey Cohen's seven theses on monstrous culture and monster theory offer insight into the foundations of teratology, the study of monsters, not least of which begin with the idea that the monster "signifies something other than itself" (4). This is in part due to the monster's inherent nature as an aberration, a hybrid being that eludes binary compartmentalization, and partly because "the monster is difference made flesh" as a constant representation of the Other. Developing this concept further, Barbara Creed calls attention to what she terms the monstrous-feminine, or "what it is about women that is shocking, terrifying, horrific, abject" in regard to the instability of the monstrous feminine body (44). While the Other Mother has indeed been analyzed as a representation of various anxieties (Rudd, Coats, Goss), these are primarily founded upon her actions within the narrative, not her visual construction. Using this foundation as a basis for the ensuing investigation, a cross-analysis of the Other Mother's visual representations will reveal what traits of the monstrous-feminine are deemed "horrific" or "terrifying" enough to illustrate, as well as those significant enough to be adapted from work to work to work. Thus, Creed's and Cohen's insights into monstrous representations offer insights into the meaning embedded in McKean's illustrations, Russell's comics, and Selick's stop-motion animation, meaning which can only be derived through visual semiotics.

Elsewhere, I have offered a working definition of visual semiotics as "a subset of semiotics primarily concerned with how meaning is constructed and represented in visual images," which allows meaning to be derived from analyzing formal elements in images writ large (Wigard 147). This correlates with Coats's insight into McKean's work as she argues his work demands active participation and interpretation, rather than passive reading (82). While noted comics formalist Scott McCloud isn't speaking directly to visual semiotics and is instead focused on comics, he argues that icons, which are basic visual representations in comics of their real-world counterparts, "demand our participation to make them work" (59). This is because, according to Charles Forceville, "unlike realistic photographs and live-action films, which more or less 'naturally' mirror real-life manifestations of emotions, comics and cartoons make use of stereotypical exaggerations using a rudimentary 'sign-system' very much like a language" (71). Essentially, formal elements in images act as signs here, signs that can only begin to be understood through active meaning-making. Under this purview, close readings of the visual semiotics at work in each of these illustrative styles will unlock new insights into the *Coraline* narrative, particularly concerning which visual elements carry forward from adaptation to adaptation.

"Big Black Buttons" and Monochromatic Surrealism

McKean's artistic style is best described as surreal, evoking a sense of unearthliness through bizarre multilayered collages, skewed perspectives, multimedia artistic approaches, and the illustrations for *Coraline*. Prior to *Coraline*, McKean created the covers for each issue of Gaiman's tremendously successful comic series *The Sandman*, as well as illustrated another children's book for Gaiman, *The Day I Swapped My Dad for Two Goldfish*, both of which feature mixed-media collages in full color. Returning to Coats's analysis of McKean's imagery, she notes that "McKean's surrealist mixed-media images engage the viewer on multiple levels but never at the level of a straight-forward representation of reality . . . the images are attempts to capture mental states and meanings that require interpretation rather than unthinking absorption" (81–82). Surrealist artwork is often "aimed at breaking the dominance of reason and conscious control by releasing primitive urges and imagery . . . [exploring] submerged impulses and imagery," and McKean's illustrations here are no exception (611). McKean's four illustrations of the Other Mother (Figures 6.1, 6.2, 6.3, and 6.4) embody these same surrealist proportions, both in terms of her own bodily depiction and of the Other World she occupies. By

Figure 6.1. Gaiman, p. 26.

exaggerating different aspects of the Other Mother's body and background without making the figure unrecognizable, McKean introduces a method of reading that necessitates interpretive work to make meaning of the image.

McKean introduces the Other Mother through a mostly innocuous illustration as she is stationed in the Other World's kitchen standing over a dinner of chicken and other assorted foods (Figure 6.1). Like his other work, McKean's image features multimedia illustrative techniques, drawing the Other Mother using pen and ink to define her strong nose, jawline, and details in her button eyes. This same technique is applied to the rest of her figure, draping her in shadows as she looks over her shoulder back at Coraline, and by proxy, the reader. The effect does not cover her completely in shadow, but acts a visual contrast point, showcasing these facial features. By comparison, the food is drawn in explicit detail, highlighting the realness of the culinary spread to the reader, while the background and the table itself are vague sketches by comparison. These light sketches suggest an ethereal quality to the Other World, lending her character a sense of gravity through visual contrast. What she has made for Coraline is real, even if the world itself feels liminal. Further, by placing the Other Mother so prominently in the foreground, she acts as the gatekeeper to the Other World before the reader, as if inviting the reader in through an upturned smile even though much of her is draped in shadows.

One key point about this illustration is that the reader is treated to the image before any textual description of the Other Mother (Figure 6.1). In the novella, the first illustration of the Other Mother appears at the beginning of Chapter III, prior to Coraline's exploration of the large house and subsequent initial foray into the Other World. This placement in the novella grants a significance to the illustration: McKean's illustration of the Other Mother is the first piece of evidence that something is truly amiss for Coraline. According to Margrit Shildrick, "the monster is something beyond the normative that stands against the values associated with what we choose to call normality and that is a focus of normative anxiety" (29). Almost immediately, this first image of the Other Mother strikes a chord of anxiety with the reader, stemming from the aesthetic weight of her monstrous eyes. She is marked as different, nonhuman even, based on this visual cue. Rudd notes that "Coraline's button replacements have the related association of giving up one's soul, the eyes being its window" (72). When the reader first encounters the Other Mother—that is, in Dave McKean's illustration—the content of the image breeds tension and anxiety: the reader hasn't yet encountered the Other Mother textually, so meaning must be made about the image with little-to-no context, and the button eyes signal monstrosity, even if the rest of her seems normative by comparison.

The second illustration of the Other Mother, however, is comprised almost solely of the Other Mother's monstrous traits, placing her button eyes, elongated fingernails/claws, and idle consumption of an insect on prominent display (Figure 6.2). The button eyes become the focal point of the illustration: their central positioning in the composition of the image demands the eye's attention, as do their black shading amidst a primarily light backdrop. Should the reader's eye follow the image down her shadowed wrinkles to the beetle trailing out of the Other Mother's mouth, which is a second main focal point, the composition keeps the eye moving counter-clockwise, trailing her hand and clawed finger back up the right side of the image back to her soulless button eyes. Here, McKean doesn't place the Other Mother against any particular backdrop, instead drawing her on top of a torn white piece of paper. As with the first, the reader may be confused as to the meaning of this specific collage, but keeping

Figure 6.2. Gaiman, p. 81.

in mind Coats's notion that McKean's work demands meaning-making and Shildrick's emphasis on the monster represents anxiety, it becomes apparent that the paper represents some aspect of monstrous foreshadowing. Kara K. Keeling and Scott Pollard emphasize the centrality of food (particularly food imagery and food symbolism) to the narrative of Gaiman's *Coraline*, arguing that food "functions as a cultural signifier" within the novel (2). As mentioned above, in the first illustration, the Other Mother has prepared a delicious-looking roast chicken, signaling the idea that eating food is normal; that is, the food that people *normally* eat. The second image, however, is centered around the Other Mother consuming a bug of some kind. Because this meal is treated normally by the Other Mother and met with disgust by Coraline, it stands to reason that, according to Keeling and Pollar, the eating of the insects associates social values of abnormality with the Other Mother. Only by progressing further into

Figure 6.3. Gaiman, p. 124.

the narrative does it become apparent that the paper isn't just paper: it's a torn fragment of a paper bag, representing the paper bag containing insects to be eaten by the Other Mother.

McKean juxtaposes the previous two sketches that spotlight the Other Mother with an image of the Other Mother silhouetted against the manor, consuming the key leading to the real world (Figure 6.3). The Other Manor dominates the bottom half of the image, a lightly drawn sketch featuring what seems to be two manors drawn over top of one another. Combined with un-finished porches and skewed window perspectives, the layering effect signals an impermanence to the Other Manor as the viewer sees the exterior merge with the interior, a combination of ghostly ephemerality. By contrast, the Other Mother is given heavy visual weight by being draped in dark shadows at the foreground of the image. These work in tandem to make the Other Mother

Figure 6.4. Gaiman, p. 159.

seem more real than the ethereal manor: her jawline, sharp teeth, serpentine tongue, and high cheekbones are all visually highlighted against these dark shadows, while her foregrounding causes the Other Mother to feel claustrophobically close to the reader.

The light splatter of ink represents the Other Manor's realness as it drifts back into the Other Mother's hand, suggesting that the longer her deadly game progresses, the more the Other World draws back into her. Lastly, a key is consumed in explicit detail by the Other Mother as she sticks out her tongue against the moonlight. Returning to Keeling and Pollard, abnormality abounds as an inanimate object is consumed, but more importantly, the Other Mother's last meal is drawn as a means of signaling the entrapment of Coraline. No key means no escape for the young protagonist, calling attention to the Other Mother's truly monstrous nature as a being that lures children in order to trap them.

The Other Mother is shown to be monstrous even from McKean's first image (Figure 6.1), as her non-normative traits are exaggerated and imbued with a surreal dread, but perhaps this is never more apparent than in the illustration of the Other Mother being attacked by the unnamed cat (Figure 6.4). The Other Mother's monstrous features are highlighted, as the reader sees her button eyes in grim detail, her unnaturally long claws, untamed hair, and sharp teeth all frozen in a shriek of terror. The composition of the image ensures that reader's eyes never stray far from the monster's eyes: the cat's claws (menacingly sharp) are poised to blind the Other Mother, while her claws return the gaze back up to the cat, whose curved body completes a never-ending loop of visual focus akin to a figure-eight, each leg pointed toward the monster's eyes, down to a monstrous appendage, and back. This image unites the three previous images, bringing together the Other Mother's unnatural eyes, overgrown claws, and pinpoint teeth into a single illustration. In this final illustration, McKean's visual aesthetic hews towards realism (or as close to realism as McKean deigns to approach in his artwork), depicting the Other Mother as hag-like, difference writ large, a hybrid being that, according to Cohen, is meant to visually signify a being just out of categorization. She is not human, but she is not a witch, or at least, not fully; McCloud notes that "by striping down an image to its essential 'meaning,' an artist can amplify that meaning in a way that realistic art can't" (30). The Other Mother, as depicted by McKean in all its surrealness, visually signals anxieties of a soulless interloper attempting to lure children out of their safe homes and into a dangerous den of her own creation. She is, from the beginning, a monster trying to lure Coraline away from her parents, prey on her desires for a more interesting life, and for this brief instant, she is no longer predator: her monstrous form is visually laid bare.

Pastel Realism, Shadows, and "Dark Red Fingernails"

Compared to McKean's surreal aesthetic, Russell's graphic novel adaptation of *Coraline* is defined by its palette of soft pastel colors and realistic drawings, both of which act as primary delineators between the graphic novel and the children's novella. Will Eisner notes that, within comics, the "comprehension of an image requires a commonality of experience," meaning that readers must be able to identify the content of the comics panel without barriers (13). Scott McCloud extends this notion by noting that the more realistically drawn a comics image is, the more recognizable that image is as something different from us; or, "the more cartoony a face is, for instance, the more people it

Figure 6.5. Russell, p. 17.

Figure 6.6. The reveal of the Other Mother in P. Craig Russell's graphic novel. Panel no. 6, p. 30, and panel no. 1, p. 31.

could be said to describe" (31). Janice Bland argues that the illustrations in the graphic novel embody McCloud's concept of amplification through simplification, wherein simpler or more universal cartoon-style artwork can offer wider meanings, particularly in the confines of Russell's adaptation. However, only looking at the visuals of the graphic novel ignores the surreal nature of McKean's original illustrations; by contextualizing the graphic novel with that of the novella, it becomes apparent that, even though Russell's illustrations do have a cartoony and somewhat universal quality to their aesthetic, they are decidedly more realistic (and thus narrow in their meanings) when compared to McKean's ethereal backgrounds, surreal figure drawings, and mixed-media collages that demand meaning-making.

When the Other Mother makes her first appearance in Russell's graphic adaptation, the reader finds a striking visual similarity to Coraline's mother (Figure 6.5). Both are wearing short-sleeved coral dresses with white accents and have short brown hair that ends before reaching their shoulders (Figure 6.6). The Other Mother's reveal takes place over two comic book panels spread across two separate pages, creating visual drama and foreboding (Figure 6.5). In the first panel featuring the Other Mother (30), located in the bottom-right corner, the reader only sees the Other Mother from behind while she is cooking;

Figure 6.7. Russell, panel no. 1, p. 31.

from this perspective, she looks similar to Coraline's very real mother, evoking a tense balance of comfort and dread in both Coraline and the reader. At this moment, before she has turned around and before the page is turned, it is unclear if this is Coraline's real mother, or something else. Upon turning the page, the Other Mother is revealed in the first panel: long teeth, with a feral and hungry look about her, pointed eyebrows, and of course, button eyes (Figure 6.7). Because this panel has zoomed in on the Other Mother's face, her monstrous elements become magnified in a comics-specific method. Whereas McKean's reveal utilizes surreal imagery to highlight her monstrosity (foreground and background, light and dark weight, detailed lines and light sketches), Russell gives the reader no other option but to take in her most monstrous feature: her button eyes. The realistic aesthetic also serves to call further attention to the black button eyes, as their round shapes are distinguished by their highlighted edges and button holes as distinctive from the rest of the soft coloring found here. Returning to Goss's analysis of the Other Mother's eyes, this monstrous facet is on display here as well as in the novella, reminding the reader that, for all of her similarities, there is still no soul behind those big black buttons, and therefore, no motherly intent.

This treatment of the Other Mother paints her monstrosity as stemming from the similarity to Coraline's real mother, comparable to McKean's first illustration of the Other Mother. Rather than accentuating her otherness through exaggerated visual characteristics or a surreal style of drawing, Russell leans into the realistic style of illustration to show how the Other Mother plays on Coraline's expectations of finding her real mother, time and again, only to be confronted with a monstrous simulacrum of what her mother should be. The monstrosity ultimately stems not from that which is different, as McKean's version does, but from the similarities between Coraline's real mother and the Other Mother (Figure 6.8). A further scene illustrates this point, as Coraline falls asleep in the liminal mirror-space, and the Other Mother picks her up, cradling the young heroine; Coraline feels a brief moment of peace, then wakes with a start upon realizing it is not her mother, but the Other Mother (Figure 6.9). Thus, when comparing the two illustrations of the Other Mother, McKean's surreal depiction has a universal otherness to it while Russell's adaptation is grounded in the realistic similarity to the real mother. Coraline's constant terror in the graphic novel stems from her inability to visually distinguish between the Other Mother and her own real mother; whereas McKean's depiction of the Other Mother becomes more monstrous over time, Russell's conception is sinisterly straightforward, always assuming a facsimile of the last time Coraline saw her mother.

"Pink, or Vermilion?" and Three-Dimensional Saturation

Selick's adaptation visually separates itself immediately from the novel through its use of color, but also from the graphic novel by imbuing the real world with rich saturation and shading. This is seen most prominently within the Other World, which features a phosphorescent and vibrant palette, to say nothing of the three-dimensionality of the stop-motion animation used. Lindsay Myers highlights Selick's *Coraline* as a wildly commercially and critically successful family film, one that deftly takes advantage of stop-motion animation production processes and digital technology. According to Scott Higgins, this is because "animation . . . both stylized and precise, has historically been an important platform for showcasing and experimenting with new visual technologies," meaning that animation is a medium built on meaningful choices when it comes to formalist elements of animation (199). Higgins suggests that the manner in which natural frame-by-frame animation for stop-motion is combined with "limited computer-generated imagery" offers

Figure 6.8. Russell, p. 69, panel no. 2, and panel no. 4, p. 68.

Figure 6.9. Russell, p. 98.

"unparalleled precision and control" unavailable in other forms of animation and film (200). However, Myers argues that in the process of adaptation, the film ultimately loses much of the progressive ideology inherent within Gaiman's original novel, resulting in a "fundamentally unprogressive vision of childhood" because the film gives agentic power to the Other Mother that she wields over Coraline's reality (247).

Ultimately, Myers finds that the film adaptation transforms the narrative from Gaiman's initial conception of empowerment into a tale grounded in contemporary fears of child abduction. The film takes visual cues from Russell's adaptation as well, initially depicting the Other Mother very similarly to Coraline's real mother (Figure 6.9). Like the graphic novel, the initial appearance of the Other Mother is something of a monstrous reveal, in that Coraline's real mother has shoulder-length brown hair, a round face, and is relatively short (compared to Coraline's real father, at least). After Coraline traverses to the Other World for the first time (in Selick's adaptation), Coraline's mother is cooking something while standing with her back to the viewer, only to turn around, fully revealed to be the Other Mother. Like Coraline's mother, this version has shoulder-length hair (black and shiny here), and is wearing a beige turtleneck and black pants. Hutcheon's notion of the palimpsestuous nature of adaptation is at play here, stemming from her claim that "an adaptation is a derivation that is not derivative—a work that is second without being secondary," seen when the multipage/multipaneled reveal of the Other Mother in Russell's graphic novel is echoed in Selick's reveal of the Other Mother, down to the pale yellow kitchen (9). The tension of the graphic novel—that Coraline's real mother has been replaced with a simulacrum virtually indistinguishable from the Other Mother—holds here as well.

As the movie progresses, the Other Mother's façade breaks down, much like McKean's original illustrations (Figure 6.10). Rather than becoming more hag-like, though, Selick's Other Mother becomes more arachnid-like. Upon her return trip to the Other World, Coraline finds the Other Mother cooking, but this time, her body has leaned out and she has adopted a different outfit: black-and-white polka dot top with red shoes and a red apron. At this point, Coraline is still cautiously intrigued by the spectacle of the Other World, visiting each of the Other versions of her real-world neighbors and laughing at the vivacious Other Parents. By the time Coraline challenges the Other Mother in order to win her parents back, however, the Other Mother is drastically distorted, characterized by her inhumanly thin limbs and impossibly tall body. This is reminiscent of McKean's surrealist illustrations for the Other Mother, skewing bodily proportions in an effort to accentuate one or two key characteristics—namely,

Figure 6.10. Selick's film reveal of the Other Mother, with comparison of Coraline's real mother.

the Other Mother's limbs. The climax of the film finds the Other Mother at her most visually monstrous, as she has become a spider, a hybrid being that "refuses any easy categorization" (Cohen 6). Any pretense of having good intentions has fallen away with this form, as she locks Coraline in, swallows the key, and distorts the living room into a three-dimensional web. Fully transformed, the stick-like legs have multiplied to give the Other Mother an arachnid-like lower body, while her arms now feature unnaturally sharp joints at the elbow. Her once-human hands are now claws comprised of sewing needles, and her clothing has melded with her body to resemble an exoskeleton. The final sequence of Selick's Other Mother reveals that each iteration was moving towards this arachnid-like being, not just in form, but in color.

As the Other Mother becomes increasingly distorted, the colors associated with her also change, reflecting her progression towards this spider-figure. Selick's sequence begins with a subtle cue: red shoes (Figure 6.11). While red shoes (flats, even) are innocuous enough on their own, reading the film intertextually with Russell's adaptation reveals a palimpsestuous correlation with the color red, as Russell's Other Mother is characterized by her monstrous claws adorned with red fingernail polish. The color red gains more prominence from form to form in the film, as the Other Mother leaves the beige turtleneck behind for form-fitting black-and-white clothing (while wearing a red apron) before wearing a tight dress of the same black-and-white polka dotted material (here with red accents). In her surreally thin and tall form, the color red comes to the forefront with a stylized red apron, as well as red high

Figure 6.11. The visual progression of the Other Mother in Selick's film adaptation of *Coraline*, and the feature of red shoes.

heels. The colors of red, black, and white might bring to mind an image of a black widow spider, but again, the monster always refuses easy categorization. Each of these depictions are shown, primarily, in the safe space of the yellow kitchen; however, upon her ultimate reveal, the Other Mother is depicted in the living room under a sinister green glow. This codifies the scene with malicious intent, as the Other Mother's embraces her arachnid heritage, molding what constitutes reality in the Other World to suit her needs. At this point, there are no other beings save Coraline, the cat, and the Other Mother. All of the color has been drained away, except for the green hue of the room, revealing what was hidden from Coraline. She returns the world into webbing, tearing away all pretense of a façade; the entire world was a trap, a snare for Coraline, and the trap has been sprung.

Selick's film adaptation represents a synthesis of McKean's surreal illustrations and Russell's graphic novel iteration, one that finds purchase in the monstrous evolution of the Other Mother. Initially, the filmic version of the antagonist hides her true form, instead masquerading as a simulacrum of Coraline's very real mother. In this form, the Other Mother suggests that, like Russell's version, the true terror is one grounded in reality: that a child may not recognize a stranger from a parent, resulting in the child going missing, getting kidnapped, or suffering an even worse fate. As Coraline uncovers more about the monstrous nature of the Other Mother, so too does the Other Mother's costume crack, crumble, and fall away. The visual semiotics at work here signify difference incarnate, a true Other, one with outwardly malicious intent. The anxiety has been externalized and reflected in the Other Mother's final form, both through the arachnid body that lurks and waits, and in her sewing needle claws which serve one purpose: "it's just a little thing; it won't hurt."

WORKS CITED

Bland, Janice. "Pictures, Images, and Deep Reading." *CLELEjournal* vol. 3, no. 2, 2015, pp. 24–36.

Coats, Karen. "Between Horror, Humour, and Hope: Neil Gaiman and the Psychic Work of the Gothic." *The Gothic in Children's Literature: Haunting The Borders*. Anna Jackson, Karen Coats, and Roderick McGillis, eds. Routledge, 2008, pp. 77–92.

Eisner, Will. *Comics & Sequential Art*. Poorhouse. 1985.

Forceville, Charles. "Visual Representations of the Idealized Cognitive Model of Anger in the Asterix Album *La Zizanie*." *Journal of Pragmatics* vol. 37, 2005, pp. 69–88.

Freud, Sigmund. "The Uncanny." *Art and Literature*. Albert Dickson, trans. Penguin, 1985, pp. 359–76.

Gaiman, Neil. *Coraline*, illustrated by Dave McKean. Harper Collins, 2002.

Gooding, Richard. "'Something Very Old and Very Slow:' *Coraline*, Uncanniness, and Narrative Form." *Children's Literature Association Quarterly* vol. 33, no. 4, Winter 2008, pp. 390–407.

Higgins, Scott. "3D in Depth: *Coraline, Hugo,* and a Sustainable Aesthetic." *Film History: An International Journal* vol. 24, no. 2, 2012, pp. 196–209.

Hutcheon, Linda. *A Theory of Adaptation*. Routledge, 2012.

Keeling, Kara K., and Scott Pollard. "The Key Is in the Mouth: Food and Orality in *Coraline*." *Children's Literature* vol. 40, 2012, pp. 1–27.

Kindborg, Mikael, and Kevin McGee. "Visual Programming with Analogical Representations: Inspirations from a Semiotic Analysis of Comics." *Journal of Visual Languages & Computing* vol. 18, no. 2, 2007, pp. 99–125.

McCloud, Scott. *Understanding Comics: The Invisible Art*. Harper Collins. 1993.

Myers, Lindsay. "Whose Fear Is It Anyway?: Moral Panics and 'Stranger Danger' in Henry Selick's *Coraline*." *The Lion and the Unicorn* vol. 36, no. 3, 2012, pp. 245–57.

Parsons, Elizabeth, Naarah Sawers, and Kat McInally. "The Other Mother: Neil Gaiman's Postfeminist Fairytales." *Children's Literature Association Quarterly* vol. 33, no. 4, Winter 2008, pp. 371–89.

Rudd, David. "An Eye for an I: Neil Gaiman's *Coraline* and Questions of Identity." *Children's Literature in Education* vol. 39, 2008, pp. 159–68.

Russell, P. Craig. *Coraline*. Harper Collins, 2008.

Selick, Henry, director. *Coraline*. Laika Studios, 2009.

Shildrick, Margrit. *Embodying the Monster: Encounters with the Vulnerable Self*. SAGE, 2002.

Wigard, Justin. "Harlequin, Nurse, Street Tough: From Non-Traditional Harlequin to Sexualized Villain to Subversive Antihero." *The Ascendance of Harley Quinn: Essays on DC's Enigmatic Villain*. Shelley E. Barba and Joy M. Perrin, eds. McFarland, 2017.

BETWEEN MIMESIS AND FANTASY
Binaries and Boundaries in *The Books of Magic*

ANDREW EICHEL

I like stories better than genres.
—NEIL GAIMAN

Plato and Aristotle are at least partially responsible for initiating the Western tradition of distinguishing realistic imitation as the goal of art, whereby "mimesis" became the standard against which literature was measured. Narratives that deviate too far from reality are dismissed as trivial by comparison. However, from the beginning, discourse around this term has been replete with disagreements. Witness, for example, Plato's banishment of poets from his perfect Republic because they speak falsehoods through their fictions, although Plato himself often refers to mythological legends and characters for his own purposes. In his monograph *Mimesis*, Matthew Potolsky explains, "Both philosophers distinguish mimesis from reality, but they take very different approaches to its natures and effects. . . . These two positions define the contours of the debate over mimesis in Western culture, and continue to inform discussions over the value of art" (7). Various philosophies and religious ideologies have since encouraged readers to view fantastic stories as entertainment only and not respectable accomplishments.

Although contemporary critics are still influenced by the pursuit of mimetic perfection, a tiny contingent holds with Kathryn Hume, who, in her seminal work *Fantasy and Mimesis: Responses to Reality in Western Literature*, argues that fantasy is as important for art as mimesis and that "it is the fantastic elements which allow literature to convey most of its varied senses of meaning" (28). I contend that Neil Gaiman's graphic series *The Books of Magic* is a refutation of the binary opposition between mimetic and non-mimetic modes of thought. Throughout protagonist Timothy Hunter's journey, reality and fantasy are offered to the audience as two ways of viewing and living in the world. As another character in *The Books*, the Phantom Stranger, puts it, a person can choose "the path of science, of rationality" or "the path of magic" (191). Gaiman may not offer a definitive resolution but that is because, as usual, he is more interested in getting readers to ask their own questions and arrive at their own conclusions. To illustrate Gaiman's arguments and mine, I will pair readings from *The Books* with some commentary from Hume, who challenges the centrality of mimesis. Along with resurrecting interest in an early Gaiman gem, this chapter will investigate the overlooked role of fantasy and its value alongside mimesis.

That Other Wizarding Wonder

Published in 1990–91, *The Books of Magic* was originally helmed by J. M. DeMatteis, who has worked with Marvel, DC, and Dark Horse. After that project dissolved, Gaiman was given the reins and, per his usual style, ambitiously undertook a multi-structured narrative concerning the division between reality and fantasy in life with each volume focusing on a different section of DC's mystical or occultist dramatis personae. Gaiman also retained different artists for each volume—John Bolton, Scott Hampton, Charles Vess, and Paul Johnson, respectively, with Todd Klein doing the lettering. This compartmentalization imbues the mini-series with a range of visual aesthetics that is as critical to its storylines and success as Gaiman's characters.

The ostensible purpose of the mini-series was simple: DC wanted to build off the success of *The Sandman*, Alan Moore's *Swamp Thing*, and James Delano's *Hellblazer* by re-integrating magic-wielding heroes and villains into their main universe. Gaiman did this by having readers traipse around behind Timothy Hunter, a bespectacled British teenager who is told by the mysterious Trenchcoat Brigade that he will grow up to become the most powerful magician of the age. Or rather that he *could* grow up to become the most powerful magician of the age *if* he so chooses. The members of the Trenchcoat Brigade are a who's-who among DC occult elite and a different character serves as Tim's Virgilian guide for the individual volumes: the Phantom Stranger for "Book I: The Invisible Labyrinth," John Constantine for "Book II: The Shadow World," Dr. Occult for "Book III: The Land of Summer's Twilight," and Mister E for "Book IV: The Road to Nowhere." In order to help Tim decide if the path of magic is for him, these guides introduce him to eldritch movers-and-shakers while providing colorful commentary on the risks—and rewards—of power, youth, and truth. Throughout his journeys, Tim is propelled both forward and backward in time as well as across dimensional boundaries, before finally being forced to confront the specter of himself as the next Armageddon.

More than a few comparisons have been made between Timothy Hunter and that other British boy-wizard, J. K. Rowling's Harry Potter. Both are male, teenaged, bespectacled, in a bad domestic situation, whisked into a hitherto unknown world of magic, accompanied by an intelligent owl, and prophesied to be a great magician someday. Visually, artistic representations of the two are similar enough to make any reader pause and consider.

Rowling's first Harry Potter novel appeared in 1997, and while Timothy Hunter's comics series was still being published monthly at that time, the character and his story had not reached near the heights of the HP pop-culture phenomenon. However, the accusations of plagiarism aimed at Rowling eventually caught Gaiman's attention to the point that he was compelled to respond. He has addressed this issue a number of times but the decisive statement is found in a 2008 journal entry on his website: "I wasn't the first writer to create a young magician with potential, nor was Rowling the first to send one to school. It's not the ideas, it's what you do with them that matters. Genre fiction, as Terry Pratchett has pointed out, is a stew. You take stuff out of the pot, you put stuff back. The stew bubbles on" ("Fair Use and Other Things"). In support of this metaphor, Gaiman has also pointed out that much of his inspiration for Timothy Hunter's character comes from T. H. White's Arthurian masterpiece, *The Once and Future King* (Richards). Yet, Gaiman's adolescent apprentice would become "nearly forgotten" (Berlatsky 1) in comparison to Rowling's boy wonder.

The Authority of Mimesis

The fetishization of authenticity is itself concomitant of our near-ontological focus on mimesis. We witness this fetishization in several ways: for instance, movie adaptations of books are often considered to be "lacking" in some essential yet indefinable way. *Of course* a movie leaves details out because there are *so many* words that layer the description in ways even special effects can't re-create; *of course* the real goal with every movie is profit and that leads to adaptation choices that rupture the narrative and introduce more inconsistencies; and *of course* technical elements like casting, lighting, editing, and cinematography will clash with individual readers' expectations, resulting in a subpar production. To suggest a movie adaptation is as good as, let alone better than, its original source material is often to mark oneself as a pariah of inferior taste.

This same line of logic leads, as another example, to the de-valuing of translations, another form of secondhand recreation. In Italian, the idiom "traduttore, traditor," meaning "translator, traitor," perfectly captures this double standard. A translator is not even mimicking by attempting to create something new and using another text for inspiration; instead, a translator is supposed to carry out the equivalent of a presumably menial literary task by lifting words from one culture/language/tradition and re-setting them in a new culture/language/tradition. The phrase "lost in translation" is synonymous for trying to explain what gets left out in any interpretation of an original but the phrase itself signals a complete lack of understanding concerning the true nature and goal of translation. The language of the original author is already at a remove from the meaning it tries to capture because of the arbitrary nature of words and their meanings. The source text of a translation cannot be any more authentic than the target text a translator aims to create because words do not embody meaning so much as they triangulate it. This linguistic axiom is at the heart of structuralism and poststructuralism, critical and philosophical viewpoints that investigate the nature of language and meaning. According to Ferdinand de Saussure, contributor to both these modes of thought, "If words stood for pre-existing concepts, they would all have exact equivalents in meaning from one language to the next; but this is not the case" (970). This is the crux of the impossibility of translation when viewed as a mathematicalizaiton of linguistic values where Term X in Language A is supposed to equal Term Y in Language B. There is no intrinsic, transcendental quality about the natural object known in English as a "tree" that gives it that label. Both the sounds and the idea they signify were already around before humans associated them in a specific system; uniting them was a happy accident. The system itself is artificial, a non-mimetic foundation upon which all language stands. In plainer terms, linguistic meaning is itself a fantasy layered arbitrarily over reality.

So, what does all this have to do with Gaiman's *The Books of Magic?* One issue Gaiman presses in his narrative is that, despite getting all the limelight, mimesis and the version of reality it depends on are simply not enough to account for all human experiences. Just as language needs a bit of non-mimetic irrationality to bridge the gap between concept and word, so too does living require more of the human mind than pure rationalization.

Gaiman's depiction of fantasy and mimesis in *The Books* aligns with elements of Kathryn Hume's critique of the artificial bifurcation of the mimetic and non-mimetic in literature. Hume argues that Plato and Aristotle found the tradition of western critical theory by "assum[ing] mimetic representation to be the essential relationship between text and the real world." However, Hume continues,

> [t]he tribute, though deserved, is not altogether a happy one. We might rather say that Plato and Aristotle between them tore a large and ragged hole in western consciousness. Ever since their day, our critical perceptions have been marred by this blind spot, and our views of literature curiously distorted. To both philosophers, literature was mimetic, and they analyzed only its mimetic components. Moreover, insofar as their assumptions allowed them to recognize fantasy at all, they distrusted and disparaged it. (6)

The oversight of these two philosophical paragons has led to an impoverishment of the Western intellectual tradition and, as Gaiman seems to hint, in how humans look at their relationship to the world. Aristotle held that the best dramatic works are those that most closely resemble real human interactions; Plato may have used fantastical mythology when it suited his own points, but he boots all such non-mimetic art from his perfect Republic because they are the shadow of a shadow, at a remove from reality and thus likely to lead unwary readers off-path. Since these elements of fiction could not be rationally—on the surface, at least—linked with common life experiences, they were denounced as not just useless but potentially harmful. Plato and Aristotle's pronouncements thereby allowed for thousands of years of crusading against non-mimetic modes of thought and creativity, creating a binary wherein all that is rational and realistic is "good" while all that is irrational and fantastical is "bad." We see this today in the general consensus that states while non-mimetic literature serves an escapist function, it cannot hope to carry as much moral or cultural value as realism—thus, the differentiation between "genre fiction" and "literature."

Dualities and Beyond

In *The Books*, the values in this binary often get flipped: rationalism is "bad" while the fantastic is "good." From the outset, the Trenchcoat Brigade makes clear that they still view fantasy and mimesis as antipodes from which only one can be chosen. Doctor Occult explains, "The boy [Timothy] is a natural force, for good or for evil, for magic or for science, and it is up to us to channel that force for good. And, perhaps, for magic" (8). "Science" and "magic" are synonyms for "mimesis" and "fantasy," or "rational" and "irrational," modes of thought.

The battle lines have been drawn and by nature of Gaiman's narration schema, readers find themselves agreeing with this viewpoint. In Book I, the Stranger provides telling details about his perspective: "Science is a way of talking about the universe in words that bind it to a common reality. Magic is a method of talking to the universe in words it cannot ignore. The two are rarely compatible" (40). Whereas science advances through force, magic relies on a more fluid dynamic, at least according to this biased practitioner. The representation of these perspectives is essential because, while the assumption is that readers should agree with the good guys, the audience, like Tim, is presented with a choice. Literature is full of unreliable narrators, and Gaiman has found a subtle, nuanced way to spread seeds of doubt about a few of his own.

Timothy is introduced to numerous other characters who express their own interpretations of the central duality of *The Books*. It is not as important whether these practitioners agree or disagree with the Trenchcoat Brigade; what matters is whether their opinions provide a nonbinary way of evaluating the choice Timothy faces. Two of the earliest opinions come during the Stranger's tour of the past, from a mage-lord in Atlantis and a young Merlin. The former expresses regret, advising Timothy, "The whole thing's a crock of dirt not worth the price I paid. Not for one second. If I had my time over again, I'd be someone happy and distant and small. Live in a hole in the ground. . . . Once you've begun to walk the path, there's no getting off it" (34). Let's pass over the blatant references to J. R. R. Tolkien's *The Hobbit* and focus instead on the mage-lord's description of choice as a one-way road. This view adheres to the fundamentalist opinions of Doctor Occult and the Stranger, presenting Timothy with the same "either/or" binary. Merlin's story is more complicated because his power allows him to see into his own future and even though he knows that the path of magic will lead him to his eventual downfall, he cannot step from it.

When Tim exclaims, "But—but if you know what's going to happen . . . why can't you change it? Do something else?" Merlin replies, "I'm sorry. I must do as I will do. Magic grants no freedoms, friend pupil. Everything it buys must be paid for" (41). Again, Merlin presents Timothy's choice as irreversible, a snuffing out of one entire world of possibility for the sake of another unknown, yet doubtless fraught, life. Given this sort of advice, it is no surprise that, at the end of this book, Tim does not yet know if he wants that power.

Despite the single-minded assessment of magic provided by most of the secondary characters in "Book I: The Invisible Labyrinth," its title—perhaps a breadcrumb from Gaiman—hints at the multiplicity of contradictory inner worlds lassoed within human consciousness. We are all "living labyrinths" where rational and irrational sides conjoin, collide, conflict, and coexist on a lattice of *both* reality *and* fantasy, not "either/or," a detail that Gaiman highlights on more than one occasion. For example, in repudiation of Doctor Fate's exposition on duality in Book II, Constantine tells Timothy, "Chaos versus order indeed. I thought everyone had heard of fractals these days. There's no chaos, no order. Just patterns of different complexity" (72). This statement also contradicts the party line put forth by the Brigade. Timothy is forced to confront these oppositions, to navigate those corridors with his eyes fully opened to the interpenetration between mimesis and non-mimesis.

For Gaiman, who is separate from his ostensibly "good" characters, the goal is not to get the boy to choose a single path but to help him see there is no real choice, only knowledge to help him live the best life possible. In Book II, Titania, the Fairy Queen, provides more insight into the role of the mind in connecting fantasy and reality:

[T]he places you will visit, the places that you will see, do not exist. For there are only two worlds—your world, which is the real world, and other worlds, the fantasy. Worlds like this are worlds of the human imagination: their reality, or lack of reality, is not important. What is important is that they are there.

These worlds provide an alternative. Provide an escape. Provide a threat. Provide a dream, and power, provide refuge and pain. They give your world meaning. They do not exist; and thus they are all that matters. (136)

There is a lot here to unpack but the main points are clear: fantasy is created by the human mind and it undergirds reality by creating recourse to alternative perceptions and means of interpretation, a fantastic hermeneutic. We do not look at the world—a conversation, an event, a relationship—and instantly understand everything about it intuitively. In a conversation, for example, we have to guess how our interlocutor might respond to what we are about to say and *then* we have to formulate a guess about what *we* will say in response to that and so on.

We can never be certain of another person's knowledge or opinion so there is a certain amount of imaginative work that is critical to allowing any communication to happen. We want patterns, so we find them, even if that means "lying" to ourselves about what we are seeing. But this is more than lying; this is storytelling, the creation of a sustaining narrative that gives us the strength and surety to continue living our life in the absence of complete existential telos. Talk to a dozen people who witnessed the same car accident and you will get a dozen different stories. Some might be more or less related to the reality of the event itself, but that does not make them lies. The truth can be found through fantastical triangulation, in this case.

What gives the fantastic hermeneutic its potency is its array of perspectives, possible only due to a distinct lack of reality which would bind it to a singular, rational mode of comprehension. Titania mentions this variety of human imagination as well, "There are, after all, as many worlds and planes, hells and paradises, as a mind can encompass" (145). Doctor Occult appears to agree with the Fairy Queen's assessment, commenting "Perhaps each of us creates his own fantasy world—a place to which we can retreat" (140). One such world the pair visits is Hell, about which the Doctor remarks, "This is a place of punishment, Timothy. Those who believe they must atone, inflict this place and its tortures upon themselves . . . until they understand that. Until they realize that they, and only they—not gods or demons—create their hell; and by this they are freed, and take their leave . . . this place is evil, Timothy. But perhaps a necessary evil" (142). Reality cannot provide a person with all the knowledge or experience that is needed to adapt and survive; cold rationality and technologic sophistication do not touch upon matters of the heart or soul or whatever you choose to label the incorporeal aspect of existence. As Hume explains, "Given that we recognize meaning as internal to ourselves, not an eternal and external fixity, we can see why realism cannot be expected to supply that sense of meaning any more. Insofar as realism concentrates with quasi-scientific disinterest on what there is in the 'real' world, it cannot validly express value judgments, they being human likes and dislikes" (50). Reality, thus, is the limitation while fantasy, for a price, offers a path to honest if imperfect liberty.

The Constant Guide

Throughout Book I, the Phantom Stranger introduces Timothy to other magical practitioners in order to help him make an educated decision about his own future, as he explains at the outset of their journey: "Our role is to educate, Timothy. To show you the path of enchantment, of the art, of gramarye and glamour. Whether you choose to walk it after that will be your own affair" (13). Note the use of "gramarye," from the Old French meaning "grammar," which makes bare the affinity between words and fantasy. Rather than follow the Phantom Stranger's insistence that these perspectives are opposed, Gaiman instead shows Timothy, over the course of the entire series, that fantasy and mimesis function together to form a continuum. Gaiman also provides the audience clues to guide them past fundamentalist assertions that cleave to dualistic interpretations of human activity. This sentiment, too, mirrors part of Hume's conclusions about mimetic and non-mimetic modes of literary production. She writes, "Fantasy and mimesis seem more usefully viewed as the twin impulses behind the creation of literature. At times, I have tried to deal with them apart from each other, but they are tightly intertwined and not readily separated. Their powers overlap, but are also often complementary and sometimes synergistic, rather than competitive, Insofar as literature gives its readers a sense of meaning, both are almost always involved" (195).

Most often, the character John Constantine serves as the voice of caution rather than the voice of reason *or* imagination. In the world of DC Comics, Constantine was traditionally a trickster character, known more for his con-man routines than his arcane might, although new changes to the DC-verse have put Constantine's powers more front stage. Shortly after the Stranger's comment above, Constantine quips, "All we know for sure is that we don't know anything for sure" (2). Constantine might best be regarded as an "enlightened" individual, one who has already made the journey upon which Tim is embarking. The audience is signaled that *something* sets Constantine apart, for instance, when he remarks, "But I'm just along for the ride. Not like these three," referring to the rest of the Trenchcoat Brigade (2). When the Stranger hands Timothy over to Constantine, the latter also jokes, "Makes you laugh, dunnit? The blind leading the blind" (54). And when Timothy asks Doctor Occult about Constantine at the outset of "Book 3: the Land of Summer's Twilight"—"I mean, Constantine, he's just a bloke, isn't he?"—the guide replies, "Yes. He dances on the edge of the known like a crazy man, pitting himself against Heaven and the Pit because he is John Constantine; and he is alive" (105). Of the Brigade, only Constantine has freed himself from the trap of viewing science and magic, the mimetic and the non-mimetic, as eternally and irreparably opposed. According to the Doctor's comment, Constantine's flouting of the dualistic viewpoint is in part a result of his mortality. He has divested himself of this restrictive outlook, the same outlook that puts Tim in danger. For while the Trenchcoat Brigade stands for the "good," their enemies, the Cold Flame, stand for the "bad" and they want Tim for their own purposes.

To complicate matters further, even the good guys have not agreed on what they should do with Timothy; the first lines readers get from Mister E are as follows:"I say that we should kill him. End the matter there" (8). He finally does attempt to murder Timothy while serving as his guide in Book IV but the incarnations of Destiny and Death intervene.

Despite the extreme views of his teammates, Constantine holds a different opinion, one that he chooses to share with Timothy and readers at certain moments. He also introduces Timothy to practitioners who offer a space between the lithic duality that seems to be omnipresent. The first such example in Book II is Doctor Fate, who holds that

> [a]ll things are divided into the twin forces of order and chaos, forever contending for dominance. Life is something that occurs in the interface; not in the writhing discord of utter chaos, nor in the flatline perfection of pure order, but somewhere in between. . . . It is the basis of magic: the imposition of order on formless chaos, the release of joyous chaos into the gray monotony of order . . . This is the true magic (71).

While he clings to a binary opposition, Doctor Fate creates room for the human experience as something that needs both order and chaos to exist. The order of rational thought and the chaos of the irrational blend and give birth to humanity. Too much of either renders life null and void of any discernable meaning. Magic, like life, partakes of both order/rationality and chaos/irrationality, just as Constantine gains confidence from and revels within that very same "interface." As I wrote earlier, Constantine responds to Doctor Fate's views by referencing fractals, self-similar patterns that repeat themselves infinitely within mathematical sets and finitely within nature. Life is not composed of opposites competing ceaselessly; rather, when you pierce the surface, you see a complex pattern, and when you observe that pattern, you see within its makeup another pattern, and so on and so on. Constantine can see that truth and it allows him to maintain sanity and liberty while other magic-users flock to one extreme or the other.

The next person Constantine introduces to Timothy is the mysterious, and passively malevolent, Baron Winter. After much insisting, the Baron advises Tim that "[m]agic is not important" and that what truly matters is "[b]eing who you are" (80). Although this is not an expanded scene, and it might be easy to pass over in favor of more action-packed sections of *The Books*, the Baron's message is similar to Constantine's own. Whether one chooses mimesis or non-mimesis, reason or imagination, you still have to be happy with yourself.

You still have to *live*. After exiting this exchange, the boy-wizard questions his guide: "Are you sure you're one of the good guys?" Constantine answers, "There aren't any good guys, and there aren't any bad guys. There's just us. People doing our best to get by" (82). Again, he rejects any attempt to portray living as something that can be neatly dissected and compartmentalized into Venn diagrams of restricted overlap.

Timothy meets another adept with a similar perspective later in Book II, when Zatanna, Constantine's friend and former paramour, escorts him to a party. Unfortunately, this is a gathering of villainous magicians who want Tim for their own ends. Their nominal leader, Tannarak, explains, "There's no such thing as black magic. It's semantic drift. Black magic is a translation of the word nigromancy, you see. And nigromancy is just a corruption of 'necromancy.' The magic of the dead. It's not black magic versus white magic. I tend to think of it as live magic versus dead magic. But even that's simplistic dualism" (95).

One of the stranger side characters Constantine introduces is Dr. Terry "The Ghost-Breaker" Thirteen, a professional debunker of all things supernatural and paranormal. Dr. Thirteen claims,

In fifteen years I haven't seen one thing which was not susceptible to rational explanation. Either it was a hoax, or a fraud, or—often—people wanting so much to believe in powerful forces outside of our ken that they'd convinced themselves of the existence of magic, taking simple coincidence or delusion as proof of their superstitions. . . . I think I can say with some certainty that if magic existed I would have found some evidence of it by now (85).

Afterwards, Constantine explains, "Now he doesn't believe in magic. And he's right. Magic doesn't exist for him." What Tim is meant to take from this meeting is: "You have to choose [magic], you see. That's what we're offering you: the choice. If you don't want magic, you'll never see it again. You'll live in a rational world, in which everything can be explained. But if you choose—well, it's like stepping off the sidewalk into the street. The world still looks the same, on the surface, but you can be hit by a truck any second. That's magic" (86).

Allowing the non-mimetic into your life creates a risk, yes, *but* it opens up your existence to a range of new experiences that are denied those who cling to rationality as the only lens through which to observe or interact with the world.

The reason I point out all these examples is to stress that Constantine—as a character and as a guide—presents Timothy with a unique range of choices for interpreting reality.Unlike his fellows in the Trenchcoat Brigade, he would prefer a hands-off approach to the boy-wizard over intervention. Experience is the surest route to gaining knowledge, a mantra for world-weary, ever-practical Constantine. When he is given no other choice, the occult con man does his best to help Tim understand the limitations of any fundamentalist interpretation of the mimesis/non-mimesis duality, even going against his compatriots to do so.

The Consequences of Extremism

In "Book IV: The Road to Nowhere," Mister E takes Timothy into the far future, where science and magic are bound together once again: "Technology has increased to the point where people no longer comprehend it. To the point where it might as well be magic, for all they know" (164). While this is a restatement of Arthur C. Clarke's well-known adage dubbed his Third Law—"Any sufficiently advanced technology is indistinguishable from magic" (Clarke 21)—it might also serve as a reminder that, like so many things in life, the compartmentalization of the rational away from the irrational relies on perspective.

According to Mister E, this blending of mimetic and non-mimetic technologies continued in the thirtieth century until the Archmage—the source of the resurgence of the arcane—broke from his prison and interrupted the normal processes and logic of science: "Science ceased to work as the irrational erupted into the mundane, subverting it, destroying it" (167). However, instead of using this power to better integrate the fantastic and the realistic, the Archmage ended up destroying all of it, and thus "science and logic and cold rationality held illimitable dominion over all" (167). It is easy to see Gaiman's warning here: balance, above all, is what is needed. Even if you are like Mister E and strive in the name of the "good," the supremacy of one ideology over all others will inevitably lead to violence, suppression, and dangerous myopia.

Continuing Mister E's tour, one of the figures Timothy runs into is the future avatar of Doctor Fate, but this incarnation is not nearly as genteel as the one he met while with Constantine. And nor is it any longer a servant of balance, announcing instead, "Order. It's offal. Chaos. It's garbage. They were just different names for the same thing: the gurgle, ooze, purl and spurt of protoplasm, deluding itself that there is meaning. There is no meaning. Just the flesh. And death" (169). Although the grotesque graphics and lexicon of this exchange conspire to turn readers against this version of Doctor Fate, if we consider the connotations of this perspective, we see that it presents a similar interpretation of reality as that espoused by Constantine and the past Doctor Fate. Constantine's many comments, delivered as jokes or afterthoughts, undercutting their significance, chip away at the logic of a dualistic approach to life. Doctor Fate's effluvial vocabulary is itself "just different names for the same thing": life is not *either* chaos *or* order—it is both, it is what happens in the "interface." Doctor Occult's earlier comment about Constantine's *raison d'être* are worth repeating here: "He dances on the edge of the known like a crazy man, pitting himself against Heaven and the Pit because he is John Constantine; and he is alive" (105). Mortality inherently supplies the meaning to life that fundamentalist ideologies attempt to force.

Before Mister E attempts to murder Timothy in Book IV, he takes him into the far future and reveals a version of reality where the boy has chosen to disregard the aid of the Trenchcoat Brigade and instead joins the opposition. He remarks, "It is sad but true that the dividing line between good and evil blurs, in the realm of magic" (157). As reasonable as this stance seems, all this interpretation does is allow Mister E to implement his own brand of vigilante justice on whomever he chooses, as his next statement makes clear: "Sometimes I think that I alone am pure." A few pages later, when Tim expresses his dislike for Mister E, the guide adds, "And I do not permit affection, or lack thereof, to influence my actions. There is good, and there is evil. The good must be protected; the evil eradicated" (159). Mister E is recognized as a potential liability by the rest of the Trenchcoat Brigade—Doctor Occult even tells Timothy that "[h]e is an extremist. He fights what he sees as the forces of darkness; but sometimes I suspect that all he ever can see is darkness" (105). Ironically, most of the Brigade have their own type of blinders on, limiting their ability to objectively consider their extreme stances. As such, Mister E stands as a particularly obvious and powerful reminder of the dangers of fundamentalist devotion to any interpretation that vilifies all opposition.

The Carousel Goes Round and Round

Finally, his long journey over—and remarkably calm given Mister E's recent murderous rampage—Tim Hunter receives the ultimatum from the Phantom Stranger:

> So, Timothy, you have seen what we have shown you. You have seen the past. You have met a handful of the present practitioners of the Art. You have glimpsed the worlds that touch your own. You have seen the beginning, and you have seen the end. Now, yours is the decision. If

you choose magic, you will never be able to return to the life you once lived. Your world may be more . . . exciting . . . but it will also be more dangerous. Less reliable. And once you begin to walk the path of magic, you can never step off it. Or you can choose the path of science, of rationality. Live in a normal world. Die a normal death. Less exciting, undoubtedly. But safer. The choice is yours. (191–92)

Tim's answer is perhaps not what the average reader expects: "I've learned a lot of things. The main thing I've learned is that it all has a price. I mean, you can get whatever you want. But it all has to be paid for, doesn't it? And I don't want to pay what it'll cost. I'm scared. I'm sorry" (192). The Phantom Stranger's reply is characteristically unhelpful: "It is your choice, Timothy. Always and forever, your choice." In a fit of panic and doubt, Tim tries to change his mind, shouting, "No! I didn't mean it. I do want it" (192). But it's too late; the Trenchcoat Brigade has already disappeared.

Yet, the story does not end there. When, in some anonymous smoky bar immediately after leaving Tim, John expresses his disappointment, the Stranger and Doctor Occult reveal that Tim had already made his choice, back when they first met and asked him if he wanted to come with them and learn about magic: "I did not lie to him, Constantine. I told him the choice was his, and indeed, it was. And he made his choice, when first we met" (195). Throughout the journey, it was implied that Tim would still be able to choose the rational world but it turns out that knowledge, like energy, cannot be destroyed, only transferred. Simply by informing Tim that there was a choice to be made, the Brigade ensured he could never again return to his previous state of mundane, rational normalcy.

Fantasy was always-already there, irrevocably. Truth, like reality, is subject to perspective bias. Constantine is appropriately upset when he learns this particular truth since he was against intervention from the beginning, when he thought they were offering Timothy an actual choice. As much as readers might want to side with Constantine, the Stranger offers a hopeful explanation that aligns with what Gaiman seems to be saying about the duality at the heart of this story: "They say humanity only gets one chance at the carousel's golden ring. But the carousel goes round and round, and round and round. And the golden ring is not going anywhere" (195). If the carousel is life, and the golden ring is the liberty made possible by letting non-mimetic modes of thought affect your worldview, then to deny Tim a chance to access that liberty whenever he wants would place more limits on his freedom, thereby proscribing him to the rational/mimetic/scientific realm of reality. If Constantine had had his way,

Tim's initial rejection of magic would be enough to forever deprive him of the joys and pains of magic. By duping him, the Stranger thereby allows Timothy a second chance, something, we are told, no other magic-user gets.

From there, the comic shows us Tim arriving back home, where everything—including his blunt, uncaring father—is as distasteful as it was before. The final page depicts Tim alone in his room and says, "I don't need you lot. I don't need anything. All I need to do is believe" (198). Suddenly, Tim's yo-yo transforms back into his owl. The last word in the comic is shouted by Tim: "Magic!" While the use of "believe" here seems a bit clichéd, it, nevertheless, accurately communicates how one can access the power of the non-mimetic. Gaiman establishes that the fantastical is, as Hume suggests, "any departure from consensus reality"; thus, to partake of that mode of thought, a person must leap away from logic and into irrationality (21). Much like religious faith, Tim's belief suspends the paradox of potential transgressions on reality. Since living in this world requires a continuum of thought processes that range from hyper-logical to hyper-fantastical, people are already well-versed in suspending disbelief.

Hume writes, "Meaning seems to be any system of values that causes phenomena to seem related according to a set of rules, and, preferably, that makes them seem relevant to human concerns" (169). Notice her repetition of the word "seem," highlighting the lack of any concrete, transcendental meaning. Magic in Gaiman's world is a material manifestation of the power of the irrational, a necessary component for mortal life in an unknowable universe. Fantasy is attendant upon meaning, as is mimetic interpretation, and humans are, among other things, telos-seeking animals; we want our lives, our actions, to have a meaning greater than the causes-and-effects that seem superficially to direct our movements and choices. Like Tim, however, when we get the chance to embark down a wholly new, wholly alien, and wholly unknowable path, fear of failure often causes us to shrink from the possibilities. *The Books of Magic* reminds readers that the Trenchcoat Brigade does not matter—Tim doesn't need them and neither do we.

The choice between mimesis and fantasy is no choice at all. We live every day caught in webs of denoted and connoted meaning, some of our own making. By forcing readers to think more critically about the vital role non-mimetic thought plays in their lives, Gaiman is attempting to rescue both fantastical literature and our own natural, fantastic hermeneutic. I might even argue this belief is one that binds together all of his fiction. Like the Brigade, however, Gaiman can merely show us the truths. What we choose to believe is up to us. And he wouldn't have it any other way.

WORKS CITED

Berlatsky, Noah. "Harry Potter's Forgotten Predecessor." *Atlantic*, 11 March 2015. https://www
.theatlantic.com/entertainment/archive/2015/03/the-other-harry-potter-that-never-was/387364/.

Clarke, Arthur C. *Profiles of the Future: An Inquiry into the Limits of the Possible*. Rev. ed. Harper
& Row, 1973.

Craig, Amanda. "Neil Gaiman: The Most Famous Writer You've Never Heard Of." *Times*, 30
October 2008. http://www.thetimes.co.uk/tto/arts/books/article2453500.ece.

Gaiman, Neil. *The Books of Magic*. New York: DC Books, 2014.

Gaiman, Neil. "Fair Use and Other Things." *Neil Gaiman's Journal*, 19 April 2009. http://journal
.neilgaiman.com/2008/04/fair-use-and-other-things.html.

Hume, Kathryn. *Fantasy and Mimesis: Response to Reality in Western Literature*. Methuen, 1984.

Hanging Out with the Dream King: Conversations with Neil Gaiman and His Collaborators. Fantagraphics Books, 2004.

Potolsky, Matthew. *Mimesis*. Routledge, 2006.

Richards, Linda. "January Interview: Neil Gaiman." *January Magazine*, August 2001. http://
januarymagazine.com/profiles/gaiman.html.

Saussure, Ferdinand de. *Norton Anthology of Theory and Criticism*. Vincent B. Leitch, et al., eds.
W. W. Norton & Company, 2001. 956–77.

INVERTED SPACES
Rising from the London Below and the Dark Lands in *Neverwhere* and *MirrorMask*

ZÜLEYHA ÇETINER-ÖKTEM

The mind of Neil Gaiman works in mysterious ways, specifically when we consider how space is employed in his works. The seamless juxtaposition of real and imaginary places that tend to overlap, create various spaces that are not simply settings where events unfold, but are almost lifelike characters in their own right that directly affect the actions of the characters as well as the production of the narrative. The major space-character is inevitably the actual location—*Neverwhere*'s London and *MirrorMask*'s Brighton, for example—which is then inverted to create a darker other and a darker story. These doppelgänger cityscapes both haunt and liberate the protagonists as they journey through mappable and unmappable spaces that enforce a reckoning of the self. Gaiman's narratives that begin in real spaces are depicted as being safe and familiar from which they are drastically altered, turned inside out, and made familiarly strange. Although the transposed city of *Neverwhere*'s London Below and *MirrorMask*'s dreamworld are quite different from one another, the functions of these spaces seem to be very similar: they allude to a metaphorical mapping of the self where there is room for transformation and change, allowing the characters to gain awareness and work out issues of self and identity.

My intent in this chapter is not to map out all the types of various spaces and places employed in Gaiman's two narratives. I aim instead to analyze how specific spaces function in Gaiman's mirror-worlds in conjunction with the main characters. Before doing so, however, I will briefly introduce the theoretical framework comparing the general aspects of the two texts, and then move forward to explore what space does in Gaiman's narratives along with how the main characters interact with specific, unique spaces.

Towards a Literary Geography

The spatial turn, the prioritizing shift from time to space, was prophetically claimed by Michel Foucault in his essay "Of Other Spaces," in which he stated that after the nineteenth century, "[t]he present epoch will perhaps be above all the epoch of space" (22). Commenting on Foucault's essay, the geographer Edward Soja wrote:

> No hegemonic shift has yet occurred to allow the critical eye—or the critical I—to see spatiality with the same acute depth of vision that comes with a focus on *durée*. The critical hermeneutic is still enveloped in a temporal master-narrative, in a historical but not yet comparably geographical imagination. (11)

Yet the spatial turn has artfully made its way into the humanities as a prevalent area of study specifically during the last decades (Kümin and Usborne 305). In their introduction to *The Spatial Turn*, Warf and Arias write that "[g]eography matters, not for the simplistic and overly used reason that everything happens in space, but because *where* things happen is critical to knowing *how* and *why* they happen" (1, emphasis original). Thus, space becomes an active element that both shapes and is shaped as "space takes for us the form of relations among sites"; moreover, "[w]e do not live inside a void . . . we live inside a set of relations" (Foucault 23). As such, the dialectic between human activity and space becomes inseparable.

Taking this a notch further, the interdisciplinary project "A Literary Atlas of Europe," carried out by the Institute of Cartography and Geoinformation, directly applies the science of cartography to the literary narrative where the main research question is: "Where is literature set and why there?" In the hunt for compiling a literary geography/cartography, as much as actual geographic sites are gathered from literary narratives, other seemingly abstract spaces, such as memories, dreams, places of longing, and other projected spaces, are also mapped.

Piatti et al., stating the obvious, say, "each literary work takes place somewhere," emphasizing that "it's impossible to even think [about] literature without any spatial context" (178). Reuschel and Hurni write: "Besides the sometimes entirely imaginary settings, common to genres such as Science Fiction and Fantasy, writers often link their stories to existing, recognisable places" (293). Although Neil Gaiman's *Neverwhere* and *MirrorMask* are both works of fantasy fiction, they begin in actual mappable geographic locations.

Mapping spaces in literary narratives requires a systematic approach and palpable categorizations that would cover various spaces and places mentioned in the texts. In dealing with specific spaces, then, the spatial designations categorized and defined by Piatti and developed further by Reuschel and Hurni is a good place to start. In their discussion concerning the relations between literary space and real space, Reuschel and Hurni discuss "invented" and "imagined" spaces: invented spaces are defined as being "an invented setting within familiar geographical reality"; whereas imagined spaces lend "no hint at all about the position of the setting, it is located 'somewhere,' with no real-world counterpart, only existing within the narration" (296). From this perspective, *Neverwhere* falls under the purview of invented space as both London Above and the London Underground have real-world counterparts, even though London Below does not exist in reality. *MirrorMask*, on the other hand, features an imagined space, although the alternative world begins in the apartment located in Brighton, the rest of the dreamworld is a semi-autonomous geography that does not actually exist in the real world.

Mapmaking, Storytelling, and the Threshold Phenomenon

Mapping spaces and places in fantasy fiction is less problematic as most of the stories occur on newly mapped locations, tailor-made for the events yet to unfold, many even include maps with books. J. R. R. Tolkien's Middle Earth, Ursula Le Guin's Earthsea, G. R. R. Martin's *Song of Fire and Ice* series are but a few examples where the physical maps enable the reader to navigate within the imagined realms. When it comes to Gaiman's *Neverwhere* and *MirrorMask*, however, things tend to get complicated. The literary maps Gaiman draws are hazy, with gaps to be filled even though the inverted spaces in both narratives are actually built on physical maps. The London Underground for *Neverwhere* and Helena Campbell's drawings in *MirrorMask* become navigational tools and points of reference where we can attempt to mentally follow and track the characters' movements through the created and imagined spaces they occupy.

But space functions oddly in Gaiman's stories. Directions in London Below often become confusing. Going down does not necessarily mean reaching somewhere underground. To get to Old Bailey's rooftop, for example, one must descend. Although already somewhere underground, Gaiman's narrator must go further "down" to reach Old Bailey's rooftop perch. Walking on Down Street literally means walking vertically down the street. Directions in *MirrorMask* also become irrelevant, especially after shadows begin to envelop spaces and lands start to fall off the face of the earth. In the film version's case, a two-dimensional map becomes irrelevant; one must envision these mapped worlds as three-dimensional templates in need of constant modifications and updates.

Maps, however, are only representations of space that contain information conveyed by images and signs (Lefebvre 233). Although maps attempt to communicate spatial information as accurately as possible, they tend to distort reality. Maps are not objective works as their purpose is to impose order upon a world. Maps convey their own reality by missing or omitting parts and they are often wrong in scale. In this sense, mapmaking is quite similar to storytelling.

Relating the act of storytelling to a sort of mapmaking, where spatial inaccuracies are what makes the stories *stories*, Gaiman writes:

> One describes the tale best by telling the tale. You see? The way one describes a story, to oneself or to the world, is by telling the story. It is a balancing act and it is a dream. The more accurate the map, the more it resembles the territory. The most accurate map possible would be the territory, and thus would be perfectly accurate and perfectly useless. The tale is the map which is the territory. (*Fragile Things* xvii; *American Gods* 589)[1]

As a literary mapmaker, following in the footsteps of other British authors such as Lewis Carroll and C. S. Lewis, Gaiman constructs landscapes and territories that fuse the known world with that of the fuzzy fantastical necessitating a transition from one space to another. These transitions—handled through portal-objects such as doors, mirrors, dreams, or walls—create a liminal space where the border of the real bleeds into the imaginary. A complete immersion into these other worlds, however, is not really possible as the existence of the inverted spaces keep seeping through, haunting the imaginary world. Farah Mendlesohn has noted that in *Neverwhere*, for example, Gaiman deliberately creates a dissonance "by overlaying the fantasy world on the familiar diagram of the London Underground system. We are never fully in the other world" (38). To this I would also add *MirrorMask*, as we are intermittently reminded of the real world via various portals (windows, doors, mirrors) spread throughout the imaginary world.

Moving from one world into its mirror-version is in itself an alteration as passing the threshold is deemed to be "a form of self-annihilation" (Campbell 91), a ritual of death and rebirth. "Crossing the threshold," then, "is transformative. The encounter may be positive or negative; it may entail risk or reward, loss or gain, but in all cases the crossing marks the cross-er of thresholds in some way" (Buck). The portal, or threshold, becomes a spatial element that establishes a dialogue between the real and the imaginary as a mediator between the two worlds. Whether in the vertical mirror-world of *Neverwhere* or in the horizontal mirror-world of *MirrorMask*, the generated territories on either side of the portal interact with the protagonists enabling them to face, or deny, their inner demons, inherently marking them.

Following the White Rabbit: The Problem of Being Richard Mayhew

Richard Mayhew's relationship with spaces is similar to his relationship with people: they are practically nonexistent. Before meeting Door, Richard Mayhew was just a regular person with a regular job trying to juggle his work life with his social life. His social life mainly consisted of Gary from the office and his fiancée Jessica whom he met in Paris. The way London shaped these characters is evident: while Jessica (possibly a true Londoner) carves her own path, Richard simply goes with the flow like a leaf in the wind. The reason behind Richard's compliant attitude may have something to do with the fact that he is not *really* from London; he comes from "a small Scottish town" (1), a place he would later remember "feeling that he was about to leave somewhere small and rational—a place that made sense—for somewhere huge and old that didn't" (4–5). Richard's Scottish otherness is not explicitly mentioned in Mike Carey and Glenn Fabry's graphic novel adaptation (which is the main version discussed in this chapter); however, the specter of Scotland seems to haunt Richard as the panels he is depicted in—coupled with Richard's own narrative voice—lends the feeling that he is not in sync with the urban space he is living in. In fact, Richard feels quite out of place as he goes through the motions of daily life that shape him, as "spatial practices," according to Certeau, "secretly structure the determining conditions of social life" (96). In "Chapter 3" of the graphic novel adaptation, Richard's narrative voice says, "London was our city" (Carey and Fabry). This remark is made in conjunction with Jessica; in retrospect, however, London was never really Richard's city. This was a city where he could only exist as a couple, as a young business man, and as a colleague, but never as an independent individual.

For John Clute, "to evoke London is to conjure a set of icons and legends of unparalleled depth in time, all set within a frame whose complex, theatrical immensity seems inexhaustible" (589). Richard finds himself in this inexhaustible, immense space that eventually chews and spits him out. London is portrayed as a harsh mistress, perhaps embodied in Jessica as she meticulously dictates how

Richard should live his life. The depicted cityscape, as far as Richard's occupied space is concerned, evolves around the office and the apartment along with the mobile space he occupies with Jessica in between the previous two spaces. It is during the movement between various points (from the office, to the apartment, to the restaurant) where Door literally falls in front of him causing Richard's gradual drift from London Above to London Below. Door actually becomes the portal that Richard chooses to metaphorically walk through. Even though it is the portal that finds Richard and not the other way around, it is still Richard who is finally able to take some sort of initiative.

Falling through the metaphorical portal causes Richard to space-shift. Although he is still physically located in London Above, his interaction with London Belowers has inevitably caused him to become a London Belower himself, as no one in London Above seems to remember or notice him. Although the spaces the two London's occupy may overlap on identical places, the people populating these spaces can never belong to both spaces simultaneously. One can only occupy one space at any given time. This inherently causes a problem in attempting to map practically unmappable spaces.

If any part of London Below is able to occupy any space in London Above, then how are we to discern between these two spaces? One way of doing so boils down to perception: London Belowers are virtually invisible to London Abovers. Hence, Richard's quest to "get back to normal again" ("Chapter 4") is not so much about space but place. Although he may be occupying the same space, he is certainly out of place as the Marquis de Carabas explains, "That's how most people come to London Below, Mister Mayhew. They fall through a crack and then they can't get back up again" ("Chapter 4").

Other unmappable instances occur as not only people but also places have the tendency of falling through the cracks: as much as people are forgotten, so too are places. One example of this occurrence is the subway entrance for the British Museum which was "closed [. . .] in 1943. And then they forgot it. It became part of the city below" ("Chapter 5"). Another is the Abbey of the Black Friars: "A church built within a temple swallowed up by the earth in another age, when London bore a different name" ("Chapter 6"). What these spaces show us is that although a place may be forgotten it does not cease to exist, it is buried in the unconscious space of the city's mind where they "still get the echoes" ("Chapter 6"). Richard's case is similar, albeit with a twist; by ceasing to exist in London Above, he is naturally forgotten.

London Below initially functions as a protagonistic space that Richard wants desperately to escape from. Once Richard is fully immersed in London Below, however, the various spaces and places he finds himself in become intimidating and menacing, causing Richard to feel entrapped. Knightsbridge, for example, which is actually Night's Bridge in London Below, not only functions as a "thematic background" but also has a "protagonistic status" both in the physical and "poetological sense" as it scares and ensnares the character (Piatti et al. 191). Although Richard is traveling with a group of people, he soon realizes that he is all alone as this antagonistic space preys on the minds of each person differently.

Passing Night's Bridge is an individual experience where the darkness thickens around Richard, "[a]nd night fell . . . like a hawk" (Carey and Fabry "Chapter 3"), alluding to the vicious nature of this particular space. Time, reality, and space are all intermingled in this abyssal place: Richard's future endeavors with the Black Friars and the Beast of London are mixed and mingled with his past initial encounter with Door lying bloodied and helpless at his feet along with Jessica's condescending voice ("Chapter 4"). Night's Bridge is literally a devouring nightmare come to life. Paying his toll, Richard eventually comes "up from nowhere into somewhere" ("Chapter 4"). Likewise, in Chapter 7, Richard will once more be subject to a protagonistical psychological space where his mind space will be invaded by the Blackfriars Station bringing him to the verge of committing suicide in a dreamlike territory. The only thing that saves him is mobility: moving mentally from the present moment to a past experience on Night's Bridge and moving physically from the Blackfriars platform onto a train car.

Mobility—or rather, the ability to navigate and move through space—continues to aid Richard on his journey, specifically through the labyrinth: a place that has mythical connotations and also acts as a protagonistic space. The purpose of the mythical labyrinth, according to Eliade, is to defend the center that represents "absolute reality, sacred power and immortality," and "to enter it was equivalent to an initiation" (*Comparative Religion* 380–81) that would free one from their bonds; so "to undo the labyrinthine knot" would rid one "of ignorance and liberate the soul" (*Images and Symbols* 117). In this sense, the labyrinth located in the depths of London Below was meant to be a space where Richard would be able to find his true inner self.

Similar to the Greek myth of Theseus and the Minotaur, Richard must also face and kill the monster at the center of the labyrinth. Reaching the center, however, is never a simple task, nor is navigating safely through the maze. Like Ariadne's thread, Richard's group is in possession of a talisman that not only protects them from the Beast but also acts as a compass enabling them to navigate through an unmapped/unmappable space. Once the talisman is broken, however, Richard replaces its function and becomes the compass himself, but only after having defeated the Beast of London. By touching the blood of the beast to his eyes and tongue, Richard is able to see a thread of light leading the way out of the maze (Carey and Fabry "Chapter 9"). The labyrinth, then, becomes a space for transformation and change, for knowledge and wisdom.

In all three encounters with protagonistical spaces (Night's Bridge, Blackfriars, Labyrinth), Richard has undergone trials that may be equated with certain rites of passage, gradually enabling him to mature and become more aware of himself. These protagonistical spaces tested him both physically and mentally, metaphorically killing him so that he was reborn each time with a stronger sense of purpose in his life.

After all the ordeals Richard goes through, he is finally able to return to London Above. Once a place of longing, London Above is now void of any meaning for Richard as he realizes that "there is no there there" (Stein 298). For Richard, London Above has become a dreary, purgatorial space, even a sort of hell, as the relations he thought he had now prove to be insignificant and incoherent. London Above is based on a capitalist social structure where the same boring routines are continuously played out with no expectation for real change. London Below, on the other hand, offers a place full of possibilities, a space he chooses to return to in the end.

... and into the MirrorMask: The Curiouser Case of Helena Campbell

Helena Campbell's relationship with space is quite different from Richard's: where he navigates through spaces, she creates them. Consequently, Neil Gaiman and David McKean's movie *MirrorMask* begins in the imaginative topography of Helena's mind. To an adoring crowd of sock puppets, against a backdrop of her own drawings, Helena declares herself to be the queen of everything, including the queen of evil, which initiates a doubleness of self that requires negotiation. The location is inside the mobile abode of Helena's camper situated on the grounds of the family circus. The circus, also a mobile entity, is another imaginative space where identities are fluid, with people permitted to shift and change into other roles through the use of masks and costumes. This is a space that allows for continuous reinvention and recreation.

Enveloped in her own world, Helena forgets her responsibilities which lead to a confrontation with her mother. Engaged in a power struggle, Helena complains that "[i]t never ends" while her mother, Joanne, attempts to console her by reminding Helena that all the kids want to run away and join a circus. The circus, as a colorful and boisterous place, is a world unto its own, where, in the minds of visiting children, the rules of the real world apparently do not apply. The circus offers a space where one can step out of the real into the imaginary. But since this *is* Helena's reality she wants to run away and join real life. "You're going to be the death of me," says Joanne. "I wish I was" mutters Helena immediately regretting her words. The confrontation ends with her mother saying, "I don't think you could handle real life, Helena" (*Mirror-Mask*). This last statement not only emphasizes that the circus is more of an imaginative territory rather than a real space, but also alludes to Helena's lack of experience and immaturity that only allows her to function in mobile and imaginative topographies.

Helena functions awkwardly in real spaces. Once Helena's mother falls ill and is hospitalized, the illusionary and colorful world of the circus is replaced with an immobile, old, and dreary apartment block located in Brighton and the sterile stationary structure of the hospital. Both stationary spaces become stable coordinates that Helena routinely weaves back and forth from. In order to break away from this grim routine, Helena transports her dreamworld, from circus to city, by hanging drawings of her light and dark cityscapes. Yet the last words spoken between mother and daughter anchors Helena in the real where she is overwhelmed by guilt and remorse. On one of her daily visits to the hospital, her mother begins telling her a story: "There was a little girl. [. . .] When she was good, she was very, very good . . ." (*MirrorMask*); although she is interrupted, the story evidently suggests that when this little girl was bad, she was very, very bad. The narrative here seems to delicately fold in on itself, subtly conjoining the doubleness illustrated with the sock puppet show and the doubleness of Helena as the possible heroine of her mother's story.

Helena slips into the otherworld on the night of her mother's operation where she unconsciously dreams of her dark self. In her dream, she sees a reflection of herself laughing at her. The possible death of her mother, coupled with the guilt that it might be her fault, leads to a fragmented self: one Helena stays in the real, while the other in the imaginary as "[d]reams are often bizarre but rarely so detached from the everyday as to offer a reliable haven of escape; what we most often find in Dreamland are distorted reflections of our anxieties" (*Encyclopedia* 297). Because the dream space, "[a]t once imaginary and real [. . .] is strange and alien, yet at the same time as close to us as is possible" (Lefebvre 209), the place of dreaming becomes a space where Helena is able to deal with her angst.

Seeing her reflection in the mirror in her dream creates a double-portal. For Foucault, the mirror as a social and cultural space, with its reflecting and inverting properties, functions both as a utopia and as a heterotopia (24), whereas for Umberto Eco, the mirror is a threshold phenomenon, a "threshold between perception and signification" that duplicates and splits the body into object and subject (210). Rosemary Jackson considers the mirror as "a different space, where our notions of self undergo radical change. . . . By presenting images of the self in another space (both familiar and unfamiliar), the mirror provides versions of self transformed into another, become something or someone else" (87). Helena's self, through her mirror image, becomes her inverted other, her dark double. The liminal space created by both dream and mirror function as a final divider of Helena's duality that is also reflected in her drawings. As the liminal borderland separates her White City from her Dark Lands, so too is she divided into Helena and other-Helena.

Helena's transition and immersion into the otherworld is almost seamless: through a window, she sees herself sleeping and surmises that she must be dreaming. These transitional portals keep interrupting the narrative, reminding us that we are in an imagined territory. A notable fracture occurs in Helena's psyche when she looks through a window and sees her empty bedroom: "I should be in there, shouldn't I, if I'm asleep?" she asks (*MirrorMask*).

This incident, following others where other-Helena is seen fighting with her father, smoking cigarettes, burning her drawings, kissing boys, are all negative rites of passage, each of which takes place in the real. Just as the landscape is split into light and shadow, so is Helena: "The sinister double [. . .] derives much of its psychological power from the fact that we all construct civilized 'social selves'" (*Encyclopedia* 285). Helena's constructed civil self is trapped in the imaginative topography while her doppelgänger is taking over her real life, the life she was told she could not handle. If a doppelgänger represents something that has been repressed (*Encyclopedia* 284), this would explain Helena's splitting of self into light and dark other. The repressed emotion of guilt that she probably caused her mother's illness entraps her in a space she can actively control enabling her to atone for her sin and find redemption.

While her sinister double is undergoing negative rites of passage in the real, Helena must pass hers in the imaginary which follows the form of the quest motif. At the crystalline and ethereal Palace of Light, Helena learns that the charm was stolen and the balance broken, causing the Queen to fall into a deep sleep. Shadows began coming from the Dark Lands, tearing down the White City. The quest is to find the charm, wake the Queen, and restore the lands; otherwise, all will be destroyed. Shadows move and expand, un-creating space by overtaking and erasing it. So, by finding the charm, waking the Queen, and restoring the lands, she will also have restored her mother.

Real and imaginary spaces in *MirrorMask* are mutually dependent: what happens in the dreamworld influences events in the real (restoring the Queen will restore the mother), and the existence of the otherworld relies on the existence of its map in the real. Since the map, in the form of Helena's drawings, is not just a representation but also simultaneously the actual imagined topography, destroying the spatial model would also destroy the dreamworld. Once other-Helena, with the intent of trapping Helena in the dreamworld, begins destroying the drawings, the dream space begins disappearing. Helena quickly realizes: "There's only one way out. The windows. The ones I drew. They're doors between our world and her world . . . and she's destroying them" (*MirrorMask*).

Other-Helena had crossed over through the double-portal of dream and mask; so must Helena. The mask as a portal object must be coupled with a secondary portal in order to function. All that was drawn on paper was destroyed by other-Helena, but one last portal remains, and that is the one she had previously drawn on the rooftop door. This window, a threshold, conjoining the real and imaginary is the liminal space that allows Helena to switch places with other-Helena while wearing the MirrorMask. With each Helena inhabiting their respective spaces once again, balance is restored on both sides of the double-portal. The White Queen awakens, and Mum's operation goes well. The story circles back to the beginning, to the circus, to a liminal, mobile space where, just like the dreamworld, anything is possible. As with Richard, Helena chooses to inhabit an imaginative topography; in Helena's case, however, this space is embodied in the circus where the real and imaginary is able to co-exist.

Moving Spaces as Places of Sanctuary

In both *MirrorMask* and *Neverwhere*, mobility demarcates spaces as both uncanny and powerful. *Neverwhere*'s Floating Market and Earl's Court are mobile spaces that operate in the in-between spaces of the two Londons, creating a dissonance in the sense mentioned by Mendlesohn, and both require a guide. The Floating Market is a space that imposes itself on another preexisting space, but to get to the market one must navigate through a different path. To reach the market held at Harrods, for example, one must pass Night's Bridge. This insinuates that although the Floating Market and Harrods occupy the same place, they do not occupy the same space. The path may be treacherous, yet the Floating Market, as a moving space, offers sanctuary. A similar accord is offered at Earl's Court which is a space that moves by following a certain order, unlike the unpredictability of the Floating Market. The court moves along the tracks of the London Underground simultaneously belonging to both Londons. Located in one of the train cars, the Earl's

Court is frozen in time if not in space, where the setting is that of a medieval court with the Earl as a powerful aristocrat within his own domain where he rules "the Underground. The bit with the trains. He's lord of the Central, the Circle, the Jubilee, the Victorious, the Bakerloo—well, all of them except the Underside Line" (*Neverwhere* 161). Ironically, the Floating Market and the Earl's Court are spaces in motion where there is a semblance of security. It seems the function of moving spaces is to offer sanctuary, a function we would generally expect from stationary spaces.

Moving spaces in *MirrorMask* also offer sanctuary, but only in the real, such as the circus, while stable places do not. As a reflection of the real, the dreamworld inverts the places of sanctuary. Drawings disrupted in the stable space of the real directly affect the dreamworld creating moved spaces such as the little white dome other-Helena rips out and places in the center of the Dark Lands. Shadows move and expand, un-creating space by overtaking and erasing it. The mobility of the shadows is a protagonistical physical element rewriting the landscape. The mobility of spaces had previously offered Helena sanctuary, but now they are working against her. Stationary spaces, on the other hand, were once mundane places that offered nothing but grief and anxiety. In this imaginative topography, stable places such as the Palace and Library are safe spaces that also provide information. Even the menacing Mask Shop does this as Helena is informed that the MirrorMask concentrates desires and wishes, giving you what you need. It is this bit of information that will enable her to re-cross the threshold from the imaginary to the real. Even though Helena navigates through the fluid topography of the mind that continuously shifts and changes, this is, nevertheless, a created space, one that she can control and manipulate.

Creating and Manipulating Space

While Richard was a navigator of space, Helena is both creator and destroyer. Her light aspect functions as the creator of worlds and portals while her dark self acts as the destroyer. Helena's artistic creations that begin in the real are transferred to the imaginary, with the slight exception of her rooftop drawing. The rooftop was a ruminative space with archetypal connotations as the act of creation (through drawing) was in a space where sky meets sea, both elements implying endlessness. Her drawings may be seen as an extension of Helena where her quasi-physical self inhabits mentally created spaces. The artist and their creations are considered to be one and the same, as Blanchot writes:

If there is anyone who is to be judged by his works, it is the artist. He is, so they say, the creator: the creator of a new reality, which opens in the world a wider perspective, a possibility by no means closed but such, on the contrary, that reality in all its forms is enlarged because of it. He is, moreover, the creator of himself in what he creates. (212)

If the artist and their creations are deemed to be the same, then the imagined topography becomes the representational space of Helena, a single body that encompasses both the dark and the light. Helena's duality is constantly weaved throughout the narrative, but it is perhaps the evocation of the biblical creation myth where these battling halves are unified as the creator is depicted as neutral, a being simply pleased with having fulfilled the act of creating:

In the beginning, she found herself in a new and empty space. [. . .] And she sat in the centre and saw a clean white sheet of void. [. . .] And when there was no more room. She turned it over and continued on the other side. So the void was filled from corner to corner on both sides. A city of front and back. A city of light and shadow. Then she rested on her bed and dreamed of her creation, and the lives that inhabited it. (*MirrorMask*)

In the fluid, color-muted, and blurry topography of the dreamworld, on the borderland Helena acts as a conductor orchestrating her creation. The borderland, located between the two realms, is a place where Helena can actively manipulate and create space. The space around her is reshaped and recreated just as she imagines it to be. Unlike her drawings of these lands in the real world, this creation takes place in real time further lending and enforcing the idea that we are in dreamland territory. This space, on the border, is an amalgamation of dreams and reality, a fluid space that can be shaped and remade. As her dark side gains agency, however, the shadows expand, making her a destroyer as well. As other-Helena tears down drawings, parts of the dark lands start disappearing. The dreamworld falls apart as the drawings are destroyed and these spaces are thrown out of balance. Whether creator or destroyer, it his Helena in both aspects that manipulates the topography.

While the fluidity of *MirrorMask* functions on the making and unmaking of spaces, *Neverwhere* operates instead on the ability to traverse space. Travel in London Below is arduous and dangerous, and those who can manipulate space itself, as House Portico can, are the most powerful beings traveling through the shifting topography of *Neverwhere*. Although Door's family members were not creators in the sense Helena was, they were nevertheless collectors and reorganizers of spaces. Door's family home, for instance, is one of the more puzzling spaces that weave various spaces in interesting ways. The spaces occupied by House Portico are strewn throughout the two Londons: any one of the rooms may occupy any space, in any time. The entrance hall is the reference point that connects the various rooms dispersed throughout space and time. "There are no doorways off it. Only paintings of the other rooms. . . . For the rest, they took what pleased them. . . . Wove it into the fabric of the house" ("Chapter 2"). They not only wove places into the fabric of the house but also "[t]heir memories are woven into the walls" where "the house tells [their] story" ("Chapter 3"). So, the spaces also act as an active archive storing emotive images of the past. As a unique family of "openers," the members of House Portico have the ability to manipulate and move through spaces as they please. Perhaps they owe their status of nobility to this exclusive relationship they have with space. Spaces and places from the perspective of House Portico become objects that may be influenced and controlled.

◆ ◆ ◆

Neverwhere's Richard Mayhew and *MirrorMask*'s Helena Campbell encounter life-altering experiences that are intertwined with the particular spaces they find themselves in. London Below in *Neverwhere* acts as the inverted landscape of London Above, and the dreamworld depicted in *MirrorMask* begins as an inverted version of Brighton only to be expanded to encompass the cityscape/landscape of the City of Light and the Land of Shadow. The urban spaces experienced by Richard and the created spaces by Helena are only different in terms of how space comes into being: one is social where the other is personal. But both spaces are mirror images of the real. "Fantasy," says Gaiman, "is a mirror. A distorting mirror, to be sure, and a concealing mirror, set at forty-five degrees to reality, but it's a mirror nonetheless, which we can use to tell ourselves things we might not otherwise see" (*Smoke and Mirrors* 2). So the distorted spatial elements within these narratives shed light on the otherwise concealed actions, desires, thoughts, and dreams of the protagonists. By tilting the mirror, we engage the world from a different angle, a different perception, one that allows for multiple perspectives to co-exist. And in the end we see what we choose to see.

As maps, or any other graphic representations or projections reduce "three-dimensional realities to two dimensions" (Lefebvre 285), they are tentative spatial projections at best and can only be used as points of reference. This gap, between the thing and its representation, allows for diverse interpretations.

Neverwhere, for example, may be read as a modern utopia of sorts: is Neverwhere a Neverland for adults, or is it a Nowhere? But, instead of speculating, we can arrive at a sounder conclusion by looking at the ways space and characters interact in *Neverwhere* and *MirrorMask*. While female characters, such as Door and Helena, are able to manipulate and create space, male characters, Richard and Valentine, can only navigate through it. This opens up another perspective that questions whether spaces in Gaiman's narratives are gendered.

Furthermore, while Richard's story ends with him rejoining the denizens of London Below creating a linear narrative, Helena's story comes back full circle to the circus where she is in the same place (but not space) she began her journey from. These endings might have something to do with the nature of the inverted worlds. Richard's path followed a vertical trajectory between the ups and downs of the two Londons, while Helena moved back and forth on the horizontal axis. While London Below presented Richard with an image of what he could be, Helena's mirror-world reflected what she was. Both end points—London Below and the circus—represent almost unmappable spaces where the characters are left with the potential to thrive. This particular quote appears verbatim twice in Neil Gaiman's bibliography: once, in *American Gods* (2001), as the epigraph to chapter 19, presented as an excerpt from Mr. Ibis's notebook, and again in the introduction to *Fragile Things* (2006), apropos of seemingly nothing, sandwiched in between the paragraph descriptions of two short stories in the collection, as the opening of an undisclosed extra story tentatively titled "The Mapmaker."

WORKS CITED

Blanchot, Maurice. *The Space of Literature.* Ann Smock, trans. University of Nebraska Press, 1982.

Buck, Stephanie. "Home, Hearth, and Grave: The Archetypal Symbol of Threshold on the Road to Self." *Jungian Society for Scholarly Studies (JSSS)*, 6 August 2004. http://jungiansociety.org/index.php/home-hearth-and-grave-the-archetypal-symbol-of-threshold-on-the-road-to-self. Accessed 10 December 2016.

Campbell, Joseph. *The Hero with a Thousand Faces.* Fontana Press, 1993.

Carey, Mike, and Glenn Fabry. *Neil Gaiman's Neverwhere.* DC Comics, 2007.

Certeau, Michel de. *The Practice of Everyday Life.* Steven Dandall, trans. University of California Press, 1988.

Eco, Umberto. *Semiotics and the Philosophy of Language.* Indiana University Press, 1986.

Eliade, Mircea. *Images and Symbols: Studies in Religious Symbolism.* Philip Mairet, trans. Princeton University Press, 1991.

Eliade, Mircea. *Patterns in Comparative Religion.* Rosemary Sheed, trans. University of Nebraska Press, 1996.

The Encyclopedia of Fantasy. John Clute and John Grant, eds. Orbit, 1999.

Foucault, Michel. "Of Other Spaces." Jay Miskowiec, trans. *Diacritics* vol. 16, no. 1, 1986, pp. 22–27.

Gaiman, Neil. *American Gods.* Headline Review, 2005.

Gaiman, Neil. "The Mapmaker." *Fragile Things: Short Fictions and Wonders.* Headline Review, 2006.

Gaiman, Neil. *Neverwhere.* Avon Books, 1998.

Gaiman, Neil. *Smoke and Mirrors: Short Fictions and Illusions.* Avon Books, 1998.

Kümin, Beat, and Cornelie Usborne. "At Home and in the Workplace: A Historical Introduction to the 'Spatial Turn.'" *History and Theory* vol. 52, 2013, pp. 305–318.

Jackson, Rosemary. *Fantasy: The Literature of Subversion.* Routledge, 1998.

Lefebvre, Henri. *The Production of Space.* Donald Nicholson-Smith, trans. Blackwell, 1991.

A Literary Atlas of Europe. Institute of Cartography and Geoinformation, ETH Zurich. http://www.literaturatlas.eu/en/. Accessed 10 December 2016.

Mendlesohn, Farah. *Rhetorics of Fantasy.* Wesleyan University Press, 2008.

MirrorMask, story by Neil Gaiman and Dave McKean. Jim Henson Company, 2006.

Piatti, Barbara, Hans Rudolf Bär, Anne-Kathrin Reuschel, Lorenz Hurni, and William Cartwright. "Mapping Literature: Towards a Geography of Fiction." *Cartography and Art.* William Cartwright, Georg Gartner, and Antje Lehn, eds. Springer, 2009, pp. 177–92.

Reuschel, Anne-Kathrin, and Lorenz Hurni. "Mapping Literature: Visualisation of Spatial Uncertainty in Fiction." *Cartographic Journal* vol. 48, no. 4, 2011, pp. 293–308.

Soja, Edward W. *Postmodern Geographies: The Reassertion of Space in Critical Social Theory.* Verso, 1995.

Stein, Gertude. *Everybody's Autobiography.* Exact Change, 1993.

Warf, Barney, and Santa Arias. "Introduction: The Reinsertion of Space in the Humanities and Social Sciences." *The Spatial Turn: Interdisciplinary Perspectives.* Routledge, 2009, pp. 1–10.

Gaiman's Brumous Boundaries and the Liminal Space

THE SHADOW OR THE SELF
The Construction of Neil Gaiman on Social Media

LANETTE CADLE

In addition to being a prolific and innovative author adept at multiple genres ranging from comics to television to novels, Neil Gaiman is a major presence on social media. Notice the verb *is* rather than *has*—social media done right creates a distinct identity, much in the way an author curates a complicated character, by selecting some details, obscuring others. Viviane Serfaty writes of this function in her book on blogging and early bloggers, *The Mirror and the Veil*, when she asserts that blogging "establishes a dialectical relationship between disclosure and secrecy, between transparency and opacity" (13), adding,

> The paradox lies in the invisibility seemingly enjoyed on the Internet by both writers and readers. Thanks to the screen, diarists feel that they can write about their innermost feelings without feeling humiliation and identification, readers feel that they can inconspicuously observe others and derive increased understanding and power from that knowledge. (13)

Serfaty points out that "the very action of bringing something to light renders other areas even more opaque, so that the screen is transformed into a mirror onto which diary-writers project the signifiers of their identity in an ongoing process of deconstruction and reconstruction" (14). This should not be surprising. A good blogger is a good writer, and good writers select what they show and what they withhold. Neil Gaiman, if anything, is a superlative writer, one who is noted for creating multiple worlds across multiple genres, from the adult fiction of *American Gods* and *Neverwhere* to the mixed mythos of *Sandman* to the skewed children's literature of *The Graveyard Book*. Even within that larger context, it could be said that Gaiman's greatest creation is

Neil Gaiman himself, aka @neilhimself, on Twitter as well as the other iterations of Gaiman on social media venues such as Instagram and his blog. Through these outlets, he manufactures a friendly and informative persona, one that reaches out to his readers and only wants to share, every bit as much as they want to know the real Neil Gaiman.

This chapter will closely examine Gaiman's intensive use of social media to create a shadow self that gives fans the access they crave to his inner processes and daily life. This means making selections, much like a curator faced with a massive archive must select pieces that form a cohesive exhibit, a process that is much more nuanced than the commercial call to create a "brand," an idea that is commonly touted within the world of business. Instead, it is a conscious construction of a shadow self, an embodiment that both is and is not the real Neil Gaiman.

The Mechanics

Before discussing the implications of social media identity construction, it might be helpful to get an overview of the mechanics of social media as shown through Neil Gaiman's example. It's not surprising that the social media identity for Gaiman is one that readers want to share a journey with, and they do it in record numbers. Virtual Neil is hugely successful in the measure that counts most for social media—followers—because he gets the mechanics right. As of this writing, Gaiman follows 853 people on Twitter, down from 907 people a year ago, and has 2.59 million followers (as of June 6, 2017). Neil Gaiman, aka @neilhimself on Twitter, gives a unique view of an author's life while artfully promoting his publications and appearances (Figure 9.1). In tandem with his tweets, he keeps a blog, which he calls a journal, that allows longer posts cross-promoted through his Twitter feed. Especially since the birth of his new son, Anthony (Ash), with wife Amanda Palmer, he increasingly uses Instagram.

The photos and occasional video document his daily life, the life that he summarizes on his blog, Facebook author page, and Twitter homepage as "[w] ill eventually grow up and get a real job. Until then, will keep making things up and writing them down." This is a longstanding motto for Gaiman, one that interestingly shifts on his Instagram homepage to: "Writes things. Changes a baby. It's a living." Instagram has both photos and video, but Gaiman also has a YouTube channel that he uses far less, despite the fact that the medium has been used effectively by others for video blogging. He is only moderately

Figure 9.1. Neil Gaiman, Twitter homepage for @neilhimself. Twitter, screenshot, 28 June 2016, 12:00 p.m. twitter.com/neilhimself.

active in other social media venues. For example, his Vimeo page has only a few entries, including his documentary, *Dream Dangerously*, which is available to rent or buy. Given the traditional film documentary form, albeit in a nontraditional marketing venue, this video biography is not really social media fodder. In the end, he seems to prefer Twitter, where followers have the advantage of seeing his tweets automatically in their Twitter feed, which may sound like Facebook's newsfeed, but functions differently. It is more driven by information itself with the goal of retweets rather than how that information will coax written responses from "friends," a major motivation on Facebook. The term Twitter uses instead, *followers*, shows the centrality of the tweets over individuals. Gaiman can and does have millions of followers on Twitter because their expectations are different than those for a Facebook friend. For new authors seeking to network within the publishing world, Facebook is unmatchable. Mentors, agents, support groups—it's all there. Gaiman already has that though and is generous enough to use the other approach, Twitter, to gather up followers and let them into his world.

Aside from Facebook and Twitter, Gaiman also uses his author blog/website for promotion. In general, blog posts are more flexible in purpose than tweets since they aren't limited to 140 characters at a time, allowing for the long thoughts of identity construction to occur. His journal is where Twitter followers can "read more about it" by following a link from a tweet. As a form of older social media, blogs were here first and one by one, the functions blogs used to have are stripped away by newer social media that specialize—Twitter, for example. Blogs that had nothing but link posts used to be common, as were photo blogs, but those two types of blogs are now rare. Walker Rettberg agrees and gives *Scripting News* or *Metafilter* as examples of these early, link-heavy blogs (14). Though Gaiman keeps the blog that started it all and utilizes it as a repository for larger, more fully formed thoughts and opinions, for him it does not hold the central place Twitter does. Rather, Gaiman uses his Twitter account as his organizing hub, even though his blog dates back to 2001, seven years before his first tweet in December 2008. Although the blog may never shift back to being his central social media place, it remains, partially because of the ability of blogs to contain more complex text, the more full-bodied expression of Neil Gaiman the character, a creation that lives both inside and outside his comics and other print media.

Digital Identity or Just Identity

As an expression of a person, Gaiman's online character generates a perceived divide between real vs. unreal, private vs. public. Fact: people are corporeal. They still have bodies and still have family and friends that they see almost every day. They touch—they can brush a stray hair from a shoulder or be pained by the off-key whistling that sometimes accompanies a man's morning shave or smell the pungent scent of Barbasol. Bodies aren't going anywhere anytime soon. This is the private self.

Along with that vision of embodiment, there is also a long history of the idea of writing as a body of work or even writing as the body *enscribed*. Easily the most central of these theories is that of Hélène Cixous and her concept of *ecriture feminine*, best stated in her essay, "The Laugh of the Medusa." Granted,

Cixous writes about what she initially positions as women's writing, but later work, especially that by Judith Butler, complicates the idea of defining a certain type of writing as being sexed, with Butler's important distinction between sex and gender in *Gender Trouble: Feminism and the Subversion of Identity* marking the change.

This concept of embodied writing has merit when considering Gaiman's use of social media for two reasons. First, Gaiman has been critically positioned as a feminist author.[1] Feminist theory, especially feminist writing theory, is full of metaphors that pair writing and the body and even writing inscribing the body. In "Speaking the Cacophony of Angels: Gaiman's Women and the Fracturing of Phallocentric Discourse," Rachel R. Martin notes that Gaiman's feminism is a planned and conscious practice rather than a theoretical stance only, that it "entices and draws in female readers through his inclusion of feminine lead characters" (11), a definite break from the past for the world of comics especially. This is not theoretical feminism; this is feminism in action and a necessary part of Gaiman's writerly identity. At the same time, when speaking of *ecriture feminine*, Cixous declares her vision for the individual when she states that "[s] he must write her self" (880), keeping that space between the terms *her* and *self* to show who is writing what. She goes on to detail why this is necessary, noting that "[b]y writing her self, woman will return to the body which has been more than confiscated from her" and that this writing "will always surpass the discourse that regulates the phallocentric system" (883), a very similar idea to Martin's claim that Gaiman's effectiveness as a writer owes much to his "feminine narratives" that break up what would otherwise be a more canonical, "phallocentric" approach (11). That said, his use of writing as the construction of a body makes sense as a sound feminist practice; taken a step further to the multimodal (text, image, audio, video) approach used in social media, Gaiman's social media empire becomes a body with Twitter as its circulatory system.

Returning to reasons why the social media Gaiman is an embodied composition, the second reason to consider this concept of embodied writing is the nature of social media itself. Done right, it grows. It is not static like print. When done long enough and done well, the result is what Neil Gaiman has: a body constructed of words and light that becomes more real to his followers than many of their next-door neighbors. That, of course, leaves the whole concept of real vs. not-to-be –dealt-with, as well as how readers value one against the other. In her 1999 book, *How We Became Posthuman: Virtual Bodies in Cybernetics, Literature, and Informatics*, N. Katherine Hayles complicates the flesh/not-flesh dichotomy with her concept of the *posthuman*. For Hayles, embodiment is both pixels and flesh, and her analysis of what that means foreshadows social media, where it is possible to have "friends" over a number of years that you may never see IRL (in real life). For Hayles, "the posthuman view privileges informational pattern over material instantiation" (2). This leads to body-housed consciousness seen as less definitive, with the body seen as "the original prosthesis" (3).

Finally, and what Hayles views as the most important feature,

> the posthuman view configures human being so that it can be seamlessly articulated with intelligent machines. In the posthuman, there are no essential differences or absolute demarcations between bodily existence and computer simulation, cybernetic mechanism and biological organism, robot teleology and human gods. (3)

Of course, in 1999, blogs were new, and Twitter was still a little less than ten years away. Nonetheless, Hayles's concept of the posthuman predicts the function of social media, that of expansion of the body rather than an erasure of the body. Not every person who uses social media takes it this far, but given enough time and skill, it is possible. Gaiman has the advantage of being active on social media from the very beginning of blogging, with his current blog listing archives as far back as September 2001. Add to that his status within science fiction and fantasy literature, and social media becomes a part of a holistic embodiment, not one end of a "bodily existence and computer simulation" (3) binary.

The Shadow Self

Neil Gaiman is far from the only author with an online presence and not all authors take this concept of an embodied posthuman self so far. Sometimes it's just about marketing. Companies and products market themselves every day through social media with varying degrees of success. Their "why" is clear: to sell more and to create brand loyalty. When it comes to authors, though, the reasons are not as clear-cut. A creative aspect can come into play. It's true that for most literary authors, Facebook, a professional site, and Twitter are increasingly important. Authors are expected to shoulder a large part of their book's promotion themselves, and the ones with the fewest resources, beginning authors, are expected to carry the largest share of their promotion—creating the author website, setting up bookstore appearances, readings, and at times, even soliciting presales from individuals and stores. Though Gaiman

Figure 9.2. Neil Gaiman, blog and homepage. neilgaiman.com, screenshot, 10 February 2017.

goes to where the money is, in this case, where the readers, viewers, concert-goers, and other consumers of the world of Gaiman can be found on social media, his work is more nuanced than that and the persona he crafts online is no exception (Figure 9.2). Granted, Gaiman still keeps a brisk personal appearance pace, but when he can't, during the times when he is actually working on a writing project for example, social media keeps him visible.

With so many years of archives, virtual Neil is so complete that his identity constructed through social media does not "feel" artificial, even though he has an assistant to schedule and at times implement the posts. This does not seem to reduce the personal "feel" to his posts. Which tweets or posts are from an assistant and which are Gaiman's never seems to be an issue. This blurring between reality and constructed reality—or as Jill Walker Rettberg asks in *Seeing Ourselves through Technology*, "people or texts?" (11)—is typical of social media, the place where people construct identities for themselves through selfies, links, and snippets of information. Gaiman compounds that by using visual rhetoric well—i.e., persuasion done through images, including selfies, and something only an author can bring, the imagined and actual images created by his work. Thus far it is strictly promotion albeit for a good cause, but he goes further with teasers and photos that make it more when he adds,

And I will do my own bit for it. I will put up something unique to this blog. Probably you are thinking, will he write about his time on the Red Carpet at Cannes for HOW TO TALK TO GIRLS AT PARTIES? It is not that. (But here are costume designer Sandy Powell, channeling Ziggy Stardust, and star Elle Fanning eating colour-coordinated macaroons.) Perhaps you are thinking, Will he perhaps post photographs of Gillian Anderson as Media in the next episode of *American Gods* incarnated as Ziggy Stardust also eating colour-coordinated macaroons? I will not. I do not believe such photos exist. Instead I will put up photos of my elf-child, Ash. I will see him on Saturday, and the Cannes red carpet would have been much more fun if he had been on it.

Of course, he intersperses these teasers with photos as described. The photo of Gillian Anderson as Ziggy Stardust is especially compelling and not a publicity still (Figure 9.3). It is a candid shot, one hauntingly evocative of the young Bowie. Of the photos of his son Ash, two are close-ups, one is a father-and-son photo, and another is of Ash laying on a bed reading. He ends the post with a schedule of upcoming appearances. On the surface, this may seem like (and at some level is) promotion, plain and simple. However, the strength of this collection of details through multiple media is not in the individual pieces, but in the massively detailed portrait it builds using an archive that literally goes back more than fifteen years.

It is in how he writes it and what details he chooses to share, a defining feature of authorship. In a tweet from June 6, 2017 he writes, "Just received this in email from @JSCarroll. The stuff of ventriloquist nightmares." The photo that goes with the pithy description is a silent audience in folding chairs, all dummies with one man, a faded black-and-white photo full of atmosphere and shockingly creepy (Figure 9.4). Another example using text more than images is from February 2012 when he was writing the pilot for the television version of *American Gods*, then intended for HBO and currently in its first season on STARZ. Through those tweets, he gave an insider view of his writing process in a series of tweets while he was in Florida in order to get some the pilot script done. He has more than one tweet in which he warns that he will be off Twitter for the day, but on the whole he still tweets, possibly using Twitter the way many others do, as fill-in activity while taking a break from work. He tells fellow author @PollySamson, "I am hiding out and writing in Florida. I can see the intercoastal water & a bird sanctuary island from my bed." On February 10, he reaches out to the hive mind, admitting, "I'm being really lazy here, but has anyone already done a playlist of the songs mentioned in American Gods? (Iko

Figure 9.3. Neil Gaiman, *American Gods* Gillian Anderson as Media (Ziggy Stardust) Photo. "The Whole Cheesecake Photo Thing Explained, with Photos." neilgaiman.com. http://journal.neilgaiman.com/2017/05/the-whole-cheesecake-menu-thing.html.

Iko etc) & can link to it?" Later, on the February 12, he muses, "Familiar weird feeling as stuff I made up & need for my story to work turns up everywhere I look/research. I need to remember it isn't TRUE." Finally, the retweets and replies add richness to the narrative, sometimes revealing things Gaiman does not, as in an April 23, 2013, tweet from @SarahDarkmagic that notes, "While writing American Gods, @neilhimself bought a car to transport the books on Florida he needed for research. That's writing as craft." It is indeed, and is a detail that would not be known without the meticulous attention to detail possible through consistent Twitter use and of course, @neilhimself retweeting it.

Through multiple streams of social media then, followers move from one facet to another and then another, forming a fragmented yet cohesive view of Neil "Himself." This multimodality is not unique to Gaiman or even to social

Neil Gaiman ✓ @neilhimself · Jun 6
Just received this in email from @JSCarroll. The stuff of ventriloquial nightmares.

↩ 118   ♺ 160   ♥ 875   ⤲

Figure 9.4. Neil Gaiman, Twitter post and retweet from @JSCarroll. Twitter, 6 June 2017, screenshot, 14 June 2017. http://twitter.com/neilhimself.

media. Jill Walker Rettberg points out in her book *Blogging* that previous generations would have compiled private writings and scrapbooks:

> self-documentation has always been both incidental and deliberate. Before digital cameras, people often kept their never-sorted photos in shoeboxes, along with other paraphernalia of their daily lives: tickets from trips they'd taken or shows they'd been to, cuttings from newspapers and so on. Only some of these would make it into photo albums and scrapbooks or be written about in diaries. Today's technology can write a story automatically from all these scraps of information about ourselves. Whether or not we want our stories told like this is another matter. (87)

This past use of scrapbooks and paper diaries was innately private—only made public when physically passed from person to person or formally shared through traditional print publication. The lines were clear. However, this blurring of public and private in sharing "paraphernalia" is a hallmark of social media use, making Gaiman an excellent case study for how authors in these deconstructed publishing days can effectively not only promote their work, but promote a well-rounded view of their life and creative process, thus creating an even stronger connection for their fans.

Embodiment Versus Use

Not all authors choose to share their creative lives, not even those who are active on social media. They could choose to use social media for expressing political views and advocating for social action. In contrast, while Gaiman occasionally passes on a charitable request or call for social justice, it is not his focus. When he does pass on a request for support for a charity or issue, he retweets it, giving the "ownership" to the individual making the request. This is quite different from direct advocacy. One of the few issues he highlights as @neilhimself is shown in a tweet that has been pinned to the top of his Twitter feed since October 27, 2014. He writes, "3 million reasons why your heart will break (& heal) in one video. If you watch 1 thing today make it this. PLEASE RT" and includes a link to the donate page with his UNHCR (the UN Refugee Agency) supporter bio and a video. Aside from this very public and consistent sponsorship, his usual approach is to pass on charity tweets from others, as in the June 8, 2017, retweet for Arts Emergency. It is a straightforward retweet with no added text, but the fact that @neilhimself is retweeting it makes for a valuable addition no matter which way you look at it. Although part of his character does include a sense of social justice, it is only one part and not the major focus.

The online shadow cast by Neil Gaiman is extensive, an embodiment so thorough that it could be said to overshadow the real Gaiman, which may be the point. There is only so much self-promotion a single person can do, and through social media, Gaiman gains an army of promoters for his projects and appearances. Beginning with his core social media outlet, Twitter, a look at his main page shows that since he joined Twitter in 2008, as of June 6, 2017, he has posted 107,000 tweets, which averaged evenly over ten years makes an average of one tweet an hour. *Fast Company*, a site that bills itself as "the world's leading progressive business media brand," uses the analytics provided by Social Bakers, a social media analysis company, to recommend three tweets a day as the optimum number for having your tweets continue to add followers without making the dreaded move from what they call "informative" to "annoying." Now, *Fast Company* targets business users trying to build their brand, which means the corporate users they are speaking to can tolerate the effects of annoyance a bit better than an individual who does not see this as a business—in other words, an author tweeting to his fans. Gaiman, with his roughly twenty-nine tweets a day, should topple over into annoyance, but somehow he does not, despite the five-to-thirty-tweet daily recommendation for companies given by *Fast Company*. However, there is a huge difference between business and pleasure. Neil Gaiman is not an unknown commodity that requires a consistent barrage of marketing. At this point, he has long been a hugely successful author with a notably loyal fan base. His tweets give new information that others will want to *retweet*, thus increasing the reach of the original. Retweeting a new tidbit of information from @neilhimself also confers on the sender additional status within the fan base in the form of "cultural capital," the glue that make social media a gift culture. This is wholly different from Gaiman "creating a brand." He is not. As James E. Porter points out in "Recovering Delivery for Digital Rhetoric," "What social networking sites, video games, wikis, and simulated worlds are demonstrating is that audiences participate enthusiastically when they are invited to become co-producers of content, when the activity is meaningful, when the content is engaging and compelling" (218). Gaiman encourages this collaboration and participates in co-production by not only curating and sharing pieces of his persona that are most interesting to those fascinated with his books, comics, and movies, but by sharing in turn the best of what they produce. That is why his retweets of calls for charities is important. He shares them as embodiments of others, not as his own, which validates the purpose of a retweet—that is, to cite and give credit to others.

Even so, Gaiman is a massively productive writer and uses social media to tell what he is working on or when a project is released. An example of that kind of tweet is the announcement for his book *Norse Mythology*, which was released in February 2017 from Norton. Hints began being dropped the day before, so followers were more than ready to retweet the announcement when it came, thus extending the reach for the announcement and the linked *New York Times* article, and not incidentally, increasing their status with other fans who heard the news first from them. Note that Twitter counts the number of retweets, and for this one, there were 300 retweets in the first two hours. Considering that each of those retweets reach other followers who may not currently be following

Gaiman, the degree of momentum generated becomes clear. Gaiman keeps that momentum alive with another tweet an hour later, when he found the book already listed on Amazon and provided the link, important information for those followers who wish to preorder the title.

Given this context, it could be argued that the series of tweets announcing *Norse Mythology* functioned as pure promotion, but that is not the case. Gaiman layers meanings and functions and uses these expected promotions to also build his online character, whether on purpose or by happenstance. In this case, a witty Twitter exchange does the trick since on Twitter, being witty increases retweets. In fact, wit is how some "celebrity" Twitter gurus are born. The "wit" factor cannot be discounted when considering the @neilhimself persona and why his social media use is more than just marketing. In a later tweet the same day as the *Norse Mythology* announcement, he comments on *The New York Times* article photo by tweeting, "I look at the photo & see a really brilliant tree with a decorative author, so no one knows the tree wrote the book." First, this gives a canny reference to Yggdrasil, the world tree in Norse mythology and at the same time, gives a very English, self-deprecating reference. Next, this tweet gives followers a chance to add wordplay in replies, the most notable coming from fellow science fiction author John Scalzi, who tweeted, "The tree's prose is usually so wooden though. Hopefully, you got it to branch out, and it will flower under your tutelage." Interactions like this are personal and engaging, allowing fans and other writers to connect with each other. They are also calculated in length so that they are short enough to be retweeted.

Even though Gaiman's social media use is not pure promotion, it still promotes well. For example, in the *Norse Mythology* tweet previously mentioned, Gaiman also includes a link to a *New York Times* article that gives more information and a photo. Along the same lines, an earlier announcement about a new book tour links to photos of the previous night's appearance in concert with his wife and her band. Finally, his tweet not only announces a concert date, but provides a link to a ticket service, making the leap from a follower's desire to attend to tickets in hand the work of a moment. Twitter, then, is the hub for Gaiman's other media and point-of-sale venues. What would otherwise be scattered media in various places on the internet is gathered up and distributed directly to an audience who has acknowledged that they are intensely interested in all things Neil: his followers.

Of course, Gaiman also has a Facebook presence, a promotional mainstay for many authors who gain likes and network through their Facebook author page. According to the most recent (2016) social media statistics gathered by the Pew Research Center:

Figure 9.5. Neil Gaiman, Facebook page. https://www.facebook.com/neilgaiman/.

a national survey of 1,520 adults conducted March 7–April 4, 2016, finds that Facebook continues to be America's most popular social networking platform by a substantial margin: Nearly eight-in ten online Americans (79%) now use Facebook, more than double the share that uses Twitter (24%), Pinterest (31%), Instagram (32%) or LinkedIn (29%). On a total population basis (accounting for Americans who do not use the internet at all), that means that 68% of all U.S. adults are Facebook users, while 28% use Instagram, 26% use Pinterest, 25% use LinkedIn and 21% use Twitter.

Statistics like these, combined with the popularity of Facebook author and book pages, raises questions as to why Gaiman does not use Facebook more often or as a hub in the way he currently uses Twitter (Figure 9.5). It is true that most people either prefer Facebook or Twitter. Interestingly, there is a script to automatically turn a tweet into a Facebook status, but there is no script that does the reverse. The reason involves methodology and goals for the two kinds of social media. Metaphorically speaking, Facebook is the hearth and Twitter is the fire. In other words, Facebook is proprietary and closed, and Twitter is open communication in the wild. Specifically, Facebook's methodology for growth is friending and the goal is to gather those friends in a conglomerate newsfeed of everyone's posts. If the user's goal is to gather around the fire with friends and limit communication to vetted people, Facebook is the place to do that. On the other hand, Twitter shouts "Look at me!" and lets tweets go out to whoever is interested, no pre-approval or friending needed.

Embodiment and the Body of Work

It is not the mandate of this chapter to assess Gaiman's embodiment within his comics and novels, but to show that this is and has been a regular part of his practice. Yet it can certainly be argued that he has written himself into some of his work. Gaiman has shadow selves he has developed over years of authorship: comic and book characters that ring a note of recognition to fans. For example, the main character of *Neverwhere*, Richard Mayhew, is described in the prologue as "a fresh-faced, boyish young man, with dark, slightly curly hair and large hazel eyes; he had a rumpled, just woken up look to him, which made him more attractive to the opposite sex than he would ever understand or believe" (2), also an apt description for Gaiman at that age. The reader carries an image of Gaiman himself through that book and its epic

Figure 9.6. Neil Gaiman. Panel close-up from *The Sandman: The Sound of Her Wings*. Vol. 8. Art by Mike Dringenberg and Malcolm Jones III. Vertigo-DC Comics, 1997.

journal through London's underground. Another example of this kind of visual carryover or blurring between identities is in the comics series, *Sandman*. Place any of the slightly different renderings of Sandman next to a photo of Gaiman and fans draw their own conclusions (Figure 9.6). In the panel close-up shown, taken from *The Sandman: The Sound of Her Wings*, the art by Mike Dringenberg and Malcolm Jones III shows a seated Sandman with his sister Death; he is drawn as a rumpled man with the hands, face, and body type of Neil Gaiman. Dream could have been blond. He could have been a redhead. He could have been short and winsome. Instead, he is the broody version of Gaiman as he ferrets out and weaves his dreams.

Thus, the stumbled-upon hero in a story that ends up being of his own making has the physical presence of the human writer, making readers more sure that they really know him the way they know a close friend. After all, they have journeyed together, adventured together, made myth together. Add to that visual characterization the ever-growing identity seen through social media and the result is extremely loyal fans, ones sure that they know @neilhimself.

Who's on First?: Only the Shadow Knows

As I have stated above, Gaiman uses visual rhetoric well, as evidenced by his comics, and this rhetorical consideration should carry over online. As mentioned before, he shares photos and art through his blog and Twitter. However, his Instagram account is still a work-in-progress, which is a shame given

Figure 9.7. Neil Gaiman, Instagram homepage for neilhimself. Instagram, screenshot, 29 June 2016, 9:46 a.m. instagram .com/neilhimself/.

that what we see is always more believable than the unseen, and the sheer visuality of Instagram is enticing (Figure 9.7). Very few readers are likely to witness baby Ash at the keyboard and singing into the microphone while seated on his dad's lap, but they can see the video on Instagram. The viewers may never be world travelers and see painfully cute animals in the wild, but Gaiman does and shares them. Events like these are one way to share via Instagram, and the Instagram link is then further shared via Twitter, extending its reach. Using Instagram like this is a good fit for Gaiman's social media identity as the author who shares his life. Unfortunately, compared to others on Instagram, Gaiman has modest numbers (statistics from June 14, 2017): 123 posts, 161,000 followers, and forty people whom Gaiman himself is following, which is up from eighty-four posts, 124,000 followers, and Gaiman himself following twenty-four people on February 11, 2017. Although rising, the numbers are still low relative to his Twitter numbers. The underlying reason for this may be that unlike his Twitter account, he still does not post often enough to attract many followers through likes and shares.

Granted, Gaiman's primary identity is that of a writer. Even though he enables great visual art through comics, television, and movies, he is still word-oriented, as evidenced by his Instagram tagline: "Writes things. Changes a baby. It's a living." Even with that textual-orientation, Gaiman's Instagram still adds to his embodiment online. Current posts are divided between obvious book publicity shots, photos taken for visual appeal or a visual connection to myth, and a few showing family life. A strength to consider here is that he is clearly still posting. That means the possibility exists for a more developed Instagram page in the future. Gaiman has always used photos on Twitter, which has its own photostream that users can choose to use. However, Twitter's photostream is archival rather than a social site like Instagram, and it certainly does not use tags or encourage following. On the other hand, shifting Gaiman's photos to Instagram would not make them invisible on Twitter. Instead, it adds another layer for his social media self, a new venue to gain followers. Additionally, this form of sharing images is more intimate than Twitter or even Facebook. Because of its strong use of "favorites" and comments for individual photos or videos, it has the potential to endear as long as it is candid rather than calculated. Luckily, Gaiman is not the Instagram cliché of a starlet making duckface in endless selfies on the red carpet. This is daily life and how Gaiman's fans and, to be truthful, most people understand daily life. A look at his Instagram shows this now and could do so more in the future.

◆ ◆ ◆

In the end, the constructed nature of social media identity using text and images is not all that different from the constructed nature of primary or bodily identity using text and images or even very different from creating fictional characters and worlds using text and images. Each are purposeful constructions made by a person, whether s/he is conscious of the choices being made or not. With that in mind, who better than Gaiman to practice the idea of an embodied self, one textually composed in virtual spaces? He certainly can write, and in the social media world of endless details and moments, has crafted, if not his best self, a very good self that is ready to be the author fans always wished they knew in real life. If authors create fictions and if the social media self is seen as a form of fictional self, then it could be claimed that Neil Gaiman's greatest fictional creation is . . . Neil Gaiman. He lives through Twitter, Instagram, Facebook, his blog, and other media as a constant story, one that never ends. In his case, the shadow-self steps out and overshadows meatspace, that place commonly known as real life. Discerning what is real is no longer a problem; it becomes an impossible yet no longer necessary distinction.

NOTES

1. See, for example, Tara Prescott and Aaron Drucker's *Feminism in the Worlds of Neil Gaiman: Essays on the Comics, Poetry, and Prose* (McFarland, 2012).

WORKS CITED

Butler, Judith. *Gender Trouble: Feminism and the Subversion of Identity*. Routledge Classics, 2006.

Cixous, Hélène. "The Laugh of the Medusa." Keith Cohen and Paula Cohen, trans. *Signs* vol. 1, no. 4, Summer 1976, pp. 875–93.

Gaiman, Neil. American Gods Gillian Anderson as David Bowie photo. "The Whole Cheesecake Photo Thing Explained, with Photos." neilgaiman.com. http://journal.neilgaiman.com/2017/05/the-whole-cheesecake-menu-thing.html.

Gaiman, Neil. Ash 36 photo. "The Whole Cheesecake Photo Thing Explained, with Photos." neilgaiman.com. http://journal.neilgaiman.com/2017/05/the-whole-cheesecake-menu- thing.html.

Gaiman, Neil. Blog and homepage. neilgaiman.com. Screenshot 10 February 2017.

Gaiman, Neil. Facebook page for Neil Gaiman. Facebook. facebook.com/neilgaiman/.

Gaiman, Neil. Instagram homepage for neilhimself. Instagram. Screenshot 29 June 2016, 9:46 a.m. instagram.com/neilhimself/.

Gaiman, Neil. "Neil Gaiman: Dream Dangerously." Vimeo. vimeo.com/ondemand/neilgaiman/.

Gaiman, Neil. Panel close-up from *The Sandman: The Sound of Her Wings*, art by Mike Dringenberg and Malcolm Jones III. Vertigo-DC Comics, 1997. Vol. 8 of *Sandman*.

Gaiman, Neil. Screenshot of Echidna photo. Instagram homepage for neilhimself. Instagram. 11 February 2017, 10:23 a.m. instagram.com/neilhimself/.

Gaiman, Neil. Twitter homepage for @neilhimself. Twitter. Screenshot 28 June 2016, 12:00 p.m. twitter.com/neilhimself.

Gaiman, Neil. Twitter post and retweet from @JSCarroll. 6 June 2017. Twitter. Screenshot 14 June 2017. twitter.com/neilhimself.

Gaiman, Neil. YouTube channel for Neil Gaiman. YouTube. youtube.com/user/Neilhimself.

Greenwood, Shannon, Andrew Perrin, and Maeve Duggan. "Social Media Update 2016." Pew Research Center: Internet, Science, and Tech. pewinternet.org/2016/11/11/social-media-up date-2016/. Accessed 12 February 2017.

Hayles, N. Katherine. *How We Became Posthuman: Virtual Bodies in Cybernetics, Literature, and Informatics.* University of Chicago, 1999.

Knop, Robert. Twitter homepage for @FatherWithTwins. Twitter. https://twitter.com/ FatherWithTwins.

Martin, Rachel R. "Speaking the Cacaphony of Angels: Gaiman's Women and the Fracturing of Phallocentric Discourse" *Death, Desire, Fury, and Delirium: Feminism in the Worlds of Neil Gaiman.* Aaron Drucker and Tara Prescott, eds. McFarland, 2012.

Porter, James E. "Recovering Delivery for Digital Rhetoric." Computers and Composition vol. 26, no. 4, 2009, pp. 207–224.

Scalzi, John. Personal tweet 29 June 2016, 7:17 a.m. Twitter homepage for @scalzi. Twitter. twit-ter.com/scalzi.

Serfaty, Viviane. *The Mirror and the Veil: An Overview of American Online Diaries and Blogs.* Rodopi, 2004.

"The Social Media Frequency Guide: How Often to Post to Facebook, Twitter, LinkedIn, and More." *Fast Company.* https://www.fastcompany.com/3029019/work-smart/the-social -media-frequency-guide-how-often-to-post-to-facebook-twitter-linkedin-a.

Walker Rettberg, Jill. *Blogging.* 2nd ed. Polity, 2014.

Walker Rettberg, Jill. *Seeing Ourselves through Technology: How We Use Selfies, Blogs, and Wearable Devices to Shape Ourselves.* Palgrave Pivot, 2014.

DAMSELS IN DEEP REST NO MORE
The Coalescence of Light and Dark in *Blueberry Girl*,
The Wolves in the Walls, and *The Sleeper and the Spindle*

DANIELLE RUSSELL

> "Keep her from spindles and sleeps at sixteen, let her stay waking and wise."
> (GAIMAN, *Blueberry Girl*)

> "'Right. I've had enough,' said Lucy."
> (THE WOLVES IN THE WALLS)

> "She's stronger than she looks . . ."
> (THE SLEEPER AND THE SPINDLE 49)

To begin an essay with an epigraph is not uncommon; three, perhaps, slightly more so. However, if one reads the invocation in the first epigraph from Neil Gaiman's poem to Natasha Amos, daughter of friend Tori Amos, it establishes a distinct contrast between passivity and activity that plays out in both *The Wolves in the Walls* and *The Sleeper and the Spindle*. Phrased as requests, the petitions in *Blueberry Girl* outline the attributes which need to be fostered in young girls in order for them to develop into confident and capable women. The path to active engagement with the world, self-reliance, and wisdom, *Blueberry Girl* insists, requires experiencing both the positive and negative possibilities of life. Rejecting the burden of chronological release of the works, I will be using *Blueberry Girl* (2009) as the theoretical framework for my discussion of two seemingly disparate texts: *The Wolves in the Walls* (2003) and *The Sleeper and the Spindle* (2014). *Blueberry Girl* can be read as an informal treatise on Gaiman's concept of girlhood—a playful and picturesque one but nonetheless a systematic consideration of what a parent might hope for his or her daughter. Collaborating with Charles Vess, Gaiman creates a complex and compelling vision of girlhood as a foundation for the future woman.

Empowerment, however, cannot come without the risk of danger. *Blueberry Girl* visually downplays this fact while still acknowledging it. *The Wolves in the Walls* and *The Sleeper and the Spindle* seemingly delve deeper into this warning but can just as easily be read as extensions of the message of *Blueberry Girl*. To varying degrees, all three employ strategic omissions and "soothing" visual content to accommodate their readership; Dave McKean and Chris Riddell have very distinctive styles and yet they achieve a similar effect to Vess. The illustrations in all the books are an integral factor in the coalescence of light and dark. Gaiman is able to address (potentially) threatening material—the stereotypically "dark"—in large part because of the illustrations; they add a much-needed "lightness." The various, and varied, illustrations also help to mask the didactic impulse of the books. Gaiman "sneaks" the feminist ideology outlined in *Blueberry Girl* into *The Wolves in the Walls* and *The Sleeper and the Spindle*; McKean and Riddell aid and abet him.

And while "ideology" might sound somewhat sinister, as John Stephens points out, it is "not necessarily undesirable, and in the sense of a system of beliefs by which we make sense of the world, social life would be impossible without them" (8). More to the point, empowering a child readership is not possible without a feminist ideology. There is a clear feminist agenda in *Blueberry Girl*: the playful tone of the poem-prayer and the visual appeal of the book make it palatable but do not erase the didactic impulse. Stephens further argues that "in taking up a position from which the text is most readily intelligible, [readers] are apt to be situated within the frame of the text's ideology; that is, they are subjected to and by that ideology" (67). While it is important to acknowledge the possibility of resistant reading on the part of any actual readers, they are nonetheless exposed to the ideology they seek to resist. *Blueberry Girl* clearly rejects a position of femininity as passivity. It offers a counter vision to the damsel in "deep rest"—the ultimate state of passivity: the sleeping beauty or silent victim. *Blueberry Girl* reveals a willingness to recognize that protection from life's darkness—as in negative aspects—is actually a disservice. Power comes from an ability to face, and to some extent, embrace the darkness. Bravery is a mere concept until it needs to be exercised.

Addressed to "ladies of light and ladies of darkness," *Blueberry Girl* seems to support the all-too-familiar oppositional relationship between light and dark. The contrast of light and dark often takes the form of a simplistic dualism—positive/negative; pure/evil; knowledge/ignorance; hope/despair; and so on.¹ The oppositional relationship between light and dark is complicated by the simple "and" which connects them: "ladies of light and darkness." The ladies may be aligned with one category or with both; regardless of how the line is read, light and dark are given equal weight in the book. A third set of ladies is also identified in the opening passage; the inclusion of the cheeky "and ladies of never-you-mind" further destabilizes the potential duality of light and dark. Gaiman signals new territory with a bit of an edge to it—"never-you-mind" can be construed as hostile but also entices the reader to "mind," as in to try to find out. The traditional pattern of opposition denies the potential intersection of light and dark. The division is more unstable than the paradigm suggests. Tim Edensor proposes "rather than considering . . . light and darkness to be opposing states . . . it is more productive and realistic to develop a relational understanding of these conditions" (435). I would argue that is exactly what *Blueberry Girl* does: in its appeals to "ladies of merciful night" and "ladies of shadows that fall," it seeks a "relational understanding" of light and dark. Coalescence is strategic in this text *and* in *The Wolves in the Walls* and *The Sleeper and the Spindle*: light and dark are united into a whole, for a common end.

Picturing Empowerment: The Play between Visual and Written Texts in *Blueberry Girl*

The gentle tone of the piece belies the rich depiction of life it provides. Throughout *Blueberry Girl*, the emphasis is on movement, growth, an engagement with the world; Gaiman and the illustrator, Vess, encourage readers to move through the world with confidence, which requires preparation. There is a strong protective impulse in *Blueberry Girl*—it is punctuated by requests to keep negative experiences at bay, "nightmares at three or bad husbands at thirty," or to diminish the negative effects of these experiences, "help her to lose and to find"—but there is also an acknowledgement of the impossibility of doing so. Instead, protection comes from preparation for life's challenges— a more productive protection than merely avoiding the complex reality of life. In this context, Vess's illustrations can seem paradoxical. He uses gentle pastel colors which have a soothing effect, and the images have a strong tendency to situate the blueberry girl in protective spaces—under the benign sight of the "ladies"; accompanied by a variety of birds and animals; or encircled by plants. The visual text is not a direct depiction of the written text, nor can it be. The relationship is more intricate than mere representation. W. J. T. Mitchell asserts such a relationship is "a complex one of mutual translation, interpretation, illustration, and enlightenment" (44). Vess's illustrations reinforce Gaiman's ideas while softening the book's didactic impulse.

Blueberry Girl can be read as a modern-day conduct book. Unlike the plethora of publications aimed at girls and young women in the eighteenth and nineteenth centuries, which prescribed the appropriate social behaviors for catching a husband (mostly looking pretty, being silent, and blushing at the correct time!), this book seeks to instill character traits which will help girls to engage with the world. The rules-to-live-by laid out in the written text focus on active engagement, self-reliance, and wisdom: "let her stay waking and wise"; "let her have brave days and truth"; "let her go places that we've never been"; "grant her your clearness of sight"; "grant her the wisdom to choose her path right"; "help her to help herself, help her to stand." Vess is particularly adept at translating the concept of active engagement in the illustrations. The various blueberry girls are depicted as marching, flying, swinging, swimming, tumbling, and exploring. They are vitality personified. Vess opts not to include detailed facial expressions—each girl becomes a kind of "every girl" figure—and yet manages to convey the impression that each girl has a distinct personality. The absence of detail opens another space for translation: the meaning the reader ascribes to the image in relation to the written text (and vice versa).

Self-reliance is a little more complicated to portray, but Vess aptly handles the challenge. The first two pages (after the title page) show the "ladies" looking down, benevolently, on a blueberry girl. They are a protective presence almost encircling her on the two-page illustration which follows. Significantly, the "ladies" leave an opening for the girl, seated on an owl, to fly: they do not restrict her movement but instead they facilitate it. The child's expression is excited and her arms are raised indicating enjoyment of the ride. The written text which accompanies the illustration is "First, may you ladies be kind." It is a plea that *appears* to have been answered. Vess's images offer the reassurance that the appeal cannot. The "ladies" will not reappear until the end of the book where they are represented by hands reaching down to another blueberry girl giving her stars and moons. Again, Vess provides the reader with the story that follows (as in comes *after*) the written text. Gaiman's requests require an answer from the "ladies"; Vess's illustrations reveal that they have been granted.

In the space between the depictions of the "ladies," readers witness a variety of blueberry girls moving through the world without adult supervision. They are independent figures but without the burden of isolation. The natural world provides any missing companionship. The dominant image in the menagerie of birds and animals is that of an owl—a choice that works well with Gaiman's emphasis on the need for the blueberry girl to acquire wisdom. It appears at least ten times, frequently leading the way, and may be interpreted as a substitute for the "ladies." Owls have a long literary tradition of being symbols of nighttime, magic, and wisdom. The Greek goddess of wisdom, Athena, was often described as being accompanied by owls.[2] Seemingly absent, the ladies—the source of wisdom—symbolically hover over the blueberry girls. The repeated presence of the owl also reinforces the insistence on the need for clarity of sight, the desire for truth, and the necessity to be wise woven throughout the written prayer.

The owl clearly functions as a familiar or animal guide for the blueberry girl; it is a presence not explicitly identified in the written text but implicitly invoked by the continuing appeals to the "ladies." Two pictures do depict a blueberry girl on her own: one has her encircled by a blueberry bush, reaching for the sky, and the other has her contemplating what the written text implies is a pearl (but looks suspiciously like a blueberry); nothing in either picture suggests that being alone is equivalent to vulnerability. The white space around each visual image, combined with the pastel colors, evokes a tranquil atmosphere. Indeed, the depiction of the girl contemplating the pearl has an almost mystical quality –the pearl levitates above her hands and her head is bowed in contemplation. She is the very picture of serenity. Vess manages to convey the written text—"Truth is a thing she must find for herself, precious and rare as a pearl"—without overwhelming the implied child reader. The blueberry girl is at peace; the serious task of seeking truth is not so cumbersome that the child cannot fulfill it. Once again, Vess moves beyond Gaiman's words and reveals the outcome rather than the process; that is, we witness the thoughtful consideration of the "pearl of wisdom," not the struggle to find it. The tactic does not negate Gaiman's story: it anticipates where it is headed.

Vess's visual texts do reinforce the written text but they do so in a complex and compelling way. As Perry Nodelman observes, a disconnect between word and image is not unusual:

> If we look carefully . . . the words in picture books always tell us that things are not merely as they appear in the pictures, and the pictures always show us that events are not exactly as the words describe them. Picture books are inherently ironic . . . a key pleasure they offer is a perception of the differences in the information offered by pictures and texts. (69–70)

At several points the illustrations are quite direct—"choose her path right," for example, has the blueberry girl approaching three paths; "words written clear on a wall" are just that. All the depictions require selection in terms of details conveyed but in the majority of the illustrations, Vess deliberately moves into a complementary but distinctive storyline. It is not a case of disruption or disharmony; Vess's images in no way undermine the prayer for the blueberry girl.

On a practical level, Vess seems to be working around the difficulty of visually accommodating lines such as "nightmares at three or bad husbands at thirty" or "dull days at forty, false friends at fifteen," but the tactic of omission signals a different kind of accommodation. In addition to the use of soothing pastels, Vess opts for non-threatening content in his illustrations; they are enticing, not intimidating. He does not depict the potential pitfalls Gaiman acknowledges. The visual journey is joyful, not perilous; the girls have expressions of mischief, interest, thoughtfulness, and joy. The written text might be construed as being aimed at the adult reader while the illustrations are directed to the child reader. Possible, but too reductive in my view: it undermines the abilities of the child—something Gaiman clearly resists in his numerous works for children—and it perpetuates the notion that adults move beyond the "simplicity" of pictures. Combining written and visual texts is actually a complex skill. Vess's reassuring images also sooth the parents contemplating their child's future. The combined texts of Gaiman and Vess work in tandem to focus on the empowerment, not the peril.

Complicating the Home: The Emergence of a Domestic Heroine in *The Wolves in the Walls*

Unlike *Blueberry Girl*, *The Wolves in the Walls* and *The Sleeper and the Spindle* do show the perilous journey in both the written and visual aspects of the books. *The Wolves in the Walls* is more visually complex than the other books. McKean utilizes a wider variety of techniques and mediums than Vess and Riddell. All three illustrators, however, employ a similar strategy, one which might be called discontinuity—not a gaping void but a provocative opening for a more complex reading experience. While the illustrations and written texts work in harmony, they reject the need to replicate each other and often border on the contradictory. *The Wolves in the Walls* in particular hinges upon a movement between fear and reassurance. Gaiman and McKean clearly recognize both the pleasure of being afraid—a kind of exhilarating brush with danger—and the need for limitations on that fear, that is, the comfort of knowing the threat is contained.

Given that the threat is literally within Lucy's home, the presence of the wolves is especially disturbing. Initially, they pose a psychological threat to

Lucy; McKean's illustrations extend that threat to the reader. The depiction of Lucy with her ear pressed to the wall is strangely compelling. She gazes directly at the reader and is clearly uneasy.

Superimposed over a realistic depiction of a young girl (and all the human characters in the book), McKean's addition of a flesh-colored mask is both disturbing and reassuring. The familiar is rendered unfamiliar—a fitting choice for a story which takes place in a disrupted domestic setting. In his work on comics, Scott McCloud theorizes the "combination" of realistic backgrounds and unrealistic characters "allows readers to mask themselves in a character and safely enter a sensually stimulating world" (43). Readers accompany Lucy on her emotional journey but retain the comfort of it being a vicarious experience.

The written text further defuses the intensity of Lucy's situation. Physical details like font type and size and the placement of the text serve several purposes in *The Wolves in the Walls*. On a practical level, they convey the story Gaiman wrote; on a psychological level, they frequently undercut the terror McKean's illustrations are building up. The darkness of the image of Lucy pressed against the wall is alleviated by the angled, white print surrounding her. That the words describing the sound of the wolves surround Lucy could suggest that she is trapped and in imminent danger. Gaiman, however, moves the reader in a different direction—the noises are "hustling," "bustling," "crinkling," "crackling," "sneaking," "creeping," and "crumpling." The adjectives are more playful than aggressive, and onomatopoeia highlights the pure pleasure of language. In this case, the devil is not in the details.

The strategy of the written text soothing readers while the visual text draws them further into the (potentially) disconcerting details of the story is used multiple times in the book. Lucy is shown cowering in her bed, her hands clutching the sheets. The description of the wolves "clawing and gnawing" briefly intensifies the scene. The continuation of "nibbling and squabbling" undercuts that tension, and the reference to wolves "plotting their wolfish plots, hatching their wolfish schemes" tips it over into the ridiculous. It is a reversal of the application of the technique in *Blueberry Girl*—Vess's images reassure, Gaiman's words demand an engagement with the complexities of life—but the technique is the same: the words and pictures are complementary, not equivalent.

In a pivotal moment in the book, Gaiman and McKean do come close to equivalency; it is a particularly evocative image. Having been chased out of their home by the wolves, the family is reduced to sleeping in the garden. Lucy is shown curled up in the fetal position in the dark with leafless trees morphing into an open-mouthed wolf about to eat her pig-puppet. It is an evocative portrait of her terrified state. Despite the presence in the picture of her sleeping (and therefore oblivious) father, Lucy is alone with her fear. Gaiman's text does nothing to alleviate Lucy's (and, by extension, the reader's) discomfort: "It was chilly at the bottom of the garden, and Lucy missed her pig-puppet. 'She'll be all alone in that house with the wolves,' she thought. 'They could do dreadful things to her.'" The refusal to release the tension through playful language—Gaiman's only concession is using "could" rather than "are"—or by McKean adding a detail like her father's arm draped reassuringly over Lucy, makes this moment in the book stand out. It is in fact a key point in Lucy's journey, motivating her to return to the home despite her fear.

The following page reveals the shadow of a wolf, mouth gaping and looming over Lucy, but *she* is also a shadowy figure. Once again, the written text diminishes the tension: the wolves "had been eating jam and toast in front of the television, and were coming back for more"—not exactly predatory carnivores pursuing Lucy. The wolves fluctuate between being comical and being dangerous; Gaiman and McKean construct them as two seemingly contradictory characters. When they burst through the walls, the wolves dominate a two-page layout—mouths open, teeth prominent. The family flees and is subsequently positioned at the bottom of the picture while a wolf, outside the abandoned home, bays at the moon at the top of the page. The darkness is once again visually broken by the white text but, more significantly, the antics of the wolves are more irritating than threatening: "the wolves were watching their television and eating the food from the family's pantry and dancing wolfish dances up the stairs and down again." The lightness of the humor undercuts the dark situation. The rescue mission is the first step in restoring domestic order. It is significant that Lucy does it alone. Concern for her pig-puppet leads her to the self-awareness that she is capable of altering the situation. In turn, that confidence will make Lucy the leader of her family.

The source of Lucy's strength is not clear; in our glimpses of the family, they are unsupportive, dismissive, and insensitive. The written text does not indicate how she got the necessary strength but the illustrations might fill in that gap. Lucy wields the pencil on the cover of the book; she is drawing wolves. Multiple framed versions of those wolves (as well as a picture of a wolf being flattened by an elephant) are displayed on the wall of the house, suggesting that her creativity is not only supported, it is encouraged (and, perhaps, that she is the author of her own destiny). In the context of the story, however, her family offers little comfort to Lucy; instead, she turns to her pig-puppet. Lucy is illustrated looking into the eyes of her doll while in the background her mother stands with her back to her. The positioning is telling; so too is the solution the mother offers when the pig-puppet is left behind in their frantic flight—to buy a new one. The family discounts Lucy's intelligence and her feelings. She does, however, have the final word: Lucy rescues her beloved pig-puppet and dismisses each family member's suggestion for relocating. Unlike her family, Lucy is not willing to concede defeat. She exercises her free will choosing action over being a passive victim. In the process, she inspires a "rebellion."

Victory is, however, deferred. Despite Lucy's successful foray into the house, the family continues to discuss alternative locations rather than reclaim their home. Calmly assessing the situation, she points out that "'there's a lot of space in the walls . . . And at least it isn't cold there.'" She is logical and determined. McKean depicts Lucy leading the reluctant, visibly cringing family into the house. Safely situated within the walls, the family witnesses mayhem. The wolves are wreaking havoc but it is distinctly human behavior—not predatory action but self-indulgent play (covering eight action packed pages). All four are outraged but it is Lucy who sparks the attack on the wolves with the statement "right. I've had enough" and the example of arming herself with a chair leg. The other family members quickly follow, and the unified group succeeds in routing the wolves. Lucy's willingness to step into the metaphorical "dark" of her fears and the actual dark of "the wall in her bedroom"—which offers very little light as McKean opts for an intensely black background—and use it to her advantage is the catalyst for change; order is restored. The reader is told "everything went back to normal," but a new sound gains Lucy's attention: "she heard a noise that sounded exactly like an elephant trying not to sneeze." A new threat emerges but McKean offers a counter image to the previous one depicting Lucy cowering in her bed; this time she looks pensive rather than apprehensive. She subsequently turns, not to her family, but to her pig-puppet who offers the pragmatic advice: "I'm sure they'll find out soon enough." The final page reveals a splattered jam sandwich, an elephant footprint, and the simple statement: "And they did." Visual and written texts combine to create a comical ending. Despite the intimidating portrait of an angry elephant squashing a wolf earlier in the book—a red stain with paws and legs sticking out suggests the rise of a new invader—the new adventure is non-threatening. Lucy has already proven that she is equipped to handle it. The traits Lucy displays—active engagement with her world, self-reliance, and intelligence—echo those outlined in *Blueberry Girl.*

The Wolves in the Walls has the potential to perpetuate the stereotype of a young girl as a victim. Lucy is physically and emotionally vulnerable for much of the book. Gaiman and McKean, however, opt for a new kind of domestic hero. Lucy emerges as "a strong female character," argues Renata Lucena Dalmaso, "that refuses to be passive in the face of difficulty or others' incredulity" setting her "apart from a tradition of submissive feminine characters in children's narratives and fairy tales" (33). She astutely observes that "the trope of the distressed heroine seeking help . . . is one that Gaiman often appropriates and subverts" (33). *Blueberry Girl* offers the steps to avoid passive femininity; the requested gifts ensure that the girl is shaped into a confident and capable individual. In *The Wolves in the Walls* and *The Sleeper and the Spindle*, Gaiman and his illustrators create two distinctive characters who consciously resist the state, and status, of being a "distressed heroine."

Thinking outside the Frame: Breaking the Tradition of the Damsel in Distress in *The Sleeper and the Spindle*

In the case of *The Sleeper and the Spindle*, the "revolution" comes from within: Gaiman and Riddell adopt and adapt several fairy-tale conventions. It is a highly stylized book with tremendous attention to fine details. Visually, it is evocative of an earlier time—appropriate for a modern-day fairy tale. Riddell's choice of a pen-and-ink effect, with limited use of a muted gold, gives the book a very "traditional" quality. But, just as Gaiman breaks from tradition by putting a new spin on two familiar fairy tales, the illustrator pushes the expectations of the reader in new, and provocative, directions. The repeated inclusion of skull imagery, the positioning of the Queen, and the relationship it creates with the reader, and the (at times ironic) border, combine to give an edginess to the visual text that fits well with the written text.

One of the more ideologically challenging illustrations is also one of the most beautiful in the book; having discovered the beautiful sleeper, the Queen releases her from that sleep. She "touched the pink lips to her own carmine lips and she kissed the sleeping girl long and hard" (49). It is a task traditionally assigned to a prince. The two-page depiction which follows offers a sensual contrast of light and dark as the Queen's dark hair cascades onto the fair-haired sleeper (50–51). It is a beautiful and potentially provocative image.

Riddell and Gaiman break from the heterosexual narrative. While the kiss is described as being "long and hard," it is actually depicted as quite chaste—the lips barely touch, their individual outlines remain distinct. Riddell's delicate touch might soften the erotic quality, but the sensual beauty of the image is evocative.

The reader's first visual encounter with the Queen complicates any interpretation of the kiss she exchanges with the sleeping girl. Again, it is a two-page, highly detailed illustration; the written text simply states: "the Queen woke early that morning" (12). At this point, it is largely uninformative; insight must come from the picture. The Queen's brow is furrowed, her face is openly hostile, and her hands clutch the skull-covered bedspread in a protective gesture reminiscent of the image of Lucy discussed earlier but the Queen reads as more annoyed than terrified. The source of her irritation is in in her direct line of vision on the second page: a dramatic dress (her wedding dress, as the written text will clarify). Seemingly discarded, or at least carelessly dropped, in the corner, are pieces of armor and a sword (almost lost in the binding of the book).

Riddell's depiction anticipates the details that follow in the written text: "The queen woke early that morning. 'A week from today,' she said aloud. 'A week from today, I shall be married'" (14). Lest there be any doubt about her feelings, both image and written text convey her dread and fears: marriage strikes her as "extremely final. . . . It would be the end of her life . . . if life was a time of choices. . . . she would have no choices. . . . the path to her death, heartbeat by heartbeat, would be inevitable" (14). Riddell depicts a pensive Queen, hand clutched to her chest while the side-panel of workmen preparing for the wedding seems to loom over her. A subsequent image of the Queen having her wedding dress/death shroud fitted, the gold ribbons almost binding her, reinforces the idea that marriage will be constricting. The written text explains that dwarves are reporting that a nearby kingdom is under a sleeping curse. The Queen's gaze is directed outward—presumably at the speakers, but in effect, at the reader—and she wears a startled expression. The image contained in this side panel is in stark contrast to that on the opposite page. In a borderless illustration, Riddell depicts an armored and armed Queen, astride her horse, moving forward with a confident and determined expression on her face. The picture reflects Gaiman's description of the Queen preparing for the adventure.

Riddell does not, however, illustrate an interesting (and comical) part of the written text. The Queen postpones the wedding, orders the evacuation of her people, ensures governance of the kingdom, and says farewell to her betrothed: "She called for her fiancé and told him not to take on so, and that they would still be married, even if he was but a prince and she a queen, and she chucked him beneath his pretty chin and she kissed him until he smiled" (21). Rather than including this seemingly inconsequential man, Riddell emphasizes the active response of the Queen. She moves towards potential danger but that danger is a welcome reprieve from the actual threat of her impending marriage. The contrast of these placating farewell kisses with the one she shares with the sleeping girl, combined with the Queen's dread of the restrictions marriage will impose, opens a space for an alternative to the heterosexual norm which dominates in children's literature. By no means is *The Sleeper and the Spindle* a lesbian text, but there is a subtext that hints at a different trajectory of desire. Readers can, of course, leave it "sub" or buried.

The written text does offer a different motivation for the Queen kissing the sleeper. Unsure of whether it worked or not, she confesses, "I feel for her, poor thing. Sleeping her life away" (52). Compassion based upon personal experience accounts for the Queen's desire to kiss the girl. In this instance, compassion overshadows wisdom and it actually renders the Queen vulnerable. She ignores the "old woman" when she says, "It's my stick. . . . I think it was my father's. But he had no more use for it" (49). A cryptic but telling clue is missed; misled by their contrasting appearances, the Queen assumes the beautiful girl is the crone's victim. She acts first and listens to the facts afterwards: the old woman provides a narrative of the past and the young girl reveals her plot: "I slept, and they slept . . . I stole a little of their life, a little of their dreams . . . I took back my youth and my beauty and my power. I undid the ravages of time and I built myself a world of sleeping slaves" (52). Beauty masks a monster. Riddell's illustration drives home the point that the "young girl" is actually a barely human figure preying on a princess.

The Queen has misread the situation but her quest is in fact successful: the old woman is sufficiently empowered to vanquish her foe who is reduced to "a tumble of bones, a hank of hair as fine and as white as fresh-spun cobwebs, a tracery of rags across it, and over all of it, an oily dust" (63). Riddell incorporates those details in the final two-page illustration of the princess with her revived subjects but, significantly, no one is looking at it. Order is restored—the princess occupies the central position in the picture, her bed is now surrounded by flowers, her facial expression is serene, and her hands rest peacefully on the bedspread. Neither Riddell nor Gaiman provide the happy ending of restoring the princess's youth and beauty "but there was a look in her eyes . . . that was the look of someone young" (62). The Queen tasks the people with caring for the princess but leaves them in ignorance: "none of the people . . . would ever understand what had happened" (63). The last image of the princess firmly establishes her as a damsel-in-deep-rest relying on the kindness of others. It is a fate the Queen actively resists in the final pages of the book.

The journey to the sleeping kingdom offers insight into how the Queen develops the courage and wisdom to determine her own fate. Undertaking the quest requires physical courage, but that trait is actually downplayed in the book. Moving through the dark of the subterranean tunnel, the group passes a sleeping monster; the Queen's sword is drawn but unnecessary. They pass by unmolested. The sleeping people will, however, become more threatening.

Sheer numbers, as Riddell's two-page illustration drives home, make the slow moving mass intimidating but the Queen's response is flight, not fight. While the fleeing Queen and dwarves might be charged with cowardice, the vacuous facial expressions render their adversaries more pitiful than predatory. A dwarf protests, "this is not honorable. . . . We should stay and fight." The Queen counters with "there is no honor . . . in fighting an opponent who has no idea that you are even there" (35). Self-preservation does not negate a sense of justice and compassion. The Queen calmly assesses the situation and reaches a logical solution—like Lucy, and the blueberry girl, she draws on "the wisdom to choose her path right" (Gaiman, *Blueberry Girl*). Riddell does illustrate the Queen wielding her sword but no opponent is in sight and the written text reveals that her target is "good kindling" (46). She uses it to vanquish the natural barrier thwarting the quest—wisdom, not brute strength, is required in this situation.

Wisdom tempered by compassion is the Queen's main strength in *The Sleeper and the Spindle*. The source of that strength oddly enough, is a direct encounter with darkness. When the beautiful girl awakens, the Queen narrows her focus to the girl's eyes and "saw what she was searching for: the same look that she had seen in her stepmother's eyes, and she knew what manner of creature this girl was" (54). Riddell's two-page illustration offers insight into the girl; there is an overwhelming presence of skulls in the image; apparently real human skulls adorn her bedframe. They are in stark contrast to the gold skull decorations on the Queen's bedspread or the grip for her sword. Given the girl's somnolent confession, linking the skulls with evil seems logical; the Queen's appropriation of the symbol, however, raises other associations: certainly death and mortality, but also, as has appeared in various cultures, in various time periods, as an emblem of protection, strength, and wisdom. The shared symbol does raise the question: what else do this creature and the Queen have in common? They do share a familiarity with "darkness," the kind of power that requires the submission of others. For the girl, the source seems nature; she observes of the Queen, "You are not of our blood. . . . but you have some of the skill." For the Queen, the source is experience (59). Past encounters with darkness prepare her for this confrontation.

The journey to the castle forces the Queen to move through a "mental fog" (40). The hallucinations it inspires are quite telling. Although "she knew [they] could not be there," familiar figures accompany the Queen: her father is given one line about diplomacy while her mother makes two brief statements about her beauty (41). Their comments frame a paragraph of boasts by her stepmpther: "My sisters ruled the world. . . . The mortal folk rose up against us, they cast us down. And so we waited, in crevices, in places they do not see us" (41). The stepmother's influence clearly overshadows that of her parents in the written text. Riddell's depiction of this page shows the sinister figure of the stepmother looming over the Queen, who gazes forward (seemingly at the reader) while looking pensive. Although it is not quite a case of a tormentor becoming a mentor, the knowledge gained from resisting her stepmother will enable the Queen to rise to the current challenge—forewarned is forearmed.

What is merely implied in the hallucinations will be explicitly stated when the Queen confronts the girl. The Queen draws parallels between the two experiences: "It's always the same with your kind. You need youth and you need beauty. You used your own up . . . and now you find ever more complex ways of obtaining them. And you always want power" (56). Defiance is fueled by the awareness that she survived "a year in a glass coffin" and that "the woman who put [her] there was much more powerful and dangerous . . ." (56). Self-confidence is based upon an awareness of her own abilities. Riddell's depiction of the face-to-face confrontation conveys the power of each adversary: they stare eye-to-eye, the girl's fair hair entwining the Queen, and the broken rose petals being blown away suggest she is in command but the Queen does not flinch, she remains steadfast (58). Threats do not sway the Queen, nor does the offer of (conditional) power. She does, however, catch herself responding emotionally: "'love me,' said the girl. All will love me, and you, who woke me, you must love me most of all.' The queen felt something stirring in her heart. She remembered her stepmother, then. Her stepmother had liked to be adored" (59). The timely remembrance of her stepmother saves the Queen. It is not the stepmother herself that influences the Queen but the hard-won lesson: "learning how to be strong, to feel her own emotions and not another's, had been hard; but once you learned the trick of it, you did not forget" (59). Emotional maturity is in spite of her stepmother, not because of her; it is precisely the weapon the Queen needs to triumph. It is fitting that she hands the spindle to the old woman to finish off the girl; poetic justice is the only justice she will receive.

The Queen leaves the princess to her fate, but the book ends with a refusal to be fated. The concluding pages reject the need for finality. Walking west means that her "wedding will be late, but it will happen . . . and the people will celebrate, and there will be joy unbounded through the Kingdom" (66). The Queen sits "on the moss beneath an oak tree and tasted the stillness, heartbeat by heartbeat" (66). In stark contrast to the earlier heartbeat sound marking the constricting life being imposed on her, the Queen draws strength from the steady beat. "*There are choices*, she thought, when she had sat long enough.

There are always choices" (66). Riddell positions the Queen gazing straight out at the reader; her body language is defensive and self-protective, but her eyes are wide open, reflective of introspection as she contemplates her future. It is clear that the Queen does desire power: power over her own fate rather than power over others. Exercising her free will, the Queen leads the dwarves east "away from the sunset and the lands they knew, and into the night" (67). The direction is interesting: the movement is away from the sunset, the conventional happily ever after.

Riddell, however, does not depict this situation. The final illustration is contained within the most detailed frame in the book. Despite the ornate frame, the picture reinforces the positive ending of the Queen's choice. The written text is specific: they walk into the night. Riddell has the group moving into the light, watching a dragon overhead. It holds out the promise of adventure, choices beyond the beautiful frame that surrounds but does not contain them.

The Queen is not a domestic hero like Lucy—their conflicts differ—but both characters reject the choices others attempt to impose on them. The central female characters in *The Wolves in the Walls* and *The Sleeper and the Spindle*—Lucy and the unnamed yet identifiable Queen—are both, initially, victims of enforced passivity. At pivotal moments, however, each girl exercises her own will by drawing upon an untapped store of courage, compassion, and cunning intelligence. In Lucy's case, she is dismissed and discredited by her family until her pig-puppet being in peril prompts decisive action on her part. Lucy will lead the family in the counterattack that reclaims their home. The young Queen's quest will also begin as reactionary; she investigates a neighboring kingdom under a sleeping spell (delaying her impending marriage). Like Lucy, the Queen quells a coup by facing the problem and her fears directly. The Queen resists and removes the threat she addresses as "your darkness" based upon lessons learnt from withstanding her stepmother (56). It is not clear what the source of Lucy's strength is; her family seems to be an unlikely source. The end of each text, however, finds the young women making informed choices: Lucy withholds the fact that elephants now lurk in the walls, and the Queen, recognizing that "there are always choices," walks with her companions away from the familiar "into the night" (68).

Both movements are revealing: Lucy's self-confidence is apparent in her wait-and-see approach which sidesteps familial (false) reassurance and the Queen opts for self-determination over the comfort of the familiar. Eyes wide-open, the pair draw upon "the wisdom to choose [their] path right, free from unkindness and fear" (*Blueberry Girl*)—two more blueberry girls engaging with the larger world.

NOTES

1. Tim Edensor discusses the history of this dichotomy in "The Gloomy City: Rethinking the Relationship Between Light and Dark." In medieval times, darkness was associated with the pagan; lightness was connected to Christianity. The division continued through the seventeenth and eighteenth centuries: the dark arts of "witchcraft and devilry, heresy, sin and death" were juxtaposed with the light provided by Christian faith and "enlightenment narratives [of] transcendent transformation from dark to light" (424, 425). The distrust of the dark lingers well into the twenty-first century; the stigma of sin may be reduced but the negative aspect—misuse of power, absence of insight/knowledge, lawlessness—tends to shape our concepts of darkness.

2. For example, see Cassandra Eason's *Fabulous Creatures, Mythical Monsters, and Animal Power Symbols: A Handbook*, p. 71.

WORKS CITED

Dalmaso, Renata Lucena. "Towards a Feminist Reading of Gaiman's Picture Books." *Neil Gaiman in the 21st Century: Essays on the Novels, Children's Stories, Online Writings, Comics and Other Works*. Tara Prescott, ed. McFarland, 2015, pp. 29–38.

Eason, Cassandra. *Fabulous Creatures, Mythical Monsters, and Animal Power Symbols: A Handbook*. Greenwood Publishing, 2008.

Edensor, Tim. "The Gloomy City: Rethinking the Relationship between Light and Dark." *Urban Studies* vol. 52, no. 3, 2015, pp. 422–38.

Gaiman, Neil, and Charles Vess. *Blueberry Girl*. HarperCollins, 2009.

Gaiman, Neil, and Chris Riddell. *The Sleeper and the Spindle*. HarperCollins, 2014.

Gaiman, Neil, and Dave McKean. *The Wolves in the Walls*. HarperCollins, 2003.

McCloud, Scott. *Understanding Comics: The Invisible Art*. HarperCollins, 1994.

Mitchell, W. J. T. *Iconology: Image, Text, Ideology*. University of Chicago Press, 1968.

Nodelman, Perry. "Decoding the Images: Illustration and Picture Books." *Understanding Children's Literature*. Peter Hunt, ed. Routledge, 1998, pp. 69–80.

Stephens, John. *Language and Ideology in Children's Fiction*. Longman, 1992.

LIMINALITY AND THE GOTHIC SUBLIME OF *THE SANDMAN*

ERICA McCRYSTAL

Clad in black and maneuvering mysteriously through both dreams and the waking world, Morpheus, The Lord of Dreams embodies the Gothic in Neil Gaiman's *The Sandman* series: both a real figure and also a metaphysical aspect brought to life. "The Gothic" is a term that is most often used to describe the romantic novel that flourished at the end of the eighteenth and beginning of the nineteenth centuries, set mostly in quasi-medieval mansions and castles developed in what is commonly regarded from an architectural view as *Gothic* style. However, as a largely symbolic mode, the Gothic has persisted and grown to encompass "a type of fiction which lacks the medieval setting but develops a brooding atmosphere of gloom or terror, represents events which are uncanny, or macabre, or melodramatically violent, and often deals with aberrant psychological states" (Campbell n.p.).

As with his haunted ancestors, Morpheus evokes the darkness in dreams, much like his sometime-namesake, the Sandman of song and lore, while retaining some of the whimsical nonsense inherent in dreaming. The series presents an overlap between the dreaming and waking worlds, dissipating clear distinctions between reality and fantasy. While Morpheus tries to keep these worlds distinct, he, a liminal body, transgresses both. However, when there is an overlap between the dreaming and the waking worlds, the border is dissolved and humans too become liminal figures who navigate both worlds. These frequent transgressions and hauntings in *The Sandman* arouse Gothic tensions. In *The Sandman*, the Endless¹ are liminal figures due to their capacity to move and exist between realms; they each exist in their own realms but simultaneously belong to the waking world. The infinite possibilities that emerge when concrete and fantastic worlds collide make the series evocative of the sublime. Gaiman and his illustrators use liminality and the sublime throughout the series through the overlapping of the Dreaming and waking world, the infiniteness of Hell, and the illusory nature of the Endless and their realms. As bodies move seamlessly through overlapping worlds that swell with uncertainty, *The Sandman* series serves as an example of a liminal fantasy that thrives on the mystery created when reality and fantasy are not distinct.

The Gothic, the Sublime, and the Liminal Fantasy

The literary Gothic tradition contains many tropes that the series embraces to fully exacerbate the uncertain nature of Gaiman's world. These include the past intruding on the present, questionable identities, and the infiltration of threats into the domestic space. Julia Round has found that the additional "processes of haunting, architecture, excess, and decomposition" as Gothic elements of *Sandman* no. 1 establish a method that Gaiman uses throughout his entire series (Round 126). The illustrations, too, create a sense of the Gothic, where there is no uniformity in panel size, shape, or layout. Perspective play makes it difficult to fully comprehend space, and looming shadows pervade the pages. The series creates characters and worlds that embody Gothic variability and make each issue mysterious and even terrifying, as mystical threats know no boundaries.

Visual and narrative Gothic uncertainties are indicative of the awe-inspiring infiniteness that makes up the sublime. Eighteenth-century philosopher Edmund Burke's definition of the sublime directly relates it to terror:

> Whatever is fitted in any sort to excite the ideas of pain, and danger, that is to say, whatever is in any sort terrible, or is conversant about terrible objects, or operates in a manner analogous to terror, is a source of the *sublime*; that is, it is productive of the strongest emotion which the mind is capable of feeling. (58–59)

Described in this way, the sublime is characteristic of the Gothic, which thrives on evoking fear and dread. Burke finds that privation, vastness, infinity, and magnificence are additional sources of the sublime. Many of these qualities create a sense of uncertainty and limitlessness of things that cannot be concretely defined or known. Vijay Mishra finds that "[t]he Gothic sublime is not a definitive form in its own right; it is a symbolic structure" (23). Likewise, Ed Cameron finds that "the Gothic's fictive excess . . . is sublime because . . . it represents that which is by nature unrepresentable" (19). Paradoxically, then, a definitive quality of the sublime is that it cannot be defined.

David B. Morris argues that "the quest for a single, unchanging feature or essence is futile. There is no essence of the sublime" (300). Given this approach—and, ostensibly, the entire purpose of this chapter—to define liminality in *The Sandman* as evocative of the Gothic sublime may also seem a futile endeavor. In this series, the Gothic sublime becomes both visible and imaginable through the liminality of time and space. Like the sublime, liminality is difficult to visualize since it is a concept noting that which is in between rather than that which is distinct. However, in the series, Gaiman and his illustrators create worlds that are simultaneously concrete and intangible, creating an essence of liminality.

Space, time, a situation, or a body is liminal when it exists in between contrasting forces. As Victor Turner defines them, "liminal entities are neither here nor there; they are betwixt and between the positions assigned and arrayed by law, custom, convention, and ceremonial" (*The Ritual Process* 95). He gives examples, likening liminality "to death, to being in the womb, to invisibility, to darkness, to bisexuality, to the wilderness, and to an eclipse of the sun or moon" (*The Ritual Process* 95). Liminal space is not concrete because it is an in-between space; it is the threshold, the borderlands. For Turner, "liminality can perhaps be described as a fructile chaos, a fertile nothingness, a storehouse of possibilities" ("Are There Universals . . ." 12). Turner's definition suggests that liminality is pregnant with opportunities. The space beyond the liminal, on the other side of the threshold, is open and vast. This suggests infinite space that cannot be charted. In this way, liminal space may be a passageway to the sublime. It also may be sublime itself, since it cannot be concretely defined as it is neither one nor the other. "Nothingness" aligns it with privation, which Burke associates with the sublime.

The Sandman specializes in liminal beings moving through liminal space. Death calls Dream an "anthropomorphic personification" (*Preludes and Nocturnes*, Part 8), which aptly describes her and their other siblings as well. The Endless are not human, but they are not gods either. To humans, they are aspects of life, but the series embodies them as physical figures that can be seen and heard. However, their embodiments are not concrete, and they shift appearances to meet the demands of the person viewing them, reverting to more or less definite forms when they are out of human observation. Their purposes mirror this gaze-reflecting embodiment: when the Endless infiltrate the waking world, it is most often to fulfill the roles designated to them by name but also for personal reasons.[2] Their designation as "the Endless" also suggests that they are figures of any and every time; their existence is infinite. Even though Morpheus's death near the end of the series suggests that he has transcended from a liminal position to a static one, Daniel replaces him as the Lord of the Dreaming; thus, the subject position is never vacant. Morpheus's death shows that his character is not an immortal deity; however, the aspect of a dream lord's subject position is immortal, or endless.

With the Endless occupying personal realms and the overlap of the Dreaming and waking world, the series may be considered a liminal fantasy. Farah Mendlesohn states that

> [i]n the liminal fantasy we are given to understand, through cues to the familiar, that this is our world. When the fantastic appears, it *should* be intrusive, disruptive or expectation; instead, while the events themselves might be noteworthy and/or disruptive, their magical origins barely raise an eyebrow. (xxiii)

Much of the action in *The Sandman* occurs in the waking world (in other words, our familiar world), but the frequent appearance of Morpheus and his sister Death do not disrupt this world.[3] While they have their own realms, they, likewise, have work to do in the waking world known to the reader to be reality. Since their actions are normal in the waking world, their physical presence is not an intrusion, which conforms with Mendlesohn's definition of a liminal fantasy.

The series positions these shifting, transitive bodies and their fluctuating worlds in liminal time, a kind of interregnum. While time markers exist throughout the series, the passage of time itself is insignificant. In "Men of Good Fortune" in *The Doll's House*, Morpheus meets with Hob Gadling in the same place every 100 years. While there are visual markers that time has passed—such as clothing, hairstyles, and the interior of the bar—the issue demonstrates that time does not necessarily matter. Hob and Morpheus will continue to meet every 100 years because they are not bound by time. Hob also notes, "I've seen *people,* and they don't change. Not in the *important* things" (*The Doll's House,* Part 4). Time is irrelevant because humanity is essentially stagnant. Boundless time may also be associated with the liminal fantasy. Mendlesohn also considers space and time: "The transliminal moment, which brings us up to the liminal point and then refuses to cross the threshold, has much greater potential to generate fear, awe, and confusion" (xxiv). This definition allows liminality to be directly connected to the sublime. While a threshold may seem apparent, the threshold is the space and time where the fantastic world thrives; the in-between is the space and time of the sublime liminal fantasy.

Dreaming and Waking Worlds

The Sandman presents two realms that seem to be polarized: dreaming and waking. However, when people in the waking world readily cross into the Dreaming, and when Morpheus, Lord of the Dreaming, readily enters into the waking world, the worlds tend to overlap and create confusion as to what is real. With this example of sublime liminality, reality and fantasy are difficult to distinguish. Events in the Dreaming also may carry into the waking world, which demonstrates the way that the real and the fantastic intertwine in a liminal fantasy[4] where borders between worlds are disrupted. For example, in Part 1 of *A Game of You*, Barbie sees the dog Martin Tenbones, who has come from the Land (where Barbie goes to when she dreams) to give her the Porpentine (a dreamstone that has the power to destroy the Land) in the waking world. While awake, Barbie recognizes Martin Tenbones and the Porpentine from her dreams. Meanwhile, in the Land, another creature, Luz, feels Martin Tenbones die in the waking world. Martin Tenbones transgresses boundaries in traveling from the Land to the waking world while his presence is simultaneously felt in both worlds because these borders are not strictly distinct. Later, when Barbie destroys the Porpentine while dreaming in the Land, it simultaneously disappears from around her neck in the waking world. The two worlds overlap with one another, making reality into a concept that is not concrete. In this volume, it also becomes difficult to distinguish what is real. While wandering the Land, Barbie finds her childhood home where she has to confront the villain, the Cuckoo, who has assumed the figure of Barbie's younger self. When Barbie enters her childhood bedroom, she asks, "[I]s this real? Or is it just my imagination?" (Part 5). Because Barbie cannot differentiate between real and imaginary, the Land cannot truly be known. Such uncertainty evokes the Gothic sublime, which thrives on absence.

Rather than positioning dreaming and waking worlds as contrasts, then, the individual dream worlds in *The Sandman* are in themselves borderless, which makes possible the overlapping of space. Sandor Klapcsik, specifically referring to Mendlesohn's liminal fantasy, argues that "[t]he fantastic is no longer interpreted as a realm different and distant from consensus reality: reality and the fantastic world overlap in a playful or 'blasé' manner, indicating the run-of-the-mill, unremarkable nature of fantastic events" (195). The overlap allows for movement between the worlds, which occurs in *A Game of You* when Thessaly, Hazel, and Foxglove travel the Moon's Road from to the Land to try to rescue Barbie. To do so, they have to enter her dream from the waking world. The practice of crossing realms is not unusual because humans often dream, but in this case, the characters physically transport themselves into another person's dream world and stimulate events that affect both the Land and the waking world. Because the other characters are able to explore the Land, it is not just a space locked in Barbie's mind.

As a liminal fantasy, *The Sandman* blurs distinctions between reality and fantasy. In *Season of Mists*, Dream says about his realm: "reality here conforms to my wishes" (Part 6). Here, a figure claims power over reality and suggests that it is malleable, which actually makes reality indistinguishable from fantasy. Reality may be morphed by the fantastic, which is a sublime occurrence itself; yet, if fantasy controls reality, then is the real actually real?

The paradoxical question is one that can only be answered by accepting that both reality and fantasy, the waking and the dreaming worlds, are not actually distinct, oppositional spaces. Instead, they readily overlap. In *Fables and Reflections,* this idea is articulated through the relationship between space and time: "Time at the edge of the dreaming is softer than elsewhere, and here in the soft places it loops and whorls on itself. In the soft places where the border between dreams and reality is eroded, or has not yet formed" ("Soft Places"). Here, "soft" time, which is perhaps immeasurable, exists in "soft" spaces that are also indistinct. There is no threshold because separate spaces do not exist; instead, spaces overlap and bleed into one another, which intensifies the Gothicity of the series.

The physical process of dreaming and questions of consciousness further complicate an understanding of distinct space. Morpheus says that "each human is connected to the dreaming. They spend a third of their lives in this realm" (*The Doll's House*, Part 2). In one sense, time spent asleep is not inactive because time spent in the Dreaming overlaps with time in the waking world. Since the dreaming is actualized into physical space in Gaiman's comics, humans, when dreaming, are transposed into the space even though the physical reality of their bodies may be in the waking world. Humans are connected to and welcome in both the Dreaming and the waking world. The crossover, though, is not always fluid. In *The Doll's House*, Morpheus meets Shakespeare in the waking world, who asks if they have met before. Morpheus replies, "We have. But men forget, in waking hours" (127). While Morpheus and man both may pass into each other's realms, their consciousness differs. Morpheus's transitions from realm to realm are fluid, whereas humans typically cannot simultaneously comprehend both the dreaming and waking world. When Rose Walker tries to remember her interaction with Morpheus in the waking world, "he fades and shimmers until he seems little more than the echo of a dream" (187). Morpheus's presence in the waking world cannot maintain tangible reality in Rose's mind because Morpheus is the embodiment of a realm that resists being simultaneously held in the mind with the waking world. As Rose falls asleep, the narration describes: "sinking, slowly, downward and inward. Enter a world where everything's going to be just fine" (188). The clearest moment of consciousness is in a physical state between dreaming and waking. In *A Game of You*, Barbie describes the transition from dreaming to waking: "there was that sensation you get on waking, as everything moved further away, and I started to become aware of the cold—and in my dream it was warm, and so I tried to stay in my dream forever, but the harder I held on the further it slipped away from me" (Part 6). Barbie is aware that she is in a transitional state but cannot control herself in it. Her mind in this moment has a liminal experience as it fluctuates on the threshold of non-definitive, Gothic sublime space. The dream world is a place where humans can forget about the troubles of the waking world. It is a place where humans seek "to belong. . . . a place to be safe" (*The Doll's House* 193). This is a way that the waking and dreaming worlds actually could be distinct spaces. In the dreaming, problems of the waking are, theoretically, nonexistent. While the space may be liminal, humans are only consciously present in one world at any given moment. Morpheus tries to maintain this distinction in his role as dream lord.

However, since Rose Walker is not just human but actually a vortex, she becomes, like Morpheus, self-aware of the simultaneity of both:

> Rose dreams. She *knows* she's dreaming. She's never had a dream like this before. Everything seems so *real*, so *vivid*; more true and more vital than the waking world. Her sense of identity has never been so certain. She can feel her sleeping body on the bed below her. It's not part of her; the essential her, the true Rose. (Part 6)

In this moment, Rose is aware of herself in two places at once, as her physical body remains in the waking world, but she is conscious of entering the Dreaming. She feels disjointed from her physical body, marking her true place in the dream world. Morpheus feels threatened by Rose because she is a vortex, what he describes as that which "destroys the barriers between dreaming minds; destroys the ordered chaos of the Dreaming . . . until the myriad dreamers are caught in one huge dream . . . until all the dreams are one" (Part 7). Rose as a vortex, rather than a human, is a liminal being, like Morpheus. She has a heightened awareness and can comprehend existing in both

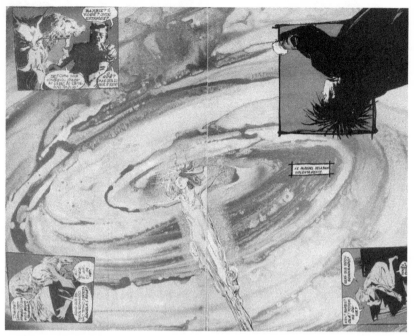

Figure 11.1. *The Doll's House*, part 6.

spaces. Her power can potentially destroy the dream world and disrupt the consciousness barrier between the two worlds that Morpheus tries to maintain (see Figure 11.1).

In Mike Dringenberg's illustration, Rose is the center of the swirling vortex. The layout of the page physically recreates the rotational movement of the vortex. The reader is required to rotate the book in order to continue reading the panels. The panels illustrate the confusion of the humans who have become self-aware of their presence in the Dreaming. If distinct space means awareness of only one realm without consciousness of the other, then in this moment, they have entered liminal space. Rose's experience as a vortex is described: "each mind creates and inhabits its own world; and each world is but a tiny part of that totality that is the Dreaming . . . and she can touch them. Touch *all* of them" (Part 6). Here, the dream world is said to be a realm that houses all of the separate worlds of individual dreamers. Dreaming, then, is entering a world within a world, which is mentally contained within a physical, sleeping body in the waking world. The worlds that individuals enter in their dreams may be considered liminal spaces that are between the waking world and the realm of the Dreaming. If dreams are the thresholds in a liminal fantasy, then humans frequently enter into liminal, sublime spaces that have endless possibilities.

The series evokes the Gothic sublime as it illustrates the instability and volatility of space. In *The Doll's House*, Morpheus describes, "the vortex, by its nature, destroys the barriers between dreaming minds; destroys the ordered chaos of the Dreaming" (Part 7). The dream world is a space of order and chaos. Morpheus needs to destroy the vortex because, in breaking the barriers, it threatens to turn the Dreaming into nothingness. While barriers create distinct space, individual dream worlds are liminal in *The Sandman* because they are not so sharply separate. The resistance to be truly known is seen through the unveiling of endless space. But since Morpheus tries to keep his world contained, the coupling makes for a liminal space. Morpheus tries to maintain a separate realm, but the frequent crossovers demonstrate that it can be simultaneously known and unknowable. The vastness and endless possibilities and the Dreaming as ordered chaos make it evident of a Gothic sublime where there is conscious access to an unknowable space.

The Cuckoo first makes us aware of countless possible dream worlds: "there must be *hundreds* of these lands . . . *thousands* of them. An archipelago of dream-islands—a glittering shoal of worlds" (Part 5). Essentially, individuals travel to these different worlds when dreaming. But the series does not present these worlds as separate from the waking world. They are often described as existing within an individual. Hazel says that the scary thing about bad dreams is "that something's going on in your head, and you can't *control* it. I mean, it's like there's these *bad worlds* inside you" (Part 3). A lack of control arouses Gothic threats in the imagination. Barbie says,

> everybody has a secret world inside of them. I mean *everybody*. All of the people in the whole world—no matter *how* dull and boring they are on the outside. Inside them they've *all* got unimaginable, magnificent, wonderful, stupid, amazing worlds . . . not just one world. *Hundreds* of them. *Thousands*, maybe. (Part 6)

The description of these countless worlds makes them awe-inspiring and full of infinite possibilities; thus, they are sublime. But since the Cuckoo manifests itself in Barbie's younger body, her dream world becomes a space ruled by a Gothic villain.

Even though these worlds are described as inside individuals, the series makes them physical places where other characters can travel. The comic book medium itself takes a dream world out of one's mind, and the illustrations physicalize the space for the reader. In this way, dream worlds in *The Sandman* are depicted as both concrete spaces and potentially imagined worlds inside

Figure 11.2. *A Game of You*, part 5.

one's mind. In *Preludes and Nocturnes*, John Dee, says, "People think dreams aren't real because they aren't made of matter, of particles. Dreams *are* real. But they are made of viewpoints, of images, of memories and puns and lost hopes" (Part 5). Morpheus's ruby, according to Dee, "seems to turn them into matter. It forces them to translate themselves into forms we can recognize in this world" (Part 5). When dreams are recognizable, they essentially become more real. The mind, when dreaming, takes these ideas and turns them into physical form, thus creating or imagining a dream world. Yet, while individuals may physicalize ideas into real forms while dreaming, there is still a Lord of Dreams on the periphery who may disrupt this process as he pleases.

Dream worlds are also potentially transient, which complicates their ability to be truly known and understood, as seen when Morpheus "uncreates" the Land in Part 5 of *A Game of You* (see Figure 11.2).

In this panel, penciled by Shawn McManus and Bryan Talbot, Morpheus holds the Land in his hand even though he, Barbie, and the others are still standing on it. This image demonstrates that there actually is no spatial reality in the Dreaming. The numerous illustrations of The Land in this volume render it a physical place, but this panel creates a visual paradox. This image also creates a unique perspective of space that allows one to see the entire land from above. Ironically, the only time anyone has access to the Land in its entirety is the moment before it is destroyed. The Land is also a very fragile space. When Morpheus lets the sand blow off his hand, it ceases to exist as the Land, though the characters are unharmed and still standing on solid ground (see Figure 11.3).

In this moment, Barbie describes, "a dead sky went on forever above us and below." The Land as a dreaming space no longer exists, and all that remains is

Figure 11.3. *A Game of You*, part 5

dead land. The humans also have no way back to the waking world. The characters are stuck in a space of essentially nothingness, which instigates Gothic terror. The dreaming and the waking worlds and their frequent overlapping make for Gothic sublime places that are indicative of a liminal fantasy.

Realms of the Endless and Hell

As with dreams, each realm of the Endless evokes the Gothic sublime and houses a liminal being who freely visits the waking world. Dream's realm (see Figure 11.4) is vast and appears to exist on the edge of nothingness.

In Sam Kieth and Mike Dringenberg's illustrations, Morpheus's journey to the gate of his realm starts from afar, and then the perspective zooms in closer. In the upper left corner, Morpheus's body is a mere shadow. The rounded panels create a distancing effect and make Morpheus's journey seem to cover immeasurable space. Morpheus narrates, "BEYOND, outside my dreamworld there is infinite dust, infinite dark. And the DREAMWORLD is infinite, although it is bounded on every side" (*Preludes and Nocturnes*, Part 2). This comment seems paradoxical since something that is infinite cannot be bound. Yet, if he perceives it as contained, then the threshold of his realm, where others dream, can be viewed as liminal. Morpheus's realm is a Gothic space that is his alone and is limited in its function as specifically for dreams. However, it contains endless possibilities in how it can affect waking world humans when they enter their individual dream worlds. The power of Dream's realm is pervasive and ubiquitous.

Figure 11.4. *Preludes and Nocturnes*, part 2.

Each realm of the Endless is disorienting, mysterious, and indefinable—thus, notably Gothic. Destiny's, in particular, is described and illustrated as a physical space that also exists as a metaphor for the paths that people take in their lives in the waking world. *Season of Mists* describes:

> Walk any path in Destiny's garden, and you will be forced to choose, not once but many times. The paths fork and divide. With each step you take, through Destiny's garden, you make a choice; and every choice determines future paths. However, at the end of a lifetime of walking you might look back, and see only one path stretching out behind you; or look ahead, and see only darkness. (Prologue)

The description suggests that people in the waking world metaphorically walk through Destiny's garden, but the illustrations of the labyrinth also turn the garden into a realized, physical place. The garden is the physicalized embodiment of choice. Yet, the space is simultaneously tangible and inaccessible: "Destiny of the Endless is the only one who understands the garden's peculiar geography, distinct from time and space, where the potential becomes the actual" (Prologue). Individuals may comprehend a space for choices, but they cannot fully know it, especially because of its infinite potential. Only a deity can understand the spatialized version of a fantastic space, which further blurs distinctions between fantasy and reality, making Destiny's garden a sublime liminal space.

This is further complicated by the accessibility to Destiny's garden. As *Brief Lives* describes: "All labyrinths are one labyrinth. All mazes meet in the center. There is a portion of space that all labyrinths share, a space common to every place in which paths fork and join and diverge once more" (Part 7). Because of this, Dream and Delirium access Destiny's realm through a carnival labyrinth All labyrinths aim to be unassailable as a first principle. Paradoxically, any individual labyrinth would not actually be unique, yet individual labyrinths do exist. This also complicates navigability. If all are one, then there would only be one path; yet, the path is actually indiscernible. Destiny's garden is also described as "not earth" and "not now" but "a place to itself" that "exists in its own time" (Part 7). However, later, the narration states, "In Destiny's garden it is always now," while Destiny reads from his book (Part 7). There is an inconsistency in describing temporality in Destiny's garden. It seems the garden is always changing and timeless. Since it cannot be logically comprehended, it is sublime, and since it still makes sense as a drawn metaphor, it illustrates an aspect of the liminal fantasy.

Figure 11.5. *Brief Lives*, part 1.

The various realms of the Endless are perfect specimens of how the Gothic sublime can be physically present in conceptual space. Desire's realm is called "The Threshold," which is described as a statue of Desire that is inhabited by Desire (*The Doll's House*, Part 1). Another paradoxical place, Desire resides within itself, which makes it more difficult to comprehend Desire's realm. Despair's realm is described as "formless and silent and still. Apathy hangs like damp mist in the chill air. No winds blow, no bird sings, nothing moves" (*Brief Lives*, Part 1). Her realm may be "formless," but it is drawn as a physical place where she resides.

Jill Thompson's illustration (see Figure 11.5) shows a place without solid ground. Instead, the ground is made of a colorless cloud-like substance. Delirium, though, is drawn crouching in it. She is not floating but steady upon the groundless ground. The realm does not seem to follow consistent laws if gravity, as she is stable, while the windows float arbitrarily.

Figure 11.6. *Brief Lives*, part 6.

Further, "in her world there are so many windows. Each opening shows her an existence that's fallen to her—some only for moments, others for lifetimes" (*Brief Lives* Part 1). Despair's realm is a place for looking into the waking world through countless windows—though it would seem only to those who have experienced despair. The windows are apparently transient depending upon how long the individual feels despair. Thus, nothing in Despair's realm is concrete.

In contrast to Despair's colorless realm, Delirium's realm swirls with colors (see Figure 11.6). Delirium's realm, drawn by Jill Thompson, is disorienting. Thompson drew Morpheus upside down for his visit. This suggests that there is no static order to the space, no up or down. The space is visible to the reader but incomprehensible.

Although the Endless occupy space that, to humans, may only be thought of as a concept, the illustrators make their essence into physical, visible places. But these realms, while drawn and colored for the comics, are still unknowable.

We can view them as places, but we must also accept that they are elusive. They are boundless spaces that are constantly changing. The medium itself also allows for the spaces to be simultaneously physicalized and unfathomable to the readers. The use of different artists throughout the series demonstrates that there is no single concrete version or vision of any place. The realms are open to artistic interpretation by artists and readers alike. With infinite possibilities, these realms are sublime, and with the acceptance of them as physical spaces, they illustrate the variety of a liminal fantasy.

Hell is yet another Gothic location in *The Sandman* series that is indicative of a liminal fantasy. In *Preludes and Nocturnes*, Morpheus calls the gate of Hell "the Naked Space" (Part 4). Nakedness suggests that everything is visible and that nothing is hidden. However, Hell is not a space that can truly be known in *The Sandman*. It is conceptualized and physicalized by artists for the content of the series, but even so, it is mysterious and unexplainable. In *Season of Mists*, Hell is a liminal space that evokes the Gothic sublime, described as "a place that wasn't a place" (*Season of Mists*, Part 1). Morpheus clarifies this idea, saying, "This is not a place, after all. It is BETWEEN places. This is nowhere" (Part 2). The between space is liminal and indefinable. However, it is never made clear what is on the other side if the liminal space. No one is able to access beyond it and, instead, is contained to Hell.

The physical size of Hell cannot be determined, which also makes it sublime. When Dream asks how big Hell is, Lucifer responds, "It's vast. Even I couldn't say for certain exactly how vast. It's almost a meaningless question" (Part 2). In the series, Hell is a place that is visible and thus, concrete. But without any conception of boundaries, it may be perceived as infinite space. If Hell cannot be bound, then we cannot determine where it begins or ends. Such a notion contributes to its liminal state. Death calls Hell, "the most desirable plot of psychic real estate in the whole order of created things" (Part 3). As "psychic real estate," Hell is simultaneously imagined and real. In Kelley Jones's drawn image, the Main Gate entrance to Hell illustrates the Gothic sublime displayed as an intricate, convoluted structure in a wide-open space (see Figure 11.7).

The top of the main gate contains a skeletal smile, and the rest of the structure looks like a monstrous body rather than a building. There is no uniformity or architectural soundness. To enter Hell appears to be like entering the body of a Gothic beast. Morpheus also mentions that here, "the doors to Hell are legion" but guarded. This simultaneously encourages and resists entrance and exit. It is not clear whether Morpheus is suggesting that the doors and guards are for those trying to gain access or those seeking to escape. Since Hell is physicalized

Figure 11.7. *Season of Mists*, part 2.

in the illustration but also described as infinite, it is a liminal space that can be seen and visited but not truly known.

Further, Charles Rowland, a boy who is killed in the volume, says, "I think Hell's something you carry around with you. Not somewhere you go" (Part 4). If Hell can be carried, then it, again, is not a fixed space. Instead, an infinite number of unique versions of Hell are possible, as each individual person can have a different notion of it. This makes Hell similar to the dream world where there is one infinite Dreaming that houses each person's unique dreams. The association of a place as a transportable mental construct also appears in *A Game of You* when Barbie says, "I don't think home's a place anymore. I think it's a state of mind" (Part 6). This is the (in a nod to *The Wizard of Oz*) lesson that she learns from her experience. Home, which is a physically real space, becomes a concept, a perception.

Gaiman complicates the idea of a Hell by contrast to a Heaven. He imagines a place that claims not to be a place, but the Heaven/Hell dichotomy is still an ethereal idea. The angel Remiel delivers a message to Dream from the Creator: "There must be a Hell. There must be a place for the demons; a place for the damned. Hell is Heaven's shadow. They define each other. Reward and punishment; hope and despair. There must be a Hell, for without Hell, Heaven has no meaning" (Part 6). The Creator establishes polarized, Gothic dichotomies of Heaven and Hell. However, the message indicates that they are not mutually exclusive. Heaven only exists in contrast to Hell and vice versa. If one cannot exist without the other, then each place cannot be defined on its own. Any conception of Heaven or Hell depends on a simultaneous understanding of the other. This makes both indefinable independent of one another. The relationship between Heaven and Hell is further complicated by dreams. Morpheus says to Lucifer, "what power would HELL have if those here imprisoned were NOT able to DREAM of HEAVEN?" (*Preludes and Nocturnes*, Part 4). Hell needs dreaming to maintain a contrast between Heaven and Hell within the minds of the inhabitants.

Ultimately, dreams establish the idea of a dichotomy and allow each space to be defined in contrast to the other. This gives power and agency to dreams but also makes them liminal as they are a point of access to Heaven.

◆ ◆ ◆

The Sandman breathlessly takes its readers through liminal time and space, overlapping reality and fantasy, and disrupting opportunities for readers to truly comprehend time and space. The brilliance of this liminal fantasy lies in its ability to seamlessly interweave reality and fantasy amidst infinite space. Space and time are not concrete but limitless and sublime. The presence of such pervasiveness evokes the transgressive power of the Gothic romance in the series, specifically the ability of the Gothic mode to broach limits and break boundaries. In highlighting darkness and uncertainty, the series embraces the Gothic and effectively makes space and narrative questionable, mysterious, and uncertain.

The visual depictions of realms, dream worlds, and Hell physicalize intangible space while the waking world is intrinsically entwined to these fantastic spaces. Ultimately, we learn more about reality from fantasy, specifically that we must accept that fantasy fuels the waking world.

NOTES

1. Dream, Death, Desire, Despair, Delirium, Destiny, and Destruction.

2. For example, Dream and Delirium set forth on an expedition to search for Destruction in *Brief Lives*.

3. In Part 8 of *Preludes and Nocturnes*, Morpheus and Death sit and chat in public while feeding birds. As they later travel through the streets of Paris, Morpheus says, "In the world of the walking, of the living, we move silent as a breath of cool wind," with humans only shivering as they pass by.

4. Mendlesohn notes that John Bunyan's *Pilgrim's Progress* creates dream sequences that serve to prophesize and engage spiritual awakening (18–19).

WORKS CITED

Burke, Edmund. *A Philosophical Enquiry into the Origin of Our Ideas of the Sublime and Beautiful.* 2nd ed. R. and J. Dodsley, 1759, Google eBook.

Cameron, Ed. "Ironic Escapism in the Symbolic Spread of Gothic Materialist Meaning." *Gothic Studies* vol. 10, no. 2, November 2008, pp. 18–34.

Campbell, Donna M. "Novel, Romance, and Gothic: Brief Definitions." *Literary Movements.* Dept. of English, Washington State University, 3 July 2014. Accessed 12 December 2017.

Gaiman, Neil. *The Sandman, Volume One: Preludes and Nocturnes,* illus. Sam Kieth, Mike Dringenberg, and Malcolm Jones III. DC Comics, 1995.

Gaiman, Neil. *The Sandman, Volume Two: The Doll's House,* illustrated by Mike Dringenberg, Malcolm Jones III, Chris Bachalo, Michael Zulli, and Steve Parkhouse. DC Comics, 1995.

Gaiman, Neil.. *The Sandman, Volume Four: Season of Mists,* illustrated by Kelley Jones, Mike Dringenberg, Malcolm Jones III, Matt Wagner, Dick Giordano, George Pratt, and P. Craig Russell. DC Comics, 1992.

Gaiman, Neil. *The Sandman, Volume Five: A Game of You,* illustrated by Shawn McManus, Colleen Doran, Bryan Talbot, George Pratt, Stan Woch, and Dick Giordano. DC Comics, 1993.

Gaiman, Neil.. *The Sandman, Volume Six: Fables and Reflections,* illustrated by Bryan Talbot, Stan Woch, P. Craig Russell, Shawn McManus, John Watkiss, Jill Thompson, Duncan Eagleson, and Kent Williams. DC Comics, 1994.

Gaiman, Neil. . *The Sandman, Volume Seven: Brief Lives,* illustrated by Jill Thompson and Vince Locke. DC Comics, 1994.

Klapcsik, Sandor. "The Double-Edged Nature of Neil Gaiman's Ironical Perspectives and Liminal Fantasies." *Journal of the Fantastic in the Arts* vol. 20, no. 2, 2009, pp. 193– 209.

Mendlesohn, Farah. *Rhetorics of Fantasy.* Wesleyan University Press, 2008.

Mishra, Vijay. *The Gothic Sublime.* State University of New York Press, 1994.

Morris, David B. "Gothic Sublimity." *New Literary History* vol. 16, no. 2, Winter 1985, pp. 299–319.

Round, Julia. *Gothic in Comics and Graphic Novels.* McFarland, 2014.

Turner, Victor. "Are There Universals of Performance in Myth, Ritual, and Drama?" *By Means of Performance: Intercultural Studies of Theatre and Ritual.* Richard Schechner and Willa Appel, eds. Cambridge University Press, 1990, pp. 8–18.

Turner, Victor. *The Ritual Process: Structure and Anti-Structure.* AldineTransaction, 2008.

QUEERING SPACE IN NEIL GAIMAN'S ILLUSTRATED WORKS

RENATA LUCENA DALMASO AND THAYSE MADELLA

In consideration of picture books, comics, graphic novels, and the like, one finds that text and illustration construct meanings together; different collaborations potentially can bring forth different possible readings, and, therefore, different forms of resistance and subversions to those readings. As such, our main question in this chapter on Neil Gaiman's illustrated works regards how heterotopias—which, in seminal French philosopher Michel Foucault's construction, are places that function as counter-spaces, those intersections between the axes of real/imagined and normal/other—function within Gaiman's work with different illustrators. That is to say, we wonder if and in which ways the writer and illustrator queer these counter-spaces and construct possible sites of resistance in their representation. By "queer," we refer to an interpretive mode which questions underlying assumptions pertaining to a topic—here, on ideas of spaces, counter-spaces, and how they interrelate—in order to better understand how these terms operate on a larger spectrum of difference.

Heterotopic spaces can be found throughout Gaiman's work. One can find examples of this motif in his picture books, such as the walls in *Wolves in the Walls* (2003); in his novels, such as the cemetery in *The Graveyard Book* (2008), the stone wall in *Stardust* (1998), the double house in *Coraline* (2002); and his comics works, such as the Roanoke colony in *Marvel 1602* (2003) and *The Sandman* series (1989–96), to name just a few. The author's collaborations throughout his career provide more than enough material for analysis. Yet, as one Gaiman critic, Tara Prescott, aptly states "[t]o be a scholar or fan of Neil Gaiman is to become okay with the fact that you cannot cover it all" (1). Thus, while acknowledging the large scope of works dealing with this issue of liminality of spaces, we opted to focus on *The Graveyard Book* and *The Sandman* as narratives that not only bring forth issues of heterotopia but situate it at the center of their stories. More specifically, we focus on the illustrated edition of the former, by Dave McKean, and its comic book adaptation, by P. Craig Russell, as well a selection of *The Sandman* series that encompasses editions of "A Doll's House" (issues 9 to 16), "A Dream of a Thousand Cats" (issue 18), and "A Game of You" (issues 32 to 37).

This chapter aims to investigate the queering of space in Neil Gaiman's oeuvre, more specifically in the body of his illustrated works, and the recurrent centrality of the liminal nature of places in these works. Liminal spaces are symbolic of two or more conflicting categories at the same time, and they may offer possibilities for subversion of imposed binarisms—such as here/there, in/out, life/death, and reality/dream. Most importantly, in Gaiman's work these spaces are most often contiguous, sharing a permeable border. These "contact zones," to borrow Mary Louise Pratt's notion of "spaces where cultures meet, clash, and grapple with each other" (34), offer opportunities to examine asymmetrical relationships and structures of power. In order to explore such liminal spaces in Gaiman's works and how those spaces may, or may not, queer binary categories, we shall borrow from Michel Foucault's concept of heterotopia. As the analyses throughout this chapter will try to demonstrate, heterotopic spaces in Gaiman's works are represented as sites rife with the potential for queering binarisms.

Spatiality and "Other Spaces": Foucault's Heterotopias

It is important to clarify how these liminal spaces can be defined and, in turn, how they can be queered. In the lecture "Of Other Spaces" (1967), Foucault argues that we are living in an "epoch of space" (13). Departing from the idea of a fixed conception of space, as an immutable axis or element within history, he claims that "[w]e are in an epoch in which space is given to us in the form of relations between emplacements" (15).[1] These types of spaces question, to a certain extent, a number of structuralist notions that have been sacralized as binaries. Foucault focuses most of his lecture on one particular type of space, the heterotopia, which functions as a counter-emplacement, as spaces that are "outside all places, even though they are actually localizable" (17). Unlike utopias, which are classified as unreal or imagined places by the philosopher, heterotopias do exist in a more concrete and everyday sense. They are, however, imbued with meaning in ways that other, more regular, places are not. Etymologically, heterotopia literally means "other" (hetero) "places" (topos), and, in Foucault's conception of the term, it is seen as the other of normal places. Foucault characterizes heterotopias as pervasive to all societies in all historical times.

So-called "primitive societies," for example, were prone to institute hetero-topias of crisis that would accommodate those individuals in a state of crisis, such as "adolescents, menstruating women, pregnant women, the elderly, etc." (18). These spaces of crisis have been replaced, in contemporary societies, by what the philosopher calls heterotopias of deviation, which, in turn, accom-modate and assign those individuals deemed non-normative: examples include rest homes, psychiatric hospitals, and, of course, prisons (18). Foucault goes on to mention a number of other types of heterotopias, such as heterotopias of time (cemeteries, museums, libraries, fairgrounds, festivals), heterotopias of illusion (brothels), and heterotopias of compensation (colonies), each of which embodies a specific social function and an intrinsic system of access/exit. One of the key characteristics of the concept is heterotopia's power to "juxtapose in a single real place several spaces, several emplacements that are in themselves incompatible," which underlines the complex and sometimes contradictory ways that these spaces relate to how individuals themselves are marked by their use and proximity (19).

The creation of spaces of exception and abnormality presupposes the exis-tence of spaces of normality and acceptance. Heteropias are, then, a response to the limits of those spaces and categories; they effectively queer the normative boundaries in which they seem to be inscribed. "Queer," used here as a rather elastic term related to non-normativity in a myriad of ways, seems to be a fit-ting way to describe the process in which liminal and contradictory spaces are constructed and how they subvert supposedly stable binary categories such as in/out, life/death, dream/awake, to name just a few. As Janet R. Jakobsen points out, "queer" as an episteme is emblematic not only in the ways that can be (as a noun or an adjective—when something or someone is queer, for example), but also in the ways it can do (as a verb—when something is queered, or when someone queers something, for instance) (516–17). In that sense, "queer" as a verb can be seen through its relation with norms and normativity, as a pro-cess of challenging normalization. The relation between norms, normativity, and normalization is, therefore, necessary in order to construct the spaces of exception and acceptance, normality, and abnormality implied in the concept of heterotopias. The possibility of resistance to these networks of norms and their normalization lies precisely in the process of queering them—a complex and critical process of acknowledging and countering the foundations for the construction of such spaces in the first place.[2]

Heterotopias are ambiguous in that they are not necessarily sites of resistance nor of obeisance. Not all heterotopias are, therefore, queering the norms and binary categories that they contradictorily juxtapose. A cemetery, for example, deals with society's complicated relations with the concepts of life and death, material and immaterial realities, experienced and imagined temporalities, but not necessarily in a manner that effectively queers those norms about tempo-rality and expectations about death. The heterotopia of the cemetery could be used, in fact, to reinforce these norms, bolstering what Jack Halberstam refers to as a "middle-class logic of reproductive temporality," which regulates a heteronormative experience conducted according to "paradigmatic markers of life experience—namely, birth, marriage, reproduction, and death" (4, 2). The queering of those spaces should not, therefore, be taken for granted.

Nobody's Home in *The Graveyard Book*

We turn now to Neil Gaiman's ode to that cemetery heterotopia: *The Grave-yard Book* (2008). When Bod first arrives at the cemetery, the inhabitants of the place need to give him "the Freedom of the Graveyard," as explained in the first chapter, "How Nobody Came to the Graveyard" (2). It means that Bod was allowed access to all the places of the graveyard and that he could access these places just as the dead could—by crossing the walls, gates, and fences—as long as he remains within the graveyard limits. Bod breaks this binary separation of life and death, as a living being finding solace within the dead. He is, for example, raised by a dead couple who could not have children in life, Mrs. and Mr. Owens, giving him their name and forming a famil-ial bond. Joseph Michael Sommers remarks about this peculiar phenomenon calling it, "a complex metaphor for the insider/outsider identity of Bod [. . .] ostensibly caught between the living and the dead" (18). While being alive is what characterizes Bod to this world, he can only survive by living as and with the dead, which, in turn, remain hidden from the rest of the breathing human beings (Sommers 18). The protagonist is the only living human who can see, talk, and have relationships with the dead, a uniqueness that puts him in between worlds. However, like the dead ones, Bod's freedom to transit into spaces is also limited by the walls and gates of the graveyard; thus, he lives by the rules of the graveyard, the same rules followed by dead people, despite not being, strictly speaking, one of them. Ironically, at the same time that Bod has the Freedom of the Graveyard, the fact that he lives with the dead, bound by the space of the cemetery, gives to gates and walls a symbolic meaning of the limitations of one's freedom (Sommers 18).

As Bod grows older, he feels the need to get to know the world outside the limits of the cemetery. In the original novel, illustrated by Dave McKean, the presence and the importance of these limitations is reinforced by the illustrations, which often depict the walls and gates that circumscribe the spaces under discussion. For instance, the image that illustrates the events in the chapter "Every Man Jack"—in which the old, and only human, friend of Bod comes back to the city—shows a bus passing by outside the graveyard (214).

The bus is portrayed at a distance, only recognizable by its contours, with thin jagged lines forming windows. Contrasting with the faded grey scale and lines of the bus, the foreground is permeated with elements drawn in sharp thick lines and dark tones—a couple of tree trunks at the edge of the frame on the left and the graveyard fence, directly in front of the bus, at the center of the page, effectively dividing the two realms. The perspective of the image is that of someone from the inside of the graveyard looking out; most likely, it reflects Bod's viewpoint.

That illustration suggests that, from that perspective, one can only see the grid walls that circumscribe the limits of the graveyard and, on the other side of the fence, the (barely distinct) bus and not much else. In this sense, the image reinforces the fact that the features of everyday life of the living, such as a bus, are kept out of these gates that protect and define the spaces here and there. For Bod, "here" is the place of the cemetery, and "there" is where all the other living people live. Thus, the feeling of "normality" for those within those fences is constructed from that apparent division between inside/outside, here/there.

However, the division between "here" and "there" receives new layers when what is considered "here" gains new "theres." In the community of the graveyard, its ground is the "normal," the rule, in contrast to the spaces beyond the cemetery. Nevertheless, the space dedicated to people whose hearts are still beating is not the only "other" in relation to the cemetery. As the cemetery is a heterotopic space from the perspective of the living human beings, from the viewpoint of the dead, new heterotopic spaces are created. Within the graveyard, spaces such as the unconsecrated grounds, the ghouls' grave, and the sleer chamber (seen in chapters "The Witch's Headstone" and "The New Friend") are among the examples of abnormalities in comparison to the rules that guide the routines of the "normal" dead (99, 35).

By contrast, in the graphic novel, adapted and overseen by P. Craig Russell (2014), and in which each chapter was illustrated by a different artist, the difference between the normality of the graveyard and these other spaces is, often, represented graphically. For instance, regardless of which illustrator depicts the sleer chamber,[3] it is consistently portrayed in dark tones, without details of the setting, and the speeches of the sleer are never represented in balloons, like those of the other characters, but always wrapped in some kind of mist with the speech written in a wavy font. In "The New Friend," illustrated by Russell himself, the page in which Bod and Scarlett—arguably, his first actual living friend—escape the chamber after going there for the first time is representative of the contrast between the normality of the graveyard and the chamber as an "other" space (57; vol. 1). In the top frames, they are still in the chamber and the frames are dark; two of the frames are completely black with only the silhouettes of the stairs, the entrance, and the two kids.

Contrasting these, the three bottom frames are brighter and full of details from nature, including birds, flowers, and trees. The narration in one of the frames states that "birds sang in the bushes. A bumble-bee droned past, everything was surprising in its normality" (57; vol. 1), reinforcing which side of these two opposing spaces should be read as normal.

Endless Sands in *The Sandman*

Heterotopias seem to abound in Gaiman's works, and one of the most emblematic uses of them can be found in the *The Sandman* (1989–96). In the series, the counter-emplacement is one of the memorable features of the narrative, i.e., the dream world. *The Sandman* narrates the story of Dream, one of the seven Endless, and his realm, the Dreaming, which is a space of many contradictions: it complicates assumptions regarding material/immaterial, reality/imagination, conscious/unconscious, and individual/collective experiences. At the same time that it is an actual concrete realm, it is simultaneously where people's dreams take place. In this narrative, dreams, which have often been thought of as expressions of one's unconscious or repressed desires, as fundamentally immaterial figments of one's imagination,[4] acquire a more material manifestation—they are indeed related to one's psyche, but that does not mean they are not as real as those experiences lived in the waking world.

Within the context of heterotopias, the dream world represented in *The Sandman* series seems to be the epitome of the concept, the ultimate counter-emplacement. It is real and, yet it contests assumptions about how genuine that reality in fact is. At the same time that it is an actual emplacement, its location is vague: it is outside as well as inside. It is not just a parallel dimension to our lived reality, in a symmetrical duality, it is both part and whole of that reality.

The dream world pertains to individual dreaming and, yet, all dreams are connected. Despite being (somewhat) spatially located, the dream world moves through time, or, perhaps, time moves through dreams, as "past and future both cast their ripples into the dreaming," breaking with a linear chronology that stabilizes itself through the axis here/present, denaturalizing, therefore, the bond between time and space (32.12). The heterotopia of the dream world, thus, brings several supposedly incompatible spaces into a single one: a real, albeit oneiric, counter-emplacement within the narrative.

The connection between the discursive and spatial features of Foucault's heterotopia appears particularly suitable when one thinks of the dream world, for in that realm language has the power to shape reality in more literal ways than in our own world. In "The Doll's House" mini-series, for example, the character Rose Walker is about to be killed by Dream, when she is saved by her grandmother Unity Kinkaid (16.14). Unity takes her granddaughter's place by urging Rose to reach inside herself and give her heart to her grandmother. Rose is understandably confused, to which Unity responds: "Rose—I'm dying. We don't have much time. You're dreaming. Anything is possible. Just do it." The subsequent three panels portray Rose, reaching with her right arm into her bare chest and pulling out a heart-shaped gemstone. In the dream world, the heart can be both literal and figurative.

Dream's gemstone is retrieved from inside Rose's body, from where her actual heart would be, but its heart-shaped form is ideographic rather than biological. The space where the action takes place interferes, therefore, with the properties of language and its performative power: in the dream world, not only can one will things into existence, but one can also play with the semantic and material values of those very things.

One of the best examples of this heterotopic characteristic of the dream world is seen in the edition of "A Dream of a Thousand Cats" (18). In that stand-alone story, the reader follows the narrative through the perspective of a house cat, who breaks away from her home to attend a secret meeting in the woods. The leader of this meeting tells of escaping from the domesticity of pet life. The human characters are portrayed as menacing shadows or shown only through their body parts or voices, thereby reinforcing the centrality of cats to the narrative. The leader tells of a revealing dream in which she encounters the king of dreams in feline form, and in his eyes, she sees the truth of a different version of time, in both the past and the future. The vision reveals a universe in which cats were lords of the Earth, much bigger than they are in our actual reality, whereas humans were as tiny as today's cats. This reversal of roles is exemplified by the expression of a "game of cat and man" (18.16).

The alternative reality where cats are lords over men, the feline narrator explains, was lost due to one man's initiative to inspire other humans to dream a universe where they were the superior species. This prophet urges his listeners to "Dream! Dreams shape the world. Dreams create the world anew, every night. Do not dream the world it is now, in thrall to our feline masters and mistresses. Dream a new world. Dream a world of human beings" (18.17). The dream lord then clarifies to the dreaming house cat that humans did not just change the future with their collective dreaming, but they changed reality throughout time: "They dreamed the world so it ALWAYS WAS the way it is now, little one. There never WAS a world of high cat-ladies and cat-lords. They changed the universe from the beginning of all things, until the end of time" (18.19). The dream world is a place that can, therefore, interfere with the linear fabric of time—a heterotopia where both time and space can be queered.

Time, then, is as material as the space in which it is experienced. If dreams can shape the world, they can also shape its history. The heterotopia of the dream world comports many paradoxes and perhaps one of the greatest is the misalignment of the axes here/there, nowhere/somewhere, and then/now/next. The obvious lesson to the cat is that "dreams shape the world" in the sense that cats should strive to dream it differently as well, to dream it back to the universe of cat-ladies and cat-lords, but the underlying notion is also that the dreaming is a place where one can alter meaning. Words and language in general can be resignified, appropriated, modified, repurposed, and so on, as the very title of this chapter illustrates, with the word "queer," used as a verb in a context radically different than one would have imagined some fifty years ago. What the story of "A Dream of a Thousand Cats" suggests is that, in the dream world, one can do that to history itself, to the fabric of the universe. The imagined "there" becomes "here," in spatial terms as well as in temporal terms, acquiring then the attributes of then/now/next as though they were always already a part of that somewhere that ceases to be a nowhere. Mind-boggling as it may be, it is the perfect synthesis of the performative power of this heterotopia, both in relation to language and in relation to space.

Toward a Queer Reading of Gaiman's Heterotopias

In general, the heterotopias of both *The Graveyard Book* and *The Sandman* seem to queer the series of rules and norms that compose and naturalize the realm of "normality" within their narratives. In *The Graveyard Book*, the heterotopia of the cemetery has, within, its own series of heterotopias, such as the unconsecrated grounds, the ghouls' grave, and the sleer chamber, with their own set of rules, functions, and contradictions. Dealing mostly with expectations and assumptions surrounding life and death, the graveyard in the narrative blurs those statuses, usually conceived as indisputable. Beyond that, it complicates these categories by showcasing a series of complex beings that embody the diversity within that space, suggesting that even the dead have their nuances.

Death, far from being the ultimate emblem of finitude, gains the contours of just another life event, as it were, and in that sense, one can see the limitations of reading the graveyard in the narrative as strictly subversive. While it does problematize binary assumptions, it also reinforces the expectations about a normative type of temporality that regulates life, death, and even life after death. And though Halberstam identifies this logic as belonging primarily to the middle class, in *The Graveyard Book*, reproductive temporality transcends class by transcending lived temporality. Even though Bod's character challenges the expectations and the fixity of that normative temporality, being at the same time both alive and dead, other characters reinforce the very rules that govern the legibility of that temporality. The couple that adopts Bod, for example, Mrs. and Mr. Owens, do so, among other factors of course, out of a sense of frustration for never having had kids during their lifetime: "'We never had a child,' said his wife. 'And his mother wants us to protect him. Will you say yes?'" (16). In this sense, never being parents is the argument used by Mrs. Owens to talk Mr. Owens into adopting the living baby, as though they would in the afterlife be able to fulfill that need. The narrative engages, thus, in the paradigm of motherhood as the "natural" step, or life event, in a woman's life, the "apex of feminine achievement," as Lindal Buchanan puts in *Rhethorics of Motherhood* (16). Mrs. Owens stands in as the emblem of the *"cult of true womanhood*, [intrinsically associated with assumptions] about women's purity, piety, domesticity" (18, original emphasis). The rhetorical collusion of motherhood and womanhood "dictated that all women should crave motherhood and become mothers" and those who did not would be seen as "deviant" (18, original emphasis). The afterlife, in this context, works as a second chance for Mrs. Owens to participate in this marker of normative temporality, reinforcing those assumptions rather than queering them.

Visually, the representation of the heterotopia of the cemetery on the one hand reinforces the divide between the space outside and the one inside, with its emphasis on the fences and walls, which delimit the boundaries of the graveyard. On the other hand, the illustrations privilege the space within, effectively placing the graveyard, and those within it, at the center, while the outside world remains at the margins. That change in perspective flips the expectations about normality and abnormality within that context, positing the heterotopia of the cemetery as the nexus of order and safety, and the space beyond the fences as dangerous and unruly. In P. Craig Russell's graphic adaptation of the novel, for example, in the first chapter, illustrated by Kevin Nowlan, the frame in which Mrs. Owens first holds baby Bod portrays precisely that reversal: the dead couple is within the boundaries of the graveyard, where Bod has wandered off, and the woman holds him in an affectionate manner (9; vol. 1). It is the first sequence of frames in which the figures of the dead are shown to the reader, and yet the contrast between their immediate embrace of the boy and the menacing human figure pursuing him (shown from behind the gates at a distance) is clear. From the beginning of the narrative, therefore, it becomes apparent that preconceived notions surrounding life/death, safety/danger, and normal/abnormal should be revisited by the reader in relation to the graveyard.

The Sandman brings forth a different process of challenging binarisms and queering expectations. In the context of this narrative, the waking life is to normality as the dream is to abnormality—an understanding shared by Sigmund Freud, who argues that dreams "lack in intelligibility and orderliness" (74). Rather than flipping the categories assigned to the heterotopia—such as takes place in *The Graveyard Book*—the narratives of *The Sandman* series actually play up that distinction and embrace the idea of abnormality of the dream world. The dream world is never not abnormal in relation to the waking world; in other words, the uncanny quality of that realm is never lifted and remains throughout a space that evokes the strangely familiar. At the same time, however, it is that very quality that grants it its uniqueness.

Throughout the series, the number of illustrators, tasked with the job of representing visually the likeness of a space wherein assumptions are questioned, seem to share the notion that the dream world is a place that defies conventions of realism in visual art and in that defiance it should stand out in relation to the "real" waking world. They come up with diverse solutions to that challenge, from abusing psychedelic scenario, to emphasizing white or black blank spaces to playing with expectations of color (such as making the sky a bright pink color) to using starry backgrounds. Perhaps one of the most emblematic examples of such experimentation can be found in Dave McKean's cover art throughout the series, which subverts expectations about the type of art one would find in a comic book, especially on a comic book cover—something the illustrator had to fight DC to be able to do (McKean). Besides not showcasing the title character on the cover, the images play with juxtaposition, collage, and digital composition in a rather abstract way that vaguely connects the content to the issue at hand, epitomizing the uniqueness of the abnormal realm within the narrative to be found inside. In "A Dream of a Thousand Cats" edition, for example, the cover portrays the painting of a silhouette of a cat jumping from a rooftop into an open space, in a frame within a frame within a frame, all of which are broken at the edge, as if the blue sky in the picture is spilling from its confines. As a painting that refuses to remain within its limits, set by the material frame, the sky and the cat of the cover are breaking free, breaking the frontier and the rules that ask them to remain representational—a challenge much like the cats in the narrative are urged to do through their dreams. In this sense, the abnormal is not necessarily a place of abjection, but rather the space where one has latitude to experiment, visually speaking.

Besides the recurrent visual experimentation with the abnormal, the queer potential of the dream realm is also explored in more specific ways within the narrative, such as in the portrayal of the character Wanda in the series of "A Game of You." In the waking world, the male-to-female pre-operation transsexual frequently deals with being called out as a non-normative sort of woman, even by her friends and neighbors; Hazel even points to the bulge showing through Wanda's panties as a "thingie" (34.7). Wanda's status as a woman is again defied by the enforced gender binary of the forces that bridge the waking and the dream world, not permitting her to go along the journey for "being a man" (34.17–22). Gender, in this context, is binary in nature, stable, and biologically defined at birth—regardless of the characters' own performative agencies. In the dream world, however, Wanda can be seen differently, as the woman she envisions herself to be. The dream that pictures her as such deals precisely with how problematic issues of representation can be for individuals like Wanda. It starts out with her vision of herself, in a dress, with a slender feminine form, long hair, and then, as a nightmare starts taking over, she is portrayed progressively in a more masculine manner throughout the sequence of frames—first as a man with short hair in a dress, then as a scared naked muscular man, forced into surgery against his will to remove his genitalia (33.12–13). The stuff of nightmares is, thus, the reversal to a biologically defined gender binary. Towards the conclusion of the mini-series, Barbie meets the now deceased Wanda in the dream world, claiming that "she is perfect [. . .] drop-dead gorgeous. There's nothing camp about her, nothing artificial, and she looks happy" (37.17). Disregarding the problematic notion that being camp or even artificial would make someone any less of a woman, the narrative seems to suggest that in the dream world one could break free from physical and biological confines in relation to perceptions of gender.

✦ ✦ ✦

In the end, the heterotopias analyzed offer a number of possibilities in terms of queering norms and challenging categories. However, the ambiguity of those spaces also points to the limits of seeing them as inherently subversive places of resistance. While the cemetery in *The Graveyard Book* shuffles binary notions around, it still reinforces heteronormative perceptions about temporality, as discussed previously. Moreover, the construction of other marginal spaces within the confines of the graveyard works to reinforce a very traditional hierarchy of normal/abnormal rather than subverting it. In *The Sandman*, the abnormal is embraced in the conception of the dream world, along with its experimental visual representation. Binary categories are also played with, in a space where one can will things into existence. Nevertheless, the extent to which individuals can will things appears bound by normative notions tied not to the dream world, but to their lives in the waking world. Thus, even if a character bends the gender norms in the dream world, those norms are still present, regardless of the possibility of waiving them altogether. Accordingly, heterotopias in Gaiman's works are as paradoxical as heterotopias can be. They queer some expectations while reinforcing others, in a complex and seemingly ambiguous process of signification that only attests to their status as the "other" spaces, that is, as spaces that break with syntax and juxtapose incompatible concepts.

NOTES

1. The translators of Foucault's lecture, Michiel Dehaene and Lieven De Cauter, note that "emplacement" in French refers to a more general site or location, whereas in English the term takes on a more specific sense. They argue, though, that in Foucault's lecture, the term should be understood in its more technical sense, as "a space or rather place in the era of the network as opposed to extension" (24).

2. We have chosen to work mainly with Foucault's concept of "heterotopia," but other authors propose similar terms that would be of use to this discussion were it not for the (unfortunate) lack of space to discuss them all adequately. If the reader is so inclined to expand the search, we suggest Edward Soja's *Thirdspace: Journeys to Los Angeles and Other Real-and-Imagined Places* (1996), Gloria Anzaldúa's *Borderlands/La Frontera: The New Mestiza* (2007), Henri Lefebvre's *The Production of Space* (1991), and Homi Bhabha's *The Location of Culture* (1994).

3. The chamber appears in the chapters illustrated by P. Craig Russell himself ("The New Friend" 55–57; vol. 1), by Gallen Showman ("The Witch's Headstone" 123–26, 155–56; vol.1), and by Scott Hampton ("Everyman Jack" 59, 82–84, 119–28; vol. 2)

4. Sigmund Freud states that his investigation into dreams "starts off from the assumption that they are products of our own mental activity" (77).

WORKS CITED

Buchanan, Lindal. *Rhetorics of Motherhood*. Southern Illinois University Press, 2013.

Foucault, Michel. "Of Other Spaces (1967)." *Heterotopia and the City: Public Space in a Postcivil Society*. Michiel Dehaene and Lieven De Cauter, eds. and trans. Routledge, 2008, pp. 13–30.

Freud, Sigmund. *The Interpretation of Dreams*. James Strachey, ed and trans. Basic Books, 2010.

Gaiman, Neil (w), and Dave McKean (a). *The Graveyard Book*. Harper Collins, 2008.

Gaiman, Neil (w), and Kevin Nowlan, P. Craig Russel, Scott Hampton, Galen Showman, Jill Thompon, Stephen B. Scott (a). *The Graveyard Book: The Graphic Novel Adaptation*. Vol. 1. Craig Russell, ed. Harper Collins, 2014.

Gaiman, Neil (w), and Mike Dringenbeg, Malcom Jones III (a). *The Sandman: The Doll's House—Part Seven*. Vol. 16. DC Comics, 1990.

Gaiman, Neil (w), and Kelley Jones, Malcom Jones III (a). *The Sandman: A Dream of a Thousand Cats*. Vol. 18. DC Comics, 1990.

Gaiman, Neil (w), and Shawn McManus (a). *The Sandman: A Game of You—Part 1*. Vol. 32. DC Comics, 1991.

Gaiman, Neil (w), and Shawn McManus (a). *The Sandman: A Game of You—Part Two*. Vol. 33. DC Comics, 1991.

Gaiman, Neil (w), and Colleen Doran, George Pratt (a). *The Sandman: A Game of You—Part Three*. Vol. 34. DC Comics, 1992.

Gaiman, Neil (w), and Shawn McManus (a). *The Sandman: A Game of You—Part Six*. Vol. 37. DC Comics, 1992.

Halberstam, J. *In a Queer Time and Place: Transgender Bodies, Subcultural Lives*. New York University Press, 2005.

Jakobsen, Janet R. "Queer Is? Queer Does? Normativity and the Problema of Resistance." *GLQ: A Journal of Lesbian and Gays Studies* vol. 4, no. 4, 1998, pp. 511–36.

McKean, Dave. "Sandman: Dave McKean's Favourite Covers—in Pictures." *Guardian*, 22 October 2013. https://www.theguardian.com/books/gallery/2013/oct/22/sandman-dave-mckean-neil-gaiman-pictures.

Prescott, Tara. "Introduction." *Neil Gaiman in the 21st Century: Essays on the Novels, Children's Stories, Online Writings and Other Works*. Tara Prescott, ed. McFarland, 2015, pp. 1–9.

Sommers, Joseph Michael. "Embodied in Name Alone: Nobody Owens and the Metonymic Estrangement from the Living and the Dead in Neil Gaiman's 'The Graveyard Book.'" *Critical Insights: Neil Gaiman*. Joseph Michael Sommers, ed. Salem/Grey House Press, 2016, pp. 17–30.

WEAVING NEW DREAMS FROM OLD CLOTH
Conceptual Blending and Hybrid Identities in Neil Gaiman's Fairy-Tale Retellings

ANNA KATRINA GUTIERREZ

Neil Gaiman understands the power in traditional stories, or well-known and frequently retold tales that endure from one generation to the next. These include folk narratives such as fairy tales, folk tales, myths, and legends, biblical narratives and related religious tales, and canon literature. Although these stories often take place in mystical worlds or in a distant past, they serve important cultural functions. They transmit knowledge about the central values, precepts, and collective experiences that are definitive of a culture, as well as convey aspects of social heritage and relationships. Traditional tales feature prominently in Gaiman's body of work (for example, *The Sandman* series [1989–2015], *American Gods* [2001], *The Sleeper and the Spindle* [2014], *Hansel & Gretel* [2014]). He knows that the most compelling modern tales have patterns from the old stories woven into them. Cognitive narratologists (e.g., Turner 1991; Herman 2002; Lakoff and Johnson 2003) call these recognizable story patterns *scripts* and *schemas*. These refer to the prototypical arrangement of plot elements towards an expected narrative outcome and the fulfillment of a *metanarrative*, or the implicit and often invisible ideologies, social systems, and beliefs that order a culture's values and experiences (Stephens and McCallum 3, 5–6). For example, "true love conquers all" is a metanarrative typically expressed through a romantic script that culminates in a heteronormative marriage. The recurrence of this scripted outcome in literary tradition influences our cognition to expect gender-specific behaviors that fulfill an idea of love.

Like the most skillful of weavers, Gaiman has the ability to pull together scripts and schemas from distinct stories and re-weave them into a "third'" narrative that is new yet old, strange yet familiar, and that is ultimately unique and meaningful. Moreover, his contemporary retellings play with readers' expectations by disrupting standard patterns of script and schema, the effect of which confronts readers with the validity of the behaviors, systems, and assumptions that fulfill the metanarrative and its underpinning ideologies. Reshaping traditional story patterns to accommodate transforming social structures has implications for representations of subjectivity, whereby the inner lives of characters develop in correlation with a range of societal and environmental discourses (McCallum 3). This chapter discusses the significance of Gaiman's creative disruptions of scripts and schemas in two of his visual retellings for young adults: *The Sleeper and the Spindle* (2014), illustrated by Chris Riddell, and the graphic novel *The Sandman: The Dream Hunters* (1999), illustrated by Japanese artist Yoshitaka Amano. In *The Sleeper and the Spindle*, Gaiman and Riddell bring together two distinct types of fairy tales, Snow White and the Sleeping Beauty, to explore contemporary shifts in feminine agency. In *The Dream Hunters*, Gaiman and Amano's intercultural collaboration reflects the shift towards hybrid identities as an effect of increased global connectivity and East-West exchange at the beginning of the twenty-first century. By weaving the old, well-worn cloth of fairy-tale narrative scripts together with new schematics, Gaiman and his collaborators present sometimes radical ideologies clothed in the comfortable garb of rehearsed, longstanding traditions. As much as this action masks the changing cultural attitudes represented by the "new cloth," Gaiman's weavings also reveal to careful readers how narratives become ubiquitous and achieve metanarrativity. To understand how our minds interpret scripts, schemas, and metanarratives, I will bring to bear conceptual blending and schema theories on my examination of the verbal and visual interplay of source texts and Gaiman retellings.

Understanding Fairy Tales: Scripts, Schemas, and Metanarratives

Fairy tales are a type of folk tale that occur within a magical reality, albeit one that is not necessarily related to fairies (Jones 9). Indeed, the genre's magical framework is grounded on codified and paradigmatic language that makes them recognizable across cultures (Warner xviii). These are character types and motifs that recur within and across fairy tales and that are symbolic and meaningful. From a cognitive perspective, motifs and types are examples of schemas and scripts. Symbolism occurs when our minds are trained to recognize the figurative or ideological significance of a script or schema through sheer repetition. A script is composed of interconnected schemas, whereby a schema is the "static element" within a set of experiences and "a script is a dynamic element, which expresses how a sequence of events or actions are expected to unfold" (Stephens 14). They present standard relations between physical things and abstract concepts.

Schemas are fundamental to memory, providing models for people, objects, procedures, and principles. Frame-like and sparse, schemas reference reality from a specific perspective and are filled out with details that are typical to what is being represented (Herman 89). These include physical features, and for people or animal schemas, social relationships and psychological attributes based on real-life experiences or drawn from fictional narratives. Development is also contingent on context, including the physical environment and the beliefs and practices of a locale, nation, group, or culture; hence, they are cultural constructs (Trites 55). The process of substantiating a mental frame with developmental details is called *conceptual blending* (Fauconnier and Turner v). Gilles Fauconier and Mark Turner coined the term to describe how new and meaningful concepts arise from our ability to identify vital relations between two (or more) seemingly unrelated concepts and combine them in interesting ways (6; Turner 10). Blending occurs through the following instantaneous steps: identification (of similarities and links between meaningful concepts), integration (through similarity recognition), and imagination. To demonstrate, the schema for a princess, at its most basic, is a woman who is born royal or marries into royalty. A fairy-tale princess arises from the fusion of our schema for a princess with our schema for a fairy tale: a magical context with a happy ending. Our brains identify points of connection between these schemas, some of which are overt and others implied. For instance, the human mind links the princess and the fairy tale through the shared concept of fate and fortune. An important contributing factor is the schema for the perfect woman: beautiful, good, and mild. The schemas for princess and perfect woman blend to justify the fairy-tale fortune bestowed upon her. The fairy-tale princess is the "emergent structure," a meaningful concept that arises from the integration of schemas that contains aspects from each of its sources but stands on its own as a singular idea (Fauconnier and Turner 42–44; 48). The entire blending process is automatic, unconscious, and instinctive. Further developments will depend on the kind of fairy tale, as well as other factors, such as the representing culture and the trends specific to a cultural moment. Yet, although fairy-tale princesses may differ across versions and traditions, our brains recognize them as part of a distinct category based on the grounding schema.

Scripts are composed of a network of "terminals," into which are entered the appropriate schemas that will complete the standardized sequence (Herman 98). The schemas are dependent upon each other, in that what is entered into one slot affects what can fill the next. Comprehension comes from the connections we make between each schematic frame; thus, the significance of a story arises from the human cognition that completes the semantic network (Trites 40). It is important to note that scripts are "narrative prototypes," which means that they do not fulfill the conditions to be a story; rather, they guide the production and interpretation of a sequence (Hogan 15). Scripts can be as simple and short as "what happens when a prince kisses a sleeping princess": (1) if it is a kiss of "true love," she wakes up and they live "happily ever after"; or (2) she remains asleep. Scripts can also involve a potentially complex set of schemas, such as "what happens in the Snow White fairy tale." Fairy-tale motifs fill in the script. These are schematic plot elements (visual and verbal) for a particular character, place, incident, or group that alert readers to predestined fates and outcomes. Motifs range from characters (the witch, the stepmother, the princess), symbolic items (apples), recurring events (three attempts to kill Snow White), and repetitive phrases ("once upon a time," "happily ever after").

The most popular fairy tales, such as the Sleeping Beauty in the Wood or Snow White, are so familiar that readers can identify them based on only a few components, allowing writers the option to play with the script's other elements. *The Sleeper and the Spindle* provides an apt example. Gaiman never refers to Snow White or Sleeping Beauty by name, but readers recognize them from the non-sequential combination of schematic elements. For Snow White, it is the mention of her "raven-black hair," a comment from a dwarf that she slept for a year and woke again, and an image of her stepmother holding an apple (Gaiman and Riddell 20, 41). For Sleeping Beauty, the words "sleeper" and "spindle" are enough to trigger the association. Scripts and motifs signify the connections and intersections between story versions from across cultures and give a sense of which prototypes and knowledge structures are salient across human experience. Motifs and scripts can also cross over from fairy tale to legend to myth to folk tale to fable, thus emphasizing the amorphous borders between folk narrative categories despite their distinct characteristics (Teverson 15).

Story-meaning thus emerges from a reader's comprehension of a combination of motifs, their associated meanings, and the rationale behind the conditions of the underlying script as well as the basic parameters of the genre. But understanding a story does not only refer to the logic of the causal chain; it also refers to ideology. Narrative prototypes serve a didactic function wherein readers are positioned to align with the ideologies of a culture or group. Stories ultimately aim to influence human beings; hence the embedded ideology "will always be attuned to the intricacies of human cognition" (Zunshine 126). Conceptual blending is, once more, the key process through which our brains combine content and ideology. A new domain of meaning arises from the integration of schema and script with ideology, whereby a reader's beliefs are directed to conform to a metanarrative, what Stephens and McCallum describe as "a global or totalizing cultural narrative schema" that dictates the logical parameters and moral precepts according to which an event is to unfold (5–6). Cultural narratives are "cognitively-stored and culturally reinforced scripts about status, power, and constructed social roles" (Trites 60). They are the belief systems that are common to a specific group and maintained through the following cognitive acts: (1) schemas and scripts that become stored in the memory through repetition, which are (2) activated by a specific cultural context (60). Thus, regularly retold fairy-tale scripts and schemas represent or align with the power structures and values that are salient in a culture, nation, or group.

Gaiman's Retellings: Dreams of Desire and Transformation

Retellings are fundamentally replications of well-known tales for the purpose of cultural reproduction and the diffusion of accepted knowledge (Stephens and McCallum 21). A cursory list of samples, however, will show they are very rarely exact duplicates, evidencing the need for a more nuanced definition. Retellings more commonly deviate from the pre-text in some manner, whether in terms of structure or form, storytelling medium, social or cultural precepts, or a combination of these (Warner: xvii). By pre-text or source text, I am not referring to an urtext, or the earliest version of a tale, but to the story version on which the focused text is based. Even when a retelling claims continuity with a specific source text, the recurring words and images may mean something specific to the representing geographical or temporal culture. For example, in Anglophone traditions, Cinderella's slipper represents her singular beauty and femininity; but Jacob Grimm has claimed that the presentation of the slipper links to an old German custom, wherein the slipper is a betrothal gift from the prince that signifies her subservience (Cox 505).

Authors develop fairy-tale scripts and schemas with details that either support enduring metanarratives, or, where there is a refusal to follow the script, challenge their continued relevance. Story versions that seek to subvert accepted norms or question the implicit, and often invisible, ideologies associated with a script are more properly called "reversions," coined by Stephens and McCallum (21). This involves the dismantling of the pre-text, which is then reshaped in ways that reflect contemporary textual, social, and ideological formations (21). The emergent meaning of a retelling or reversion, then, is not self-contained but is understood within an intertextual context, or through "the interaction of various retellings" (3). It arises from the interplay between the focused text, the underlying script and schemas, and the most relevant retellings and versions in a fairy-tale network. As a system based on similarity-recognition, it is possible to use the network to trace emergent links between story versions from across genres and modes, whether these replicate the prototypical script in its entirety or merely allude to its salient elements or features. In Gaiman's *Dream Hunters*, for example, readers recognize that the two unnamed Asian men are Cain and Abel, two recurring characters in Gaiman's *The Sandman* series that are based on the doomed brothers in the Bible, by virtue of their roles and values and despite differences in physical and ethnic attributes and circumstances. Characters from different tale types can also be cross-linked when they contain the same motif. In *The Sleeper and the Spindle*, Gaiman and Riddell link Snow White and Sleeping Beauty scripts through the enchanted sleep motif, among others, to emphasize overarching models for passive femininity.

The meta-level at which *The Sleeper and the Spindle* and *Dream Hunters* operate demonstrates a trend in contemporary reversions for young readers, in which several fairy-tale scripts are integrated through their shared motifs and schemas to create a third narrative that departs from traditional storytelling logic, thus encouraging readers to question the validity of cultural narratives and schematic conventions. Source texts are transformed into scripts and merged with one another, along with the intertextual and politically charged meanings embedded within each script, to create a new text that reflects contemporary ideologies (Stephens and Geerts 193). *The Sleeper and the Spindle* and *Dream Hunters* are excellent examples of blended or third narratives, whereby the disruption of preordained story and generic scripts signal contemporary shifts in structures of power, gender, and identity. As illustrated texts, meaning-making comes from the mind's comprehension of blends on visual and verbal levels and in relation to an intertextual network. In the following sections, I demonstrate how Gaiman, through his collaborations with Riddell and Amano, uses conceptual blending to break away from traditional patterns for subjectivity and power in order to reflect changing values and diverse realities.

The Sleeper and the Spindle: Waking Women from the Fairy-Tale Dream

In *The Sleeper and the Spindle*, Gaiman and Riddell's fusion of scripts critiques the idea of the fairy-tale romance, generated from the combination of romance and fairy-tale that convey a metanarrative of heteronormative love, and the sociocultural assumptions this creates in young readers. The text was originally published as a short story in the anthology *Rags and Bones: New Twists on Timeless Tales* (2013). Riddell's illustrated version adds a visual dimension that reinforces as well as extends Gaiman's twisting and reweaving of the source scripts. Their imaginative retelling focuses on how a woman's success and happiness have become measured according to the fulfillment of cultural stereotypes, which involve making judgments for or about others based on standard patterns rather than on critical and individualized experiences, and which are devoid of emotional empathy (Trites 41). Both verbal and visual narratives work in concert to confront readers with society's need to perpetuate stereotypical forms of femininity, judged against a particular feminine ideal for which marriage is the ultimate goal and the ultimate reward.

Conventions for women and marriage are challenged at five pivotal points. The first, coming at the beginning of the tale, introduces the queen as a woman engaged. The joy and romance associated with a fairy-tale wedding is immediately overturned in Riddell's dramatic spread, which shows the queen sitting up in bed, her body turned away from the wedding dress that looms above her. The queen's jet-black hair provides a sharp contrast to the rest of Riddell's ink illustration, combining with symbolic motifs distributed throughout the story that identify her as Snow White, including her three dwarf companions and her mother saying her beauty is like "a crimson rose in the fallen snow" (41). Her bleak gaze and the slightly downward tilt of her head draws a vector from her eyes to the bedspread she clutches, printed with golden skulls that make it look more like a shroud. The skull-printed bedspread and her gaze extend beyond the bottom corner of the right-hand page, guiding readers' minds to predict a narrative future marked with death (Figure 13.1).

Gaiman's text completes the story-meaning. The queen reflects upon her impending change in status:

> It would be the end of her life, she decided, if life were a time of choices. In a week from now, she would have no choices. She would reign over her people. She would have children [. . .] But the path to her death [. . .] would be inevitable." (14)

Figure 13.1. Gaiman and Riddell question the automatic pairing of marriage and "happy ever after."

The terms by which Gaiman and Riddell redescribe marriage challenge the cultural narrative underlying all fairy-tale romances wherein marriage is the happy ending that all women desire. Emphasizing "ending" over "happy," and beginning the story at the point where it traditionally closes, prompts readers to reflect, first, upon stories as constructs that can be changed and transformed, and, second, about what marriage truly is beyond the perfect picture shown at the end of the Disney films, and what it might mean to different people. It challenges the uncritical equation of marriage and social power with the higher, more rewarding state promised in the prototypical fairy-tale script.

Gaiman further comments on the artifice of narratives when the dwarfs are shown to have, upon crossing the border into the next kingdom, entered into the Sleeping Beauty script. He casts a playful light on the fluidity of fairy tales, in the sense that retellings are influenced by what is salient to the storyteller and the narrating culture, by likening storytelling to gossip. A plague of sleep is spreading across the land, and various folk (an allusion to the *Volk*, the purported source of folk tales) recount the familiar script but also argue about the accuracy of some details, thus retaining the tension between source scripts and reversion. The dwarfs return to the queen on the day before her wedding to tell her what they heard and that the curse will soon be upon her own kingdom. This is the second pivotal point, and Gaiman and Riddell overturn gender stereotypes when the queen decides to postpone her wedding and undertake a quest to break the curse. In claiming the quest/rescue motif for herself, she gains the agency typically reserved for Sleeping Beauty's prince, whereby she becomes integrated with schematic masculine performance and breaks away from the passive Snow White role. She "called for a map" (21) and marks a defensive strategy for her kingdom. She bid her first minister to keep house—a reversal of the script, in which the woman is usually the one who waits at home. In another reversal, she told her "pretty" fiancé "not to take on so" and "kissed him until he smiled" (21). Finally, she "called" for a mail shirt, a sword, provisions, a horse, and rode out of the palace in the manner of a fairy-tale hero (21). Riddell's illustrations brilliantly focalize the queen's transformation from fairy-tale princess to hero. The dwarfs bring her their news as she is being fitted for her wedding gown. The stiff and heavy dress constrains her movements, and invisible attendants pull at the laces that entwine her waist (20). The image alludes to the motif from the Grimm pre-text in which the evil queen attempts to asphyxiate her in a similar manner, and also underscores the slow suffocation she endures within the limitations of the schema. It contrasts sharply with the movement afforded her when she enacts the hero schema, and Riddell shows this in the image on the opposite page where, dressed in chain mail and trousers, the queen rides away from her story and into one in which it is she who awakens a sleeping girl (Figure 13.2).

and then she rode
out of the palace,
towards the
east.

Figure 13.2. The queen frees herself from the limitations of the Snow White schema.

Figure 13.3. Subverting schemas of femininity.

The queen's agency, however, is not entirely dependent on masculine performance; rather, her power emerges from the blending of hero and Snow White
schemas. She does not succumb to the sleeping sickness, unlike the heroes who
went before her, because as Snow White, she has already been awakened. Upon
reaching the castle, she and the dwarfs overwhelm the old woman guarding the
princess, whom she wakes with a "long and hard" kiss (49) according to the
hero's script. Riddell's composition also follows the traditional script, except the
rose in the queen's flowing black hair emphasizes her femininity (50–51). This
is the third pivotal point, wherein the combination of words and pictures, as
well as the fusion of schemas, forces readers to confront cultural beliefs about
feminine passivity and "true love." But the other sleepers do not wake with the
girl. Instead, the old woman speaks with sudden clarity and remembers that
she was once a young princess who pricked her finger on a spindle, and the girl
reveals that she is the evil fairy—the villain in the Sleeping Beauty fairy tale. In
this fourth pivotal point, Gaiman fuses the three women with the Triple Goddess archetype, a model that represents and limits feminine creativity within
concepts of Virgin, Mother, and Crone, to challenge assumptions of virtue, age,
and beauty. The fusion underscores the hybridity of each woman. The queen,
mother to her people but also a hero, recognizes in the fairy the same desire for
adoration that filled her stepmother. Cross-linking villain schemas from both
fairy-tale scripts allows her to discern that to defeat the fairy, she must "feel her

own emotions and not another's" (56). In other words, she must interrupt the cultural narrative that equates beauty and youth with power and benevolence. The girl, also an ancient fairy, controls the sleepers, who are zombie-like, based on the adoration they hold for the Sleeping Beauty schema—a beautiful, passive princess. The influence she exerts over her sleeping slaves is an effective metaphor for society's mindless obsession with status and beauty. The queen disrupts this metanarrative and the associated stereotypes when she passes the spindle to the old woman. Realizing that the yarn wrapped around the spindle is the life that had been stolen from her, the old woman literally takes her life into her own hands and stabs the girl-fairy with the sharp spindle (Figure 13.3). That the sleepers awake with this inversion of the hero schema cleverly represents a society disabused of stereotypes.

The image of three women with a spindle between them also evokes the Three Fates. Riddell complicates the blend when he illustrates the crone-princess drawing the thread—her life—towards her heart while it unravels from the spindle thrust into the girl-fairy's chest (60-61). Whereas the crone typically snips the thread of life, Gaiman's crone-princess returns life to herself, to the sleepers, and to the queen, who chooses a vagabond existence in a refusal to fulfill the romantic expectations of the Snow White script. Gaiman has invoked the blended image of Triple Goddess and Three Fates many times throughout his opus (as "the kindly ones" in the *Sandman* series, the Norn in *American Gods*, and most recently in *The Ocean at the End of the Lane*), suggesting a persistent examination of predestined scripts and schemas vis-à-vis reversions in which subjective agency emerges from the disruption of narrative conventions. In *Dream Hunters*, the blend is used to illuminate the continuity between the focused text, which has a Japanese aesthetic, and the greater *Sandman* universe, which draws largely on Western myths and popular culture. The Japanese incarnation of the fused Triple Goddess/Fates alerts readers to hybridity in the characters, context, and narrative scripts.

Dream Hunters: Reflecting a Hybrid Global Culture

Dream Hunters is styled as a retelling of the Japanese folk tale "The Fox, The Monk, and the Mikado of All-Night's Dreaming" within the larger syncretic mythology of *The Sandman*. In the Afterword, Gaiman narrates the experience of finding the folk tale in the Rev. W. B. Ashton's "Fairy Tales of Old Japan," but in fact neither book nor collector exists and the embedded tale is a Gaiman original (Wagner et al. 130–31). This playful use of paratextual space encourages a critical reading of the text. It reveals how our minds automatically classify information as truth or fiction based on scripts repeated across human experience, such as, in this instance, the concept of the Afterword as a space where the author's description of "the book on the table in front of me" and the close nature of the "encountered" folk tale to the "Sandman analogues" are understood as truth. More informed readers recognize that the fictional fairy-tale collection associates Gaiman's adaptation of Japanese scripts and imagery to *Japonaiserie*. *Japonaiserie* refers to an art style that reflects Japaneseness but from a Western perspective. A critical reading of *Dream Hunters* thus reveals that Gaiman appropriates Japanese motifs to enhance or replicate the Western experiences that run in the background of the *Sandman* series. This suggests that there are experiential scripts that are shared across cultures, and that these can be contextually developed. That Amano's illustration style is reminiscent of *sumi-e*, or Japanese ink painting, is an ideal match. The aim of *sumi-e* is to capture the spirit of a subject rather than its exact likeness using bold brushstrokes and white space (Sato 9–10). This style of painting emphasizes the essence (or script) that the Japanese motifs and the *Sandman* analogues share. It guides reader cognition to operate within the East-West blend rather than outside of it.

Positioning readers to interpret *Dream Hunters* from this blended, cross-cultural perspective reveals the effect of increased global connectivity on narratives and identity formation. In other words, intensified East-West exchanges enable greater instances of similarity recognition and adaptation, resulting in creative and multicultural expressions of cultural narratives. Ultimately, the effect of the East-West blend transforms the entire *Sandman* series and invites readers to reconsider any boundaries (shape, nationality, and the like) that they might have imposed upon the Dreaming and all who dwell within it. Moreover, cognizance of diegetic doubling prompts readers to examine Gaiman's statements regarding the origin of *Dream Hunters* in a new light, for although the illustrated narrative is not a strict retelling, it demonstrates how new stories emerge from already existing tales.

The dream landscape in *Dream Hunters*, for instance, is one where a relationship of interpenetration and blending exists between dreams, the waking world, and the land of the dead, such that the events that occur in a dream world can flow into and transform the waking world, and dreams are pathways to the underworld. This concept is central to both the dream motif in Japanese folk tale (Kawai 17–18, 21) and the Dreaming, the kingdom of the Sandman (the title character in the series), and thus implies a cross-cultural belief that dreams represent a desire for transformation in our conscious reality. Gaiman strengthens the fusion by filling the landscape with a combination of Japanese dream imagery, such as the nightmare-devouring *baku* (dream eaters), along with the Japanese counterparts of characters from the *Sandman* mythos (the kindly ones, Matthew the Raven, Cain, and Abel) that occupy the Dreaming that until now had only been represented in Western forms. Because these characters are recognizable even in Japanese form, readers who are unaware of Gaiman and Amano's contextual illusions still understand that the East-West blend emphasizes the amorphous quality of the Dreaming, which is representative of a universal conceptualization of blending and change that has local expressions. The Sandman, in the course of the seventy-five issue series, was a shapeshifter also known by the names Dream and Morpheus, and this allows readers to extend to his kingdom the metamorphosis inherent to his character. In *Dream Hunters*, Morpheus shifts from Japanese Emperor, punk rock star, and Great Black Fox (fox spirits are shapeshifters in East Asian folklore), while in the background run his various incarnations in the entirety of the series. The play of Eastern and Western forms within the universal idea of Morpheus/ Dream alerts readers to the cross-cultural development of subjectivity, in which the Dreaming approximates a global network.

Dream Hunters adapts a combination of Japanese fox-girl schemas (the seductive trickster and the tragic lover) to create a fairy-tale quest that mirrors the overall exploration of mutable narratives and realities in the *Sandman*. The motif of the metamorphosing fox easily fits into Gaiman's mythology, since shape-changing is a familiar attribute of Morpheus. A fox-girl falls in love with a monk who is cursed by an *onmyoji* (a master of divination) to dream dreams that lead him to his death. She finds a way to dream them for him, but the monk learns of her sacrifice and arranges to reenter his dreams to save her. He makes a pilgrimage to the Dream King, in a journey that parallels the Orpheus myth as it is retold in Gaiman's own comic book reversion, *The Song of Orpheus* (Gaiman et al. 1991). Like Orpheus, the monk travels to the place where death and dreams intersect. Amano employs a Japanese aesthetic, but his emphasis on essence over detail lays bare the visual schema through which the monk's journey and Orpheus's quest can be cross-mapped (Gaiman and Amano 89) (Figure 13.4). This connection, and the idea of the Dreaming as a concept that is contextually developed, is reinforced when cross-referenced with Talbot's illustration of Orpheus at the gates of Morpheus's palace (Gaiman et al. 14) (Figure 13.5).

Like Orpheus, the monk asks for the fox-girl's return to the living world. The Dream King allows it, but because the curse must be completed, the death dream returns to the monk and he dies. The fox-girl vows revenge. Here,

Figure 13.4. The monk at the gates of the palace of the King of All-Night's Dreaming draws from the same schema as Gaiman's *Song of Orpheus* (see Figure 13.5).

Figure 13.5. Orpheus at the gates of the palace of Morpheus, this time in Ancient Greece.

Gaiman fuses the Orpheus myth with the seductive fox-girl script, in which she bewitches powerful men and feeds on their life force (Casal 28–29). In *Dream Hunters*, the fox-maiden exacts her revenge in a similar vampiric manner. She seduces the *onmyoji* and convinces him to abandon his duties, to burn his house to the ground while his wife and concubine slept within it, and to give all his magic and possessions to her. She resumes her fox form and bites off his eye, which sends him into madness. The fusion of scripts from Greek myths and Japanese folk tales into a third story, and the mirroring of Japanese, Greek, and *Sandman* imagery expand and extend the *Sandman* mythos. However, even though the East-West blend operates through similarity recognition whereby interpretation is anchored on the *Sandman* text, neither is completely subsumed into the other. Instead, the emergent hybridity of Morpheus and the *Sandman* narrative emphasizes a trend towards the cross-cultural development of subjectivity, whereby the cognition of modern readers is shaped from the interplay between cultures.

Dreams that Alter Reality

In both *The Sleeper and the Spindle* and *Dream Hunters*, Gaiman's deliberate play with fairy-tale structure—the intermixing of scripts and shapeshifting schemas echoes the fluidity of dreaming. Warner states that one of the central characteristics of fairy tales is its capacity to "express hopes" (2014: xviii) through both its formulaic form (overcoming hardship, a happy ending) and the mutability of that form. The amorphous quality of fairy tales and other types of folk narrative allow humanity to narrate a persistent longing "to transform the world and make it more adaptable to human needs, while we also try to change and make ourselves fit for the world" (Zipes 27). In other words, genres that are persistently retold are essentially predisposed to respond to shifts in temporal and sociopolitical circumstances—to express a society's desires, dreams, as well as their fears. Gaiman anchors his blended reversions on that shared quality of fairy tales and dreams to challenge stereotypical patterns and imagine new ways of being—new shapes for heroism, for women, for love—that, as Zipes said, are reflective of changing realities. Illustrators such as Amano and Riddell reinforce Gaiman's reconceptualizations on a visual dimension, thus encouraging critical thinking and innovative cognition on several levels. In motivating cognition to follow new story shapes, Gaiman underscores the need to have a historical understanding of narrative patterns and the need for such patterns to respond to a more interconnected and dynamic world.

WORKS CITED

Aarne, Antti, and Stith Thompson. *The Types of the Folktale: A Classification and Bibliography.* Stith Thompson, trans. Academia Scientiarum Fennica, 1981.

Casal, U. A. "The Goblin Fox and Badger and Other Witch Animals of Japan." *Folklore Studies* vol. 18, 1959, pp. 1–93. nirc.nanzan-u.ac.jp/nfile/268.

Cox, Marian Roalfe. *Cinderella: Three Hundred and Forty-Five Variants of Cinderella, Catskin, and Cap O'Rushes, Abstracted and Tabulated, with a Discussion of Medieval Analogues, and Notes.* Introduction by Andrew Lang. Publications of the Folklore Society 31. David Nutt, 1893.

Fauconnier, Gilles, and Mark Turner. *The Way We Think: Conceptual Blending and the Mind's Hidden Complexities.* Basic Books, 2002.

Gaiman, Neil, and Yoshitaka Amano. *The Sandman: The Dream Hunters.* DC Comics, 1999.

Gaiman, Neil, and Chris Riddell. *The Sleeper and the Spindle.* Bloomsbury, 2014.

Gaiman, Neil, Bryan Talbot, and Mark Buckingham. *The Song of Orpheus (Sandman Special 1).* DC Comics, 1991.

Herman, David. *Story Logic: Problems and Possibilities of Narrative*. University of Nebraska Press, 2002.

Hogan, Patrick Colm. *Understanding Indian Movies: Culture, Cognition, and Cinematic Imagination*. University of Texas Press, 2009.

Jones, Stephen Swann. *Fairy Tales: The Magic Mirror of Imagination*. Routledge, 2002.

Kawai, Hayao, and Reece Sachiko, trans. *The Japanese Psyche: Major Motifs in the Fairy Tales of Japan*. 2nd ed. By Hayao Kawai. Spring Publications, 1996.

Lakoff, George, and Mark Johnso. *Metaphors We Live By*. University of Chicago Press, 2003.

McCallum, Robyn. *Ideologies of Identity in Adolescent Fiction: The Dialogic Construction of Subjectivity*. Garland, 1999.

Sato, Shozo. *Sumi-e: The Art of Japanese Ink Painting*. Tuttle Publishing, 2014.

Stephens, John. "Schemas and Scripts: Cognitive Instruments and the Representation of Cultural Diversity in Children's Literature." *Contemporary Children's Literature and Film*. Kerry Mallan and Clare Bradford, eds. Palgrave MacMillan, 2011, pp. 12–56.

Stephens, John, and Sylvia Geerts. "Mishmash, Conceptual Blending and Adaptation in Contemporary Children's Literature Written in Dutch and English." *Never-ending Stories*. Sara Van den Bossche and Sylvia Geerts, eds. Academia Press, 2014, pp. 193–214.

Stephens, John, and Robyn McCallum. *Retelling Stories, Framing Culture: Traditional Stories and Metanarratives in Children's Literature*. Garland, 1998.

Teverson, Andrew. *Fairy Tale*. Kindle ed. Routledge, 2013.

Trites, Roberta. *Literary Conceptualizations of Growth*. John Benjamins, 2014.

Turner, Mark. "The Cognitive Study of Art, Language, and Literature." *Poetics Today* vol. 23, no. 1, Spring 2002, pp. 9–20. Project Muse, muse.jhu.edu/article/27895.

Turner, Mark. *Reading Minds: The Study of English in the Age of Cognitive Science*. Princeton University Press, 1991.

Wagner, Hank, Christopher Golden, and Stephen R. Bissette. *Prince of Stories: The Many Worlds of Neil Gaiman*. St. Martin's Press, 2008.

Warner, Marina. *Once Upon a Time: A Short History of Fairy Tale*. Kindle ed. Oxford University Press, 2014.

Zipes, Jack. *The Irresistible Fairy Tale: The Cultural and Social History of a Genre*. Princeton University Press, 2012.

Zunshine, Lisa. "Rhetoric, Cognition, and Udeology in A. L. Barbauld's *Hymns in Prose for Children* (1781)." *Poetics Today* vol. 23, no. 1, Spring 2002, pp. 123–39. Project Muse, muse.jhu.edu/issue/1631.

"The World Always Seems Brighter When You've Just Made Something That Wasn't There Before"

Afterthoughts, Filters, and Interviews

CODA
"A Walking Shadow": Life as a Reader and Author of Neil Gaiman

JOE SUTLIFF SANDERS

Let me tell you my favorite Neil Gaiman story. It's partly a story about the history of Gaiman as an author, partly about the history of scholarship on Gaiman, and partly a chance for me to settle a very old score.

First, pick up your copy of *American Gods*. Look all the way in the back, on the second page of the acknowledgments. There, right after the name of little-known comics author Alan Moore, you'll see my name.

Now, you would think Neil's recognition would make me happy. He had worked on *American Gods* for a long time, and in many ways it was his first major step as a novelist in his own right: he had a novel with Terry Pratchett, but that was co-authored; he had *Neverwhere*, but that was really a novelization of the BBC miniseries of the same name; he had *Stardust*, but that was conceived as an illustrated story with Charles Vess, not precisely a novel. *American Gods* was proof that Neil could work in a medium with no pictures and that he could do it by himself. When it became a bestseller, it validated him as a novelist. It was a major event in his career, and there he was, mentioning my name as someone who had played some part in making this dream of his come true. Here's the problem: he's not talking about me. In fact, he's pointedly *not* talking about me. Look closer at that line in the acknowledgments: Neil thanks "the original Joe Sanders" (464).

Why the qualifier? Is there some other Joe Sanders whom he is *not* thanking?

I first met Neil when I was a graduate student, delivering a paper at the International Conference on the Fantastic in the Arts about his use of language in his *Death* mini-series. Neil was one of the special guests at that conference, and he very sweetly attended my session, acted interested, and even asked a question at the end. Later, we walked out to the pool together for a photograph that would later appear in the industry magazine *Locus*, along the way discussing comics, language, analysis, and all the other things that two new best friends talk about. After the conference, we stayed in touch sporadically, and from time to time we exchanged emails, usually about matters having to do with our children.

But at that very panel where we first became—or so I thought—bosom companions, there was *another* scholar named Joe (note the lack of middle name) Sanders. That was no accident: he and I had discovered the previous year at the same conference that we had interests as similar as our names, and we thought it would be funny to have a Joe Sanders panel at the conference. Joe was an established scholar and very well known within the field (he had actually received an award in recognition of a lifetime of generosity to the profession one year before I met him), so he knew how to propose a special session that was more likely to get picked up, and thus the double Joe Sanders panel was born. That Joe also gave a paper on Gaiman at our panel, when Neil was in the audience. In fact, it was a really good paper.

In fact, it was so much better than mine that Neil and Joe kept talking about it after the conference. In fact, that conversation became the seed of *The Sandman Papers*, the first book of collected scholarship on Gaiman, edited by Joe and including one little paper by me, a book that happened in part because Neil pushed behind the scenes to get not-me Joe the support he needed.

As part of that blooming friendship, Neil sent not-me Joe drafts of his own manuscripts while he was working on them, and not-me Joe gave helpful advice.

Advice for which Neil was, it turns out, grateful.

Therefore, when you see in the acknowledgments page that Neil, in writing this book that would be so consequential for his career, thanks "the original Joe Sanders," he is not thanking me. He is instead thanking the Joe Sanders who was born first and is, hence, original.

Indeed, one might say that he is *going out of his way* not to thank me.

"You know that bald Joe Sanders with the misspelled British middle name?" the acknowledgment seems to ask. "Screw *that guy*, he did *bugger all* to help me, and I've got *exactly zero thanks* for him. No, let the record show very plainly exactly which Joe Sanders I am thanking, and it is 100 percent not that guy."

In the years that have followed, I have had the joy of pointing out to wave after wave of students who notice my name in the back of this book—or in *The Graveyard Book*, which won the highest award in my field, and to which the original Joe evidently also contributed some precious morsel of help—that no, Mr. Gaiman is not thanking me. Yes, he knows me, but he has not the slightest bit of gratitude toward me. He's talking about someone else, someone he likes better.

It's an annual tradition that always helps lower me in my students' eyes, a service for which I am deeply grateful. Perhaps I should put something about it in my own acknowledgments page.

Don't worry, there's a point to all this self-flagellation.

The subtext to this story—the text being, of course, how horribly I have been wronged in not having been thanked for not in fact helping—is easy to miss, but it is one that follows hot on the heels of a theme that has wound through all of the essays that you have just read.

Throughout, every single chapter in this collection has been arguing in one way or another that to understand Gaiman best, one must think about Gaiman as *between* two points that at first appear incompatible. Recounting them all would be tedious, but let me point to a few of the most obvious theses as examples: in *The Books of Magic*, mimesis and anti-mimesis intertwine; in his adaptations of fairy tales, Gaiman creates a tension between original and adaptation by emphasizing their interconnectedness; in his collaborations with Dave McKean, Gaiman hovers in a space of hesitation between fantasy and reality; in his essays, Gaiman asks us to step between one subject position and another to create empathy; in his social media posts, Gaiman is both himself and a character he creates for those posts. In her chapter, Eric McCrystal uses exactly the word that I have been dancing around: for her, Gaiman's is "a liminal fantasy that thrives on the mystery created when reality and fantasy are not distinct" (186). This fuzzy space between, which overlaps with and connects two ideas that we generally take to be separate is the *liminal* space. In their introduction, the editors of this volume point out that they have created a special section for chapters on the liminal, but I think that the liminal has—and perhaps this is inevitable—slipped the boundaries that the editors set for it, tiptoeing into the other sections and whispering in the ears of the other authors. It is in the in-between spaces that all of the essays have been saying one can best understand Gaiman's work.

The concept of liminality hit literary studies when I was in graduate school (in fact, at exactly the time that I met and signally failed to impress the floppy-haired author in question). I remember coming up with jokes about how far everyone wanted to stretch this new concept with Theodora Goss, who was also a graduate student and then went on to become a brilliant fantasy writer who also never thanked me in any of her books. Dora and I were, again, sitting next to the pool at the Fort Lauderdale hotel for the conference at which I gave my paper on *Death*. It's important to keep in mind that *American Gods* had yet to appear, and Neil Gaiman was not yet, if I may put it so obtusely, quite "Neil Gaiman." Those of us who were reading comics in the 1990s knew who he was, of course, but outside of comics, he wasn't yet the public figure whose emergence Lanette Cadle so ably portrays. To those who weren't reading comics or hadn't stumbled across the promising short stories that had begun appearing, he was more likely to stand out as the fellow rather foolishly insisting on wearing black jeans and a black leather jacket in the Florida humidity.

But the fact that he was there—indeed, that he was a special guest of the conference—was an early sign of how important liminality would be to the identity of Neil Gaiman when he eventually became Neil Gaiman. The conference was an academic conference, founded by literature professor Bob Collins decades earlier, and academic conferences are rarely a place to find living authors (dead ones, sure: we grind them up to make into the ink with which we print our programs). This conference, however, is rare in that it emphasizes scholarship as well as the reading and production of original works of drama, poetry, and prose. Academic sessions run alongside panels of authors reading forthcoming stories or poetry, and once, a fellow academic and I joined Brian Aldiss (who counts as an academic or novelist, depending on whom you're trying to impress) in performing a play written by Sydney Duncan (a playwright who eventually became the president of the academic organization that puts on the conference), a play I admiringly described as "*Waiting for Godot* after the apocalypse." I often reflected in my many happy years attending that conference that it was as though the scholars of fantasy and science fiction had found themselves in the academic gutter, then looked over at the *writers* of fantasy and science fiction in their own gutter, and said, "We should really party together." It is a conference built on liminality, and Gaiman's presence there as a special guest signaled early on that his career should best be understood as a career built in the seams that stitch together communities that the larger world insists must be kept separate.

Since then, Gaiman's profile has only become delightfully messier. As Sarah Thaller demonstrates in her contribution to this volume, even Gaiman's works that are most clearly for either children or adults are difficult to prove as exclusively belonging to one group or the other, a point on which Joseph Michael Sommers and Kyle Eveleth expand in their introduction.

Thaller's provocative conclusion is that the works most explicitly for children are dark works that actually draw from fears more closely associated with adult experiences, not child experiences. Sommers and Eveleth's conclusion is that Gaiman prods us to question the boundaries between child and adult on which the grown-up world so anxiously insists. Thaller points out that Gaiman's fantastic children's books are therefore horror books for adults, and if we put her conclusion together with that of the introduction, we might wonder whether one of the reasons they play upon the fears of adults is that if we insist on the overlap between—the liminality of—these books, they quietly argue that when adults talk about what childhood is, they don't know what they're talking about. And they know that it's only a matter of time before children figure them out.

The Graveyard Book, surely the most recognizable of Gaiman's books for young readers, again marks his place among and between. As the only book ever to have won both the Carnegie Medal and the Newbery Medal, it was an instant classic of children's literature, but of whose children's literature? The Carnegie is a British award founded by the British Library Association, and although it is open to non-Brits, the list of winners is heavily dominated by British writers, including four of the five authors preceding Gaiman—the fifth, incidentally, is an American long based in London. The Newbery, of course, is a profoundly American institution, emphatically for American books almost since the time it was first conceived.[1] However, like Susan Cooper before him (both have lived in the US for decades), the organization behind the award— the American Library Association—determined that Gaiman was British, yes, but American enough for its highest award. Therefore, British and American librarians seem to think of Gaiman as British and sort of American.

I have been suggesting that the essays in this collection argue that the best position from which to understand Gaiman's work is one staked out in liminal spaces, but I might also add that this advice is important not just for those of us reading his work, but for the author himself. A review in the *Economist* of his most recent book, *Norse Mythology*, recommends the book as "an excellent introduction to the stories that wield such great cultural influence."

However, the review also complains that Gaiman's "retelling is almost tentative, restricting itself to the core of the corpus." The stories are, the reviewer argues, too beholden to their original category, of myths told by someone else for another time, and they go on to argue that not enough of the retellings blur the boundaries between yesteryear and "modern times." When the reviewer complains that too much of Gaiman's "typical style" is absent, it might be that what they are missing is the Gaiman who lifts the fence enough for ideas to stray from their intended pastures.

Compare these complaints, though, with Sarah Hunter's review of Gaiman's most recent work in comics: 2016's *How to Talk to Girls at Parties*, a graphic adaptation of a signature (indeed, award-winning) short story originally published in 2006. Hunter has many positive things to say about the artwork provided by the extraordinary Brazilian comics team of Fabio Moon and Gabriel Ba, but her highest praise is reserved for Gaiman writing in the mode that the reviewer from the *Economist* linked to Gaiman's signature style. Hunter singles out

Gaiman's, as she puts it, "particular brand" of horror wedded to science fiction, two genres that Gaiman has made a career of blending. Horror and science fiction both draw from traditions variously dubbed as the fantastic or speculative, but when Gaiman brings this energy to his story, he does so by blurring the genre boundaries on which contemporary marketing relies. He does so here in this edition of the story, he did so earlier in his previous edition of the story, and, as Hunter points out, he does so routinely throughout his body of work. "Most enchanting" in the story, Hunter suggests, is how Gaiman positions his tale right on the edge of knowing the full details of the action. The viewpoint character hovers at the edge of the action, glimpsing the outlines of the tale's sublime villains and overhearing suggestions of but never witnessing the dark liaison at the center of the conflict. The story works, this reviewer argues, because it is so firmly rooted in the places between: between genres, between knowledge and ignorance. The story succeeds because it is liminal, because it fits Gaiman's "particular brand."

What the essays in this collection reveal, then, is that the quintessential voice (to return to another idea expressed in the introduction) of Neil Gaiman is one that pointedly borrows from different fields, ideas, age categories, epistemological subjectivities, and periods that should not, we have been told, be allowed to mix.

This realization can, as these essays demonstrate, make us better readers of Gaiman. It might also, if these reviewers are right, make Gaiman a better writer of stories that are in the mode of Gaiman.

Not, as he will be quick to point out, that he takes advice from me.

NOTES

1. For the full story on the birth of the Newbery, see Leonard Marcus's indispensable *Minders of Make-Believe*, p. 87.

WORKS CITED

Gaiman, Neil. *American Gods*. William Morrow, 2001.
Gaiman, Neil. *The Graveyard Book*. HarperCollins, 2008.
Hunter, Sarah. Rev. of *How to Talk to Girls at Parties* by Neil Gaiman, Fabio Moon, and Gabriel Ba. *Booklist*, 15 September 2016, p. 44.
Marcus, Leonard. *Minders of Make-Belive: Idealists, Entrepreneurs, and the Shaping of American Children's Literature*. Houghton Mifflin, 2008.
Sanders, Joe, ed. *The Sandman Papers: An Exploration of the Sandman Mythology*. Fantagraphics, 2006.
"Stories from the Top of the World; Norse Mythology." *Economist*, 4 March 2017, 72.

Interviews

A SHORT CONVERSATION WITH NEIL GAIMAN ON COMICS

JOSEPH MICHAEL SOMMERS

It goes without saying that Neil Gaiman is an incredibly busy man of late. Between acting as executive producer on the television adaptation of *American Gods* and performing similar duties on *Good Omens*—in addition to writing all the scripts for the BBC adaptation of his and Terry Pratchett's much-beloved 1990 novel, crafting sequels to *Neverwhere* (*The Seven Sisters*) and *American Gods*, among his many other writing projects, speaking engagements, and humanitarian concerns (not to mention enjoying time with his youngest child, Anthony)—coming by a moment of his time to do little more than to talk about comics is incredibly rare. Fortunately, Neil Gaiman is also very generous with his time, and that's why his fan base frequently has to be patient when awaiting forthcoming work.

Gaiman took a few moments to sit down with me and shed some light upon the state of comics and the comics industry, adaptations, and his some of his favorite collaborations . . . in addition to discussing his own future in comics. He was honest. He was forthcoming. And he likely will make quite a few comics fans quite pleased with where he sees his future within the industry. However, they will have to remain patient.

This interview was conducted 26 July 2017, the date of which signifies nothing in particular save the fact that Neil Gaiman had time to speak.

Joseph Michael Sommers: If I may ask you a few questions on comics: recent data has shown that comic *book* sales have been on the downturn for quite some time, but greater comics media—movies, television programming, video games, merchandizing, toy sales, etc.—has grown just tremendously.

As someone who has dabbled in all these things, do you see this trend as an evolution of the form, or even problematic, or an issue of the direct market . . . too many crossovers?

Neil Gaiman: You know, I think that you've got so many things happening. I don't think that . . . There's no point where there's ever been an A and a B where comic movies, movies from comics, feeding in particularly healthy ways to the comic book stores and the comic book direct market. I think you have this problem now where the comics are generally regarded, rightly or wrongly, by the entities that actually own them as places that are feeding grounds for movies. [They think]: "These are properties on which movies can be based."

And I think that's sad. I think you have some fantastic media out there. I think you've got more interesting and more different and more diverse works being done in the medium of comics that ever before, but, at the same time, you're also fighting everything for an entertainment dollar. It's like the cost of printing, the cost of paper, the cost of color—the cost of all of this stuff—goes up. And how many pages of entertainment, how much time does your dollar buys you drops in comic [books].

And I also worry the same thing that I've been worrying about for twenty-something years, that there aren't the on-ramps to comic [books]. You always need, you need the comic [books] for kids to exist in order . . . and then you need to make comic [books] for young adults, and then you need to make comic [books] for adults, and you need to keep people. And one of the weird things that happened in the days of Alan Moore and me and Frank Miller and so forth was you've got people who would normally have stopped reading comic [books], and they stuck around. And that was great, but you can't just service an audience of thirty-five-year-old comic [books] fans; you've always need to have a really good on-ramp. And they have to be affordable.

Alan Moore used to point out that one of things that comic books had going for them that the movies didn't was an unlimited special effects budget.

JMS: [*laughter*]
NG: You know, he would say [back then], "Well, in comic [books], you actually have no special effects budget," and the problem is, now, *the movies* have an unlimited special effects budget. Ya know, it's like . . . It's *probably* not going to cost you more than two million dollars a minute [both laugh] to CGI [computer generated image] anything in the world! Which means that you can do anything—you can do *Thor: Ragnarok*. You can do [*Marvel's*] *The Avengers*. You can do all this stuff and it's really using an unlimited special effects budget. Now, you can see these people flying around and talking and hitting each other through buildings and getting up and saying, "Now, you've made me really angry!"

And having said all that, I think that it's definitely not—you know, it goes weird. *Watchmen*, for a good year before, the year of, and at least the year after the movie came out, probably several years after the movie came out, became the bestselling graphic novel, kind of ever. The movie didn't set the world on fire, but enough people found it, and it raised the awareness of people who went and found that there was something here to see, and the graphic novel was getting read again. And I love the fact that the graphic novel was getting read.

JMS: Part of a good comic book, of course, is the collaboration between the writer and the artist. You have a stable, if you will, of artists that are simply incredible: Dave McKean, P. Craig Russell, even Chris Riddell, who's done done of your graphic novels, Chris Bachalo, J. H. Williams III, certainly. What makes collaboration with these folks work so well, particularly given, in some cases, very, very disparate styles?

NG: Mostly it's trying to match the right person to the right story, and then shutting up and getting out of the way.

JMS: Hmm—really?

NG: Finding out what an artist likes to draw is huge. With *Sandman: Overture*, I knew that it was going to be a space operate which meant that I knew that I needed to find an artist who could give me a space opera. And it did not take much prodding around to ask J. H. Williams III, and that was a relief because I couldn't really think of, you know . . . I think I might have had a tentative conversation with Karen Berger about whether Jim Lee would be interested and her saying, "Well, he would be, but he's so tied up, we can't even go and ask him." And you go, "Okay. Well, who else have we got?" And J. H. became the obvious other candidate, and we were relieved that he said yes.

But, there are things that I would not ask J. H. Williams III to do. Not many of them because he's really, really amazingly talented. But, probably for the same reason, I wouldn't have asked Dave McKean to do a space opera—that's not Dave's strongpoint. And it's also not his enthusiasm; he would get very little joy from doing it. It's the kind of thing he would endure, and that would be a terrible thing. For me, the biggest and most important thing is just doing that [finding the right artist].

JMS: You mentioned three specific names there that brings up a couple of different questions: Dave McKean, Karen Berger, and, of course, Alan Moore.

Thinking about two of the collaborators, P. Craig Russell and Dave McKean, it occurred to me while you were speaking that P. Craig Russell and Dave

McKean both drew, to some degree or another, different versions of the same project. Russell, of course, orchestrated the graphic novelization of *The Graveyard Book*, and McKean provided the illustrations to the prose version. When you look at those types of projects, and we can see it in a few different places: certainly *Neverwhere*, *How to Talk to Girls at Parties*, even the graphic novelization of *American Gods* and *Coraline*—when you see these different artists working with your words to craft different interpretations, how do you view them? Are they now different books? Are they now new through the collaboration?

NG: Wow, what a great question! In my head, it's a lot closer to going and seeing a play based on one of my stories. You know that it's not the story; you know that it's somebody's interpretation; and you know that the thing you saw that night will never happen again. And, even if it runs for a couple of weeks, and then it's done, and then it's done again in a different city by a different cast—it'll be completely different.

So, having said that, it's shading. I couldn't imagine *The Wolves in the Walls* or *The Day I Swapped My Dad for Two Goldfish* or whatever being done by anyone else. I couldn't imagine giving those books to any other artist besides Dave McKean. What Dave and I made feels like half and half. Whereas, I loves Dave's illustrations of *Coraline*; I love the Chris Riddell illustrations of *Coraline*; I love the Craig Russell illustrations of *Coraline*. They're all different, but they're wonderful.

JMS: Karen Berger is coming back to comics with Dark Horse Comics with her imprint of Berger Books, and Alan Moore has said that he has a finite set of pages left within him, and it feels like we're seeing one giant return to comics and we're saying goodbye to another. I suppose the question is . . . and I don't want to ask how you feel about it, but . . . Alan has meant so much to your career, and in a different manner, so has Karen, and both seem like they still have a remarkable bit left to say. There's just such a wealth of stories in, for example, *Jerusalem*, to the point where I wonder if Alan used them all up. But, how do you feel about the returns and farewells of these giant voices in the comics industry?

NG: I'm thrilled that Karen is editing again. Because she is a wonderful, amazing, and brilliant person who is also . . . just nice and good and all of the adjectives. With Alan, I guess I think about Alan retiring in the same way as I think about [Hayao] Miyazaki retiring, which is—I do not think that Miyazaki has ever lied about retiring. I have also observed Miyazaki retire and then do films after retiring. And then retire again. [*laughs*] And then do films after retiring.

And I think you're allowed. You're allowed to come back to work. So, if Alan *is* retired—does retire after the next book—then we are the universe that has had thirty-to-thirty-five years of Alan Moore comics which is better than *anybody* since . . . 1976 or within, and we have all of these amazing comics. If he comes back that will be wonderful too.

And, you know, if he decided to go off and become a chaos magician or a stage tycoon, [*both laugh*] or decides that actually he wants to go in and take his art skills, the old *Maxwell the Magic Cat* art skills, and start doing chalk drawings on sidewalks for money . . . You know that whatever Alan Moore is going to do is going to be brilliant. He still is the best thinker about comics I've ever run into. And despite having a reputation for being huge and terrifying and such, he's ones of the politest, kindest, nicest people that I know.

JMS: If I may, I would like to end our time on you. I know you have something like the next six, seven years of your life planned out with projects, and future prognostications are just that, but do you think we'll see any new comics from you? I recall *Miracleman* possibly being something that you wanted to finish up—

NG: *Miracleman* is definitely on the way back. It got derailed by contractual issues that were not Marvel's fault and were not our [Mark Buckingham] fault, and just were . . . nothing with *Miracleman* is ever simple. [*both laugh*] So, at the point where we're ready to go, *of course* we had to find a bunch of contract stuff that needed to be sorted out, and it got pushed out, but [*Miracleman*] *will* happen.

And then there's one big project for DC that I plan to start writing relatively soon . . . which may take a very long time to come out because I don't know how long it's going to take me to write and I don't know how long it's going to take to be drawn. So, it a . . . [*pauses*] I do know that I learned my lesson with *Sandman: Overture* on letting anything come out before the whole thing is done. So, I think it may be quite a while before this is actually announced. It will probably be announced once it's finished.

JMS: That's all right! I don't recall who said to always leave the audience wanting more, but I think it's safe to say that with the prospects of something new at DC or within the DC universe, that's probably as good a place to leave the reader as any. [*both laugh*] Thank you so much!

NG: You're so welcome! I always figured . . . one of the reasons I stopped doing *Sandman* when I did was, as I explained at the time, I think I'd rather leave while I'm in love. And, there's a good thing about leaving while you're still in love which is that, when you come back, it's like going and spending time with an old girlfriend who you haven't seen and are still incredibly fond of. And, so far, such as it were, I have never got up in the morning, looked gloomily in the mirror and gone, "Oh God. I've got to go and write some comics today."

And I have definitely got up, looked gloomily in the mirror and gone, "Oh God. I have to sort out backstage politics on a TV show today." [*both laugh*] That stuff, that feels like work.

Life in comics still feels like a joy.

JMS: It is a wonderful life, indeed. Thank you, Neil.

THE ART OF ADAPTATION
An Interview with P. Craig Russell

KYLE EVELETH AND JOSEPH MICHAEL SOMMERS

Collaboration is a key component to Neil Gaiman's visual media. Having learned the trade of visual scripting from Alan Moore, Gaiman has crafted a variety of techniques for working with his pool of handpicked artists across comics, pictures books, and other adaptations of his otherwise written word. However, this discussion has largely gone overlooked in *auteur* examinations of Gaiman's narrative style and in critical examinations of his works generally. Unlike many authors, who either turn to visual artists or are assigned to them by a press to illustrate their texts, Gaiman frequently provides significant latitude for his collaborators to have a hand in the narrative plotting to the point of encouraging them to take liberty with the visualizations as their familiarity with each other grows.

Gaiman has featured many collaborators over the course of his career, most frequently Charles Vess, Dave McKean, and Chris Riddell. Powerful storytellers in their own right, to this list we must add the most frequent Gaiman collaborator in recent memory, the lauded comic artist Phillip Craig Russell, who since illustrating *The Sandman* no. 50, has worked with Gaiman on projects including *Coraline, The Graveyard Book, Murder Mysteries*, and *American Gods*. Born on 30 October 1951, Russell is a multiple Eisner and Harvey award-winning artist and educator who is possibly best known for *Killraven* and his work with the adaptation of *Elric* with Roy Thomas (as well as his work with Gaiman). He has also been lauded for his inks and pencils on works such as *Doctor Strange: What is it that Disturbs You, Stephen?, Fairy Tales of Oscar Wilde*, and *Robin 3000*.

We caught up with the artist at his home and studio in Kent, Ohio, to discuss Gaiman, comics collaboration, and admire his astonishing and thorough collection of classic Fiestaware dinnerware.

Joseph Michael Sommers: So, you've been in this industry for over forty years now.

P. Craig Russell: Forty-four this spring.

Kyle Eveleth: How would you characterize your visual style? And what do you suspect it was about that style that may have attracted Neil Gaiman in the first place?

PCR: Well, in relation to Neil, it was the illustrations for *Thief of Baghdad*, which has that very much turn of the century [look]; obviously, I'm influenced in some sense by Rackham, Dulac, Klein, Neilson, and all those guys, so that was there in the artwork and that is what he was looking for. I think several things of my own style, as clear as I can see it—trying to look at your own style is like being a fish in water, you are not even sure what it is. But there is a level of realism to the characters but also a level of fantasy. So, the twin poles would be the Oscar Wilde fairy tales, [which] tend to be much of it just made up out of my head, almost like the classic animation style, to something like Lois Lowry's *The Giver*, which I'm adapting right now, is dead-on realism through almost the whole thing.

JMS: How have you seen your work change? Is there some sort of evolution in the field of comics you palpably feel in your work, something that you adjust for?

PCR: No, actually. I've always approached my work pretty much the same every project in that I'm telling a story and hopefully that has evolved over the years. There have been times when I've made a real sudden, conscious change—when I did *A Voyage to the Moon*. That was so different from the previous three stories, *The Gift of the Magi*, *Golden Apples of the Sun*, and *H. P. Lovecraft from Beyond*. And this was done in a really cartoony style that just came out of nowhere. That was a significant conscious break, but mostly it's not and most artists don't . . . but if you look at their work one month to the next you can't tell any difference. You look at Jack Kirby 1945, '55, '65, '75, or Carl Barks in '44,' 54,' 64—there is this evolution that they're not aware, I don't believe, of doing, it's just happening. Either your handwriting can change over the years, and it's all the other influences that have been brought to bear. You are learning things. Hopefully you're still learning every year or at least at certain one point you hope you plateau and don't go down from that, as you see also happening.

But I do make sometimes a conscious effort to pursue a different approach like once I started working with Laverne and once digital came in—it changed that way I drew in that, previous to that, especially working with newsprint comics, the spotting of blacks was much more important. If it was a night sky, you did it black, and painted on little white stars. Once you have color, now you can have a midnight blue, you can do all this, so there were a lot of places where I would have put in solid black that I'll be thinking, no, we are going to do this for color, so I'll leave it open and the color will produce the shade and tone and all of that.

KE: Something I love about your style is its accessibility. It's very classically styled, easy to read.

PCR: I've evolved a very clear sort of user-friendly look. You've seen Dave McKean's illustrations for *Coraline*—just stunning. He's an amazing, amazing artist. When Neil was talking to me about my doing this, I'm pretty sure it was Neil and not one of the editors, about having me do it instead of Dave McKean, he was sort of hemming and hawing about it.

I said, "You want a more user-friendly artist." He laughed and said yes, that style might overall be too scary for children or a little too sophisticated or whatever and I have just a simpler, more realistic fantasy style. McKean is in a whole other category.

KE: I love Dave McKean, and that book was absolutely terrifying.

PCR: A friend here in town, Josh, showed *The Graveyard Book* to his eight-year-old. She saw the first page and started crying, and he had to assure her that it gets better after this.

JMS: And yet your version is totally different. Much more of a maddening unease. McKean starts with the image of the knife, which sets a tone to emulate that incredible first line of the novel. You start with the Man Jacks, which complements Gaiman differently, giving access to subtler suggestions.

PCR: It's like Hitchcock. It's what you don't show, until you finally show it.

It's like that in *Murder Mysteries* too. I believe that you should always be bringing something to it that is not in the original without being unfaithful to the original. This is an extremely faithful adaptation but there are things like when he says, "I'll buy a cigarette," and he offers him a quarter. I drew that closely so that you saw the Liberty on the quarter, and then at the end as he's leaving town and his airplane, which is just a tiny thing in the sky and the overhead things, the street sign is Liberty because this is what this angel has giving him.

That's not in the prose at all; it's just what things unfold as you are laying out the story and you start making connections.

When he murders this woman and her little girl, it's Christmas. Now, if Neil hadn't told me it was Christmas, I might not have thought of this, but he says, "She shrugged and I pulled her to me one last time," and you see this little Christmas tree in the back and an angel. This imagery isn't in the prose but it underscores it. It illuminates the prose and if you are doing this as an artist, that's the difference between just cutting and pasting bits of like EC style text and doing an illustration.

KE: It seems like one of your greatest aims is to make interior monologues interesting visually.

PCR: Right. When Neil gives his introduction here—"looking around today parts of my life left over from those days I feel uncomfortable"—okay, parts of my life left over from those days, so I thought of this dresser with the drawer open and this T-shirt. Then Neil describes him in this cell waiting to be awakened, and here we see him in this kind of cell and he ends up in the elevator in a cell.

Here's another part: "I feel as if I have received a gift unasked from another person, a house, a wife, a child, a vocation, nothing to do with me," and so we see his children playing and there he is back there and in the background this church with a graveyard. Then back into here—every seven years each cell dies and his replaced—he comes up and pulls this thing out. When he says, "I've truly inherited my life from a dead man," now he is looking at this shirt and holding it even though he's forgotten all of this, he knows something is missing—misdeeds of those times have been forgiven and buried with these bones. This is when we come in and we see a blood stain on this shirt from another part of his life that he can't remember. And then come in close up for this little girl, and now the cemetery closer. So, you have this combination of childhood and murder and death, and in a sense, this is foreshadowing the murder will come pages later, which in fact happened years before, so that is sort of foreshadowing of a flashback, but I think that is what an adapting artist should be doing: finding a visual structure that doesn't just repeat the prose but amplifies it in some way.

JMS: Many of your opuses are adaptations of primarily musical works, and your art has a very synesthetic quality to it. How does the music weave into the visualization?

PCR: I always bring classical music references into everything. I grew up from kindergarten listening to classical music. There was something about the drama of it. One was about the Tortoise and the Hare from some salon piece called "The Golden Wedding" or something that used to be well known, but there was a moment there when it went from a major to a minor key, and at five years old, the hair stood up on the back of my head. This was a dark, scary place it went into and then it comes back into a major key.

JMS: So in many ways, the quality of the music plays into the qualities of the visualization.

PCR: There's that, but especially in the nineteenth century, almost all classical music has a constant flow, an unfolding, a transition of ideas and drama that's just like storytelling. You get into the idea of transition and juxtaposition. Juxtaposition is much more twentieth century, a sudden sharp change. I use that and everyone uses that. You have transition and juxtaposition and transition is almost just juxtaposition in extreme slow motion. Because it's still one picture put next to the other but I think I got this unfolding of a story by listening to classical music. You listen to a symphony, it's an unfolding, constant flow through the whole thing, and I think that I just internalize that in a way that I can't exactly describe but I think it has influenced the way I tell a story. So, it's a symphonic narration sort of thing. You are taking an oral structure and turning into a sort of visual palate, telling a story in a way that builds the same way as operas go.

JMS: If we could pivot: What began your relationship with Gaiman?

PCR: Gaiman pretty much started my relationship with Gaiman. He, as I recalled, called me. He had written the script, or was in the process of writing the script for *Sandman* 50. The previous year he had seen a book that I had illustrated called the *Thief of Baghdad*, and he liked those illustrations and this story was obviously *Thief of Baghdad* material. So, he asked me if I was interested in doing it and, if I was interested, to do it just *like Thief of Baghdad* but only more so. So that was right up my alley and that's what started it.

JMS: So that's probably the late 1980s?

PCR: Early '90s. I had read the *Sandman* series, and that was pretty much it. The novels hadn't come out yet, and his very early work I didn't know. I had inked one issue of *Sandman* that Kelly Jones did with the splash page with Morpheus coming through with all the robes, but to me, at that time, it was just an inking assignment.

JMS: What is it about your collaborations together? It feels as if you've taken over Dave McKean's role as primary collaborator in recent years, so what is it about your relationship with Neil that works so well?

PCR: Well, part of it is that I can be sort of liaison between the original prose and the visualization. Some artists just simply want to be told panel by panel, give me a script, panel this and panel that. They aren't interested particularly in adaptation, they just want to do the illustration, which is fine but to me, that's the most fun part, is taking this thing and literally taking it apart sentence by sentence and putting it back together again with fifty percent of it left on the floor or however.

I've never done a percentage of how much script is left. I'd like to do that sometime just to see how much of the original prose is in the adaptation. But one of the first things Neil said to me when we were talking about *Sandman* 50, and one of the reasons why he asked me for that also, is that he had seen my adaptation of Rudyard Kipling's adaptation of the *Jungle Book* story, "Red Dog," and he thought very highly of it, thought I did a very good job, one of the best adaptations he had seen. So that was nice to hear, and I think because of that he trusts me with his original material of making that leap from one form to the other. I'm sort of the middleman. I can script and visualize at the same time. That's actually how I do it; there is no final script. It's all written out in little squiggles on the pages and then on the full-size layout pages.

KE: When you do adaptation with Neil Gaiman, does he give you the text and say: "Go make something"?

PCR: Yes, pretty much. Yes. Now, don't get that confused with the two original scripts he gave me *Sandman* 50 and *Venice*—those were original scripts— everything else is an adaptation of a prose piece that he wrote.

So, those are two different things. We'll talk in the beginning, like in *Murder Mysteries*, he sent me a cassette tape of the radio version on the BBC. So, there are things in this adaptation that are not in the prose short story, like the little tinkling bells in the beginning and the end—that's from the radio play. So, I had the short story and the radio play to listen to and to work with both of those to make that. But, anyway, at the beginning he will say, like in *Murder Mysteries*, he just reminded me that yes: this is LA and it's hot, but don't forget it's Christmas. So there are elements of this, and of course LA being the City of the Angels and this whole thing being about angels, so he will give me some pointers in the beginning.

When I was working on *Graveyard Book*, I think I had a half a dozen questions, I sent to him just to clarify what is happening here or there and different questions. And he'll get back to me about that. That's pretty much it. In the *Dream Hunters*, there was one page where he asked for a caption to be removed; usually it's the other way around [a silent page of the fox waking up and heading down to get some water]. People want their words in there, and so I sorted painted over that and filled in the drawing.

KE: What were some of the challenges you faced in adapting something like *The Graveyard Book* or *Coraline*, which wasn't necessarily scripted to be visualized?

PCR: It's just . . . you could say writing a screenplay; it's the same discipline. The easy stuff is either dialogue, that's just there, and you are staging it, or the prose description of a scene, painting a visual picture or a prose picture. And that is easy to just cut, because I am drawing the picture of the descriptions of the characters. All of that is pretty easy to do.

The challenge then becomes on like an interior monologue where there is no dialogue, no events are happening, but this is an important part, and you just don't want to leave it as words on a page. You have to show something. That's the fun part—coming up with something, a visual structure that may go along with some of the prose you leave in. That is an advantage you have over visual mediums like movies or television, of course; they can use some narrator voiceover, but really you can't do much at all without it being really obtrusive. But this, we can still leave in a lot of the author's voice, but you have to be careful of course that you don't end up with just talking heads. I always tell students to just watch Hitchcock for those long, conversational scenes because it's anything but talking heads. There's dynamic things going on all over the place, like power relationships and such and whether you are looking at the back of a person's head or front or why? Or why you are looking at this person who is not talking when the other person is talking because this person's expression is more important than what's being said. So, there is a lot to learn, you can glean from movies about story telling.

JMS: *The Graveyard Book* is especially interesting because you and a group of other artists crafted it, and the visualizations change a bit. Some are these very classic Bela Lugosi-style vampires, werewolves, and mummies, and some are very abstract. What kinds of archetypes were you pulling out to create these characters?

PCR: Well, I was doing the same thing as Neil does, casting artists because I was in the position of editor. I don't know how I got cornered into that, but I ended up subcontracting all the artists for that book: making the phone calls, tracking them down. Some people said yes and then months later would drop out, and I would have to find someone else. I was trying to assemble a group that had certain aspects in common, certain illustrative approach, as opposed to say *Endless* [*Nights*], all of those artists were picked to be opposed to one another. Those were all disparate styles for a certain effect.

The concern with *The Graveyard Book* is that they did not *want* that. They wanted a more homogenous style. Having me do the layouts of the whole thing, and to have a distinctive layout style, helped to knit it all together and keep a certain similarity, the same voice even then though these artists all have different approaches. I did character design for Silas and sent that out to everyone because part of the problem was continuity too. Certain backgrounds had to remain the same, certain characters. If one artist designed a character that appeared somewhere else, then you had to follow that artist's design. So, I did some of them, like Silas. Tony Harris, who did the Hounds of God, designed Ms. Lupescu. That was his design.

The problem with designing Bod is that he ages just like Mowgli, from infancy to around seventeen years old. I knew a guy, who is actually the nephew of my original Mowgli [from Russell's *Jungle Book* adaptation], who was about seventeen years old. So, I took photo references of him for the last couple stories in the book. Scott Hampton came up from North Carolina and took pictures of this kid. Then, I went through his family photo albums and I got pictures of him from every couple of years and I assembled them on a sheet, made copies of those, and sent them to all of the artists so they could see what this kid looks like at various ages, and they have to go from there. And even then, sometimes Bod would look significantly different one from the other.

JMS: Were there any reasons for a particular order of artists?

PCR: I asked Kevin Nolan to do the first story for his architecture. Originally, I thought since I was doing the adaptation and was doing all of this, and was going to do one of the stories, that I would do the opening story. But the more I thought about it and looking at Kevin Nolan's work, the way he draws a room, a doorway—it's just plain lines around the door but it's unmistakably Kevin Nolan. That first story is one of the few that takes place mostly in a house, in this architecture, and he's just so good at that. I said, "No, I'd rather you do the opening story, and I'll do the second one," which is almost all nature in the graveyard and is what I prefer doing.

JMS: It is a great juxtaposition of a fairly recent house with this millennia-old graveyard. It's a remarkable representation of what it looks like if you could walk into it.

PCR: Well, I had a book, by coincidence, that I've had for decades on Highgate Cemetery, which is what *The Graveyard Book*'s graveyard is based on. Neil would take his little boy into Highgate Cemetery, you know, just in the stroller, and he talked about that sometimes, and that was sort of the genesis of the idea. I made sure I sent notes to all of the artists that this is a cemetery in London based on Highgate. Especially the artists in the South, Scott and Tony, [who had] hanging moss [in their] local graveyards for reference material. I said, "Make sure this is a northern hemisphere sort of thing," and everyone was aware of that. We all did a lot of research material; I had stacks of it. I went up to the cemetery in Cleveland [Lakeview Cemetery], a very famous one, I think [James] Garfield or [William] McKinley is buried there.

KE: Did you review other artists' work on Gaiman's books, like the illustrations in *Coraline* and *The Graveyard Book* or Yoshitaka Amano's version of *Sandman: The Dream Hunters*?

PCR: I definitely don't want to see anyone else's version. And I think when I saw Amano's, it was early on, before I thought I would ever be doing this story. Neil sent me his rough draft of *The Dream Hunters*, and that was I think before I even saw Amano's. When the book came out, I didn't realize it was the rough draft [I had read], and that is what I adapted *The Dream Hunters* from.

After it was done, there were a couple places where he made minor changes like instead of choking on a peach, he choked on a rice cake, things like that. And Neil had then put in a scene with Morpheus and Jeremy at the end, which was not in his rough draft. So, I didn't even have that in there. It went straight through to the end, and I got a call from either Shelly Bond or Karen Berger, saying, "Where's the scene with Sandman?" And I said, "What are you talking about?" The whole thrust was this sort of rush to the end and then Sandman making his appearance on the last page and then I had to work out a structure to get him back into it.

KE: If I recall correctly, the Sandman was the Fox in Amano's version. It was supposed to put Morpheus in ancient mythology. But Amano's version was much more visual than yours as well.

PCR: The purely visual is something that, even though I would avoid, I don't think would have influenced me because our approaches are pretty significantly different. When I was doing the *Ring of the Nibelung*, I wouldn't allow myself to look at Hall Caine's version. Even when it first came out, and I was nowhere near beginning mine—it was still a future dream—I wouldn't look at it.

KE: So there isn't much influence from other artists on your storytelling then?

PCR: No, because in doing an adaption, there aren't many adaptations that are out there, not many people working with solving the problems of visualizing things. I think that is what I specialize in. I trained myself [to find] any visual solution I can come up with. I'm always trying to get the grammar of the prose into a visual grammar. Like in the Oscar Wilde books, it's the only place that I do this but I leave in the "he said, she said" in that. So, you can read it almost completely without the visuals at all. Oscar Wilde is so arch that leaving that grammar in seems to work for those stories. I wouldn't use it for the *Dream Hunters* or any of the others.

KE: You called your version of *Dream Hunters* a graphic play after a screenplay.

PCR: Yes.

JMS: How did you match the style to achieve that kind of stand-alone "graphic play" approach, rather than an "adaptation"?

PCR: Well, it gave me a great excuse to buy stacks of Japanese articles when I had a number of them already. I'd been working with Danny LaVerne at DC and had seen what he could do with color. Actually, that's probably the most collaborative thing in my career, working with LaVerne and going back and forth on the coloring. But, from the very beginning, when he started coloring my work and I stopped doing it all myself, I said the look I wanted on anything we did was more like a Japanese woodblock print. So, when it came to the *Dream Hunters*, I think it was LaVerne's idea to introduce this texture like it's on sort of a grainy rice paper or something. Among all the other things we'd done with the style, we selectively introduced texture, or as he calls it "noise," in the coloring.

In *Dream Hunters*, I'd been sort of evolving a layout style in which I'm looking at both pages together, and gutters are running across both pages and matching up. Starting with *Coraline*, I was fascinated or just simply interested in playing very large panels against very small panels on a page, finding one that was the most important panel and really focusing on that; that approach just fit with the style of Japanese architecture or screens. If you look at a classic Japanese house with sliding rice paper screens and the tatami mats, it's very flatly geometric. I really concentrated on that in the *Dream Hunters*. Very different than, say, the Baghdad style for *Ramadan*, which was very curvy and flowing.

JMS: You mentioned *Coraline*. *Coraline* is one of those great Neil Gaiman books where he tells us he doesn't write for kids or adults, but just writes. Both the Laika film adaptation and your graphic novel capture that ability to unnerve both audiences beautifully. How did you achieve that?

PCR: Well, Neil addressed that. He was talking to me about the issue, and he said that adults find *Coraline* much more upsetting than kids. Kids are not as freaked out by this because there is this clunky, smart, confident little girl that they are with and her whole attitude is, "I'm an explorer, and I'm going to figure this out." They feel pretty confident that she is going to work her way out of it. It's very scary for an adult to see a child in that situation, so there was that.

JMS: I agree, *Coraline* is one of those mischevious little works that reads delicately but scares me as a father. As an artist, when you are drawing something like that, do you feel the need to shift your visual palate for a younger audience?

PCR: No, I just do the best I can to tell the story. If the story is sort of aimed at middle school, I'm just not thinking of them. If the author has written this in such a way that it is scary, I am going to draw it in such a way that it is scary. I'm not going to second guess his approach to the audience I am just looking at if this is a story I want to do, and let's do it.

KE: And yet you really captured the sort of dry, dark aesthetic of the book.

PCR: I was very aware of how these large panels aesthetically play one against the other. Sometimes it is more storytelling effect, and, other times, it's just for the design of the page, what looks good. But let me show you something here. This is the challenge in doing a scene like this. It's two people in a kitchen having a conversation; how do you make that interesting? Here is where Gaiman has the Other Mother yawn and then start tapping her finger. So I don't have to say that's what she's doing, it's just the "tap tap tap," but while she is doing this, I can segue into the tapping of the water in the sink. This younger girl and this older woman are playing a game with each other, and it is very low-key, just solving these little problems while the other one is thinking that there is no way the girl will get it. The challenge and the fun is making that sort of dynamic on the page.

KE: Were there any really difficult scenes to achieve, then?

PCR: A writer can come up with something that works perfectly in the reader's mind. Then when you try to visualize it, you see that doesn't work. When Coraline goes down to the basement where her other father has been relegated to now, and basically he's devolved into a slug with sticks for arms and legs, he starts chasing her around the basement. You can't really chase someone around with little sticks so, I came up with a more anthrophomorphized character that's just dissolving and falling apart and decaying, but he was a least able to chase her around. Then when Neil saw it, we were talking on the phone and he said, "You didn't give me my slug dad." I said, "I'm sorry, I could not ambulate that thing. I couldn't do it." Then the film came out, and they didn't even try, so I felt vindicated. But at the same time I sunk down in my seat and said, "Ah, Neil still didn't get his slug dad."

JMS: There are so many little visual winks, like brilliant puzzle boxes within puzzle boxes scattered about your work. When I read it, of course, I don't notice it at first, but if I reread it becomes much clearer.

PCR: I think people don't know. If this is the first time you've read the story, you haven't read the original ones. You don't know what the adapting writer has done. You're just sort of accepting it on its own level. When I reread some of this stuff, I have a hard time now remembering what I left out. Now, if you have an unlimited number of pages, you can theoretically put in absolutely everything but sometimes there are just barriers or whatever and you only have this amount of pages. I think on *Sandman* I asked for extra pages and got it. A number of things, I've asked for extra pages because a lot of times the writer will write something so rich they don't even know all of the visual possibilities that are in this. I've had the last paragraph of *One Life, Furnished in Early Morecock*—I turned into three pages because it was just so rich with the visual things and that. In "Death and Venice," he had written one page as a four-panel page, which I did as fourteen panels, because there was just so much stuff there that you could just spin out so I asked for more pages.

JMS and KE: Thank you for your time, Craig.

CONTRIBUTORS

LANETTE CADLE is a professor of English and teaches rhetoric and creative writing at Missouri State University. A longtime editor for *Computers and Composition Online*, she does scholarship in the area of computers and writing, including her Kairos article "Why I Still Blog." This will be her second publication on Gaiman and his work with "The Power of the Perky: The Feminist Rhetoric of Death," included in *Death, Desire, Fury, and Delirium: Feminism in the Worlds of Neil Gaiman*. Her poetry has appeared in a variety of literary journals, including science fiction/fantasy poems in *Star*Line*, *Yellow Chair Review*, *Young Ravens Literary Review*, and *Menacing Hedge*.

ZÜLEYHA ÇETINER-ÖKTEM is a full-time lecturer at the Department of English Language and Literature of Ege University, where she has been teaching courses on comparative mythology, medieval literature, and science fiction and fantasy since 2002. Her work on medievalism, graphic novels, science fiction, and fantasy has appeared in various international publications. She has recently edited a collected volume titled *Mythmaking across Boundaries*, published by Cambridge Scholars Press in 2016.

RENATA LUCENA DALMASO is a professor at the Universidade Federal do Sul e Sudeste do Pará (Unifesspa, Brazil). Before that, she was a postdoctoral fellow at the Universidade Federal de Pelotas (UFPel, Brazil). Her research interests include graphic memoirs, autobiographical writing, representations of disability, queer theory, and feminisms. Over the past years, she has presented papers in conferences covering those fields of interest in Dublin, Boston, San Jose, New Orleans, Utrecht, Rio de Janeiro, São Paulo, and Taipei. She also considers herself an (aspiring) comics artist.

ANDREW EICHEL (PhD, University of Tennessee) joined the faculty of the Georgia Institute of Technology as a Britain Postdoctoral Fellow for the 2016–17 cohort. At GT, Andrew serves as an ELL-specialist professional tutor in the Communication Center while teaching themed composition courses on topics as diverse as monstrosity, science fiction, and fantasy. He also assists with workshops, advising, and assessment. Andrew's teaching and research focus on ELL writing, composition, Old and Middle English literature, translation studies, critical theory, and speculative fiction. He has published critical examinations of Sir Gawain the Green Knight, Augustine, Neil Gaiman, and a personal translation of Old English poetry. When he is not reading, writing, or teaching, Andrew is spending time with his cat, playing video games, devouring too much media, and generally enjoying life in Atlanta, Georgia.

KYLE EVELETH is a McNair Post-Baccalaureate Fellow, summer research fellow, and PhD candidate in English at the University of Kentucky, where he lectures in rhetoric, literature, and film. An alumnus of the King-Chavez-Parks Future Faculty Fellow program for the state of Michigan, selected for his work on the Scott Pilgrim transmedia franchise, Kyle specializes in children's and young adult literature, contemporary literature, and graphic narrative. His recent publications include an essay on *Lumberjanes* for the Ohio State University's Billy Ireland Cartoon Library and Museum's exhibit, "Good Grief! Children and Comics," on Exit Wounds in *disClosure: A Journal of Social Theory*, on *Fun Home* in the *South Central Review*, and on the Bronze Age of American superhero comics in *Critical Insights: The American Comic Book*. He has also published on the decay of player control in indie video games like *Braid* and *Actual Sunlight*. His dissertation re-examines the creation and proliferation of literature for adolescents in the United States during the twentieth century.

His other research projects include an examination of the subversiveness of new Cartoon Network animated series like *Adventure Time* and *Steven Universe* alongside their Boom! Studios comics counterparts *Lumberjanes* and *Bravest Warriors*, a long-term excavation of comic-strip and comic book musical accompaniment, and a longitudinal study of the representations of redheads in children's and young adult literature.

ANNA KATRINA GUTIERREZ is a children's literature expert from the Philippines. Following a PhD in Children's Literature at Macquarie University, she held fellowships at the Swedish Institute for Children's Books, the Hans Christian Andersen Centre, and the International Youth Library in Munich. Her publications include *Mixed Magic: Global-Local Dialogues in Fairy Tales for Young Readers* (John Benjamins, 2017) and numerous articles and book chapters.

Katrina is the communications and project manager of Lantana Publishing, where she pours her academic energies into producing books all children can enjoy. Neil Gaiman went to the Philippines twice to empower young writers to tell stories and write. Everything she writes is in response to his call.

DARREN HARRIS-FAIN received a BA in philosophy from the Honors Tutorial College of Ohio University and an MA and PhD in English from Kent State University. After one year as a freelance editor and adjunct instructor, two years as a reference book writer and editor, and fifteen years teaching English at Shawnee State University in Portsmouth, Ohio, he moved to Alabama in 2011 to teach at Auburn University at Montgomery, where he is a professor of English. He edited three volumes on British fantasy and science fiction for the *Dictionary of Literary Biography*, and is the author of *Understanding Contemporary American Science Fiction: The Age of Maturity, 1970–2000* (University of South Carolina Press, 2005). He has also published nearly thirty essays and articles about science fiction, fantasy, and comics and graphic novels.

KRYSTAL HOWARD is an assistant professor of children's literature in the liberal studies program at California State University, Northridge, where she teaches courses on children's and adolescent literature, integrated teacher education, comics, and multicultural children's literature. Her research focuses on form and cultural studies in literature for young readers, and her scholarship has appeared or is forthcoming in *Children's Literature Association Quarterly*, *Graphic Novels for Children and Young Adults*, *The Lion and the Unicorn*, and *Critical Insights: Neil Gaiman*, among others. For more information, please visit www.krystalhoward.com.

CHRISTOPHER D. KILGORE has published on narrative theory, graphic narrative, and interdisciplinary writing instruction and support, including an article on Gaiman and McKean's *Signal to Noise*, which appeared in *JNT* in 2015. He currently serves as writing resource coordinator for the School of Social Work at the University of Texas at Arlington, where he also teaches for the English Department. In his spare time, he runs a serial online fantasy novel, *The Adasir Project* (www.adasir.com).

KRISTINE LARSEN received her PhD in physics from the University of Connecticut and has been an astronomy professor at Central Connecticut State University since 1989. Her teaching and research focus on the intersections between science and society, including gender and science; the links between pseudoscience, misconceptions, and science illiteracy; science and popular culture (especially science in the works of J. R. R. Tolkien); and the history of science. She is the co-editor of *The Mythological Dimensions of Doctor Who and The Mythological Dimensions of Neil Gaiman,* and the author of *Stephen Hawking: A Biography, Cosmology 101,* and *The Women Who Popularized Geology in the 19th Century.*

THAYSE MADELLA has a MA in English Literature from UFSC (Universidade Federal de Santa Catarina), in Brazil. Her research interests range from post-colonial texts by women to graphic novels that deal with issues of displacement and Orientalism. She has presented in conferences covering the fields of gender, feminism, comics, and popular culture, in Oxford, New Orleans, Buenos Aires, São Paulo, and Florianópolis. She has also published scholarly work on those topics. She is now an assistant professor of the English Department at Unicentro, Paraná, Brazil.

ERICA MCCRYSTAL earned her PhD in English Literature from St. John's University, where she focused her research on Gothic supervillains in urban multiverses. Her research interests include Gothic literature and media, Victorian crime fiction, and comic book studies. Erica has published articles on nineteenth-century Newgate and detective fiction, the posthuman Gothic in *True Blood,* and liminality in representations of fin de siècle London and Gotham City. Her podcast, *Villains 101,* launched in fall 2017 (www.villains101.com).

TARA PRESCOTT is a lecturer in Writing Programs and Faculty in Residence at UCLA, where she teaches "The Art of Neil Gaiman." She is the author of *Poetic Salvage: Reading Mina Loy* (Bucknell University Press), editor of *Neil Gaiman in the 21st Century* (McFarland), co-editor of *Feminism in the Worlds of Neil Gaiman* (McFarland), and co-editor of *Gender in the Superhero Narrative* (University Press of Mississippi). She recently wrote and performed "Hike Your Own Hike" for TEDxUCLA (available online).

DANIELLE RUSSELL is an associate professor in English literature at Glendon College, York University. She specializes in American and Victorian literature. She is the author of *Between the Angle and the Curve: Mapping Gender, Race, Space and Identity in Cather and Morrison.* Her publications include chapters on *The Song of the Lark, The Color Purple,* the critical legacy of *The Madwoman in the Attic, Anne of Green Gables,* Neil Gaiman's fiction, the *Hunger Games* trilogy, and a forthcoming chapter on Morrison's *Beloved, Song of Solomon,* and *Paradise.*

JOE SUTLIFF SANDERS is university lecturer in the faculty of Education at the University of Cambridge. He is the author or editor of five books, including most recently *A Literature of Questions: Nonfiction for the Critical Child* (University of Minnesotra Press, 2017) and *The Comics of Hergé* (University Press of Mississippi, 2016).

JOSEPH MICHAEL SOMMERS is a professor of English at Central Michigan University, where he teaches courses in children's and young adult literature as well as courses in modern and contemporary Anglophone literature, visual narratives, and popular culture. He is an associate editor for *Children's Literature Quarterly*. He has published work on figures such as Alan Moore, Robert Kirkman, Ray Bradbury, Dav Pilkey and, of course, Neil Gaiman. Over the past several years, he has brought out academic essays on the culture of childhood in nineteenth-century lady's journalism, the maturation of Marvel Comics' characters in the post-9/11 moment, Hellboy amongst the Melungeon People, Dialogism in Bradbury's *Fahrenheit 451*, Christopher Nolan's *The Dark Knight*, a revisionary examination of C. S. Lewis's Narnia, and posthumanism in *The Walking Dead*. Likewise, he has produced several book-length collections: *Sexual Ideology in the Work of Alan Moore, Game on, Hollywood—Essays on the Intersection of Video Games and Cinema* (2012 and 2013, both McFarland), *The American Comic Book, Critical Insights: Neil Gaiman* (2014 and 2016, both Grey House/Salem Press) , and *Conversations with Neil Gaiman* (2018, University Press Mississippi). At present, he is working on still further work on Neil Gaiman, as it's good work if you can find it, as well as completing his first monograph, a project he's been putting off, seemingly, since time immemorial.

JUSTIN WIGARD is a PhD candidate in English and university distinguished fellow at Michigan State University. His forthcoming essay with Dr. Ted Troxell utilizes visual semiotics to examine the Street Fighter series as a point of convergence for international forms of professional wrestling, embodied in characters such as E. Honda, Zangief, and El Fuerte. His scholarship and more recent publications focus on the visual evolution of superheroic figures across a variety of media as they move from comic to television to video game. He wrote his contribution while listening to We Are Scientists' entire discography because they're silly rock 'n' roll lads.

INDEX

CPSIA information can be obtained
at www.ICGtesting.com
Printed in the USA
FFHW020310030419
51445480-56893FF

9 781496 821652